OKANAGAN UNIV/COLLEGE LIBRARY

02457471

OKANAGAN UNIVERSITY COLLEGE
LIBRARY
BRITISH COLUMBIA

V

THE WORLD OF
Ngũgĩ wa Thiong'o

D0793085

Edited by
Charles Cantalupo

General Editor of *Paintbrush*,
Ben Bennani, Northeast Missouri State University

Africa World Press, Inc.
P. O. Box 1892
Trenton, New Jersey 08607

Africa World Press, Inc.

P. O. Box 1892
Trenton, NJ 08607

First Africa World Press, Inc. Edition
Copyright © 1995 Africa World Press, Inc.

Copyright © 1993, 1995 by *Paintbrush*

Paintbrush: A Journal of Contemporary Multicultural Literature is published annually by Northeast Missouri State University, Kirksville.

This collection of essays poems and interviews comprised Vol. XX, Nos. 39 and 40, the Spring and Autumn 1993 edition of *Paintbrush.*

All rights reserved. No part of this publication may be reproduced, stored in a retrieval system or transmitted in any form or by any means electronic, mechanical, photocopying, recording or otherwise without the prior written permission of the publisher.

Cover Design: Carles J. Juzang
Cover and Interior Illustrations: Lawrence F. Sykes

ISBN: 0-86543-458-1   Cloth
          0-86543-459-X   Paper

THE WORLD OF
Ngũgĩ wa Thiong'o

CONTENTS

CONTENTS (contd.)

Introduction

THE PHILOSOPHER THOMAS Hobbes wrote in 1651 that in his writing he felt "beset with those that contend, on one side, for too great Liberty, and on the other side for too much Authority." The situation described by Hobbes seems no more settled today. The basis for this collection of essays, interviews and poetry is the liberty and authority embodied in the work of Ngũgĩ wa Thiong'o.

Hobbes also observed "if there be not powerful eloquence which procureth attention and consent, the effect of reason will be little." Since his exile from Kenya in 1982, the elo-els, essays, and plays has nearly all the geographi-ters in the world of arts tragic exception of Kenya and his writings have in *Moving the Centre*, ing out the mainstream (8) and of "moving to-tures, literatures and lan-rality of centres all over provided the testimony to move the centre from

Since his exile from Kenya in 1982, the eloquence of Ngũgĩ's novels, essays, and plays has rung out and echoed in nearly all the geographical and intellectual centers in the world of arts and letters, with the tragic exception of Kenya itself.

quence of Ngũgĩ's nov-rung out and echoed in cal and intellectual cen-and letters, with the itself. Quite simply, Ngũgĩ exemplified, as he writes the "possibilities of open-to take in other streams" wards a pluralism of cul-guages" (10) and "a plu-the world" (11). He has of a witness to "the need all minority class estab-lishments within nations to the real creative centres among ... working people" (xvii) of equal status, regardless of any conditions of gender, race, religion, sexuality, economics, intelligence, and physical ability. He has testified to

> Moving the centre in the two senses—between nations and within nations— ... [to] contribute to the freeing of world cultures from the restrictive walls of nationalism, class, race and gender. In this sense, I am an unrepentant universalist. For I believe that while retaining its roots in regional and national individuality, true humanism with its universal reaching out, can flower among the peoples of the earth, rooted as it is in the histories and cultures of the different peoples of the earth.

No time in human history more than now has needed such powerful reason and eloquence to be effective.

Corresponding to Ngũgĩ's ideal of a worldwide and truly democratic "pluralism of cultures, literatures and languages" (10) the contributors to this collection represent no one critical school, party, age, or social group, nationality, race, or genre. Furthermore, their works represent a plurality yet only a sampling of centers—and by no means all—to be found in the world of Ngũgĩ's writings. Since he is a writer of strong views strongly expressed, both Ngũgĩ's work and the abundance of writing about it have developed, as he has observed about culture in general, "within the process of … people wrestling with their natural and social environment. They struggle with nature. They struggle with one another" (*Moving* 27). As he also writes, "Cultures that change to reflect the ever-changing dynamics of internal relations and which maintain a balanced give and take with external relations are the ones that are healthy" (xvi). Although struggling and changing on a smaller scale, the contributors to this collection have this principal of trial and error, vision and revision, and liberty and authority in common. They seek neither to correct Ngũgĩ's writing for any kind of excess, deficiency, or sin of commission or omission, nor to substitute themselves for his work; yet they speak critically and vigorously about many of the same controversial and complex issues which Ngũgĩ himself addresses. Like many forms of African sculpture, Ngũgĩ's work becomes a site of accumulation. It is added to, embellished, and encrusted, and in places even obscured, by those who seek to communicate to or through it. Still, there is no loss or lessening of beauty, while the text does not remain untouched, pristine, or static. It is vibrantly answered. One needs the other; neither needs a dictator. As Ngũgĩ begins *Matigari* "To the Reader/Listener" (ix), the contents of this collection begin with the response "To Ngũgĩ/Reader/Listener." Also in agreement about the inseparability of political action and the action of writing, all of the contributors to this collection testify to, in John Keats' words, Ngũgĩ's abiding "anxiety for Humanity," and they ask if he "has in truth epic passion, and martyrs himself to the human heart, the main region of his song."

The genesis for this collection was a conjunction of the passion for literature and Ngũgĩ's "powerful eloquence." Just after Ngũgĩ had visited Penn State Schuylkill to read from his work and to meet with students, I was talking with *Paintbrush*'s founder and editor, Ben Bennani, who had just completed *A Grain of Wheat* with his introductory World Literature class at Northeast Missouri

State University. The book had inspired Ben and his students, and when I told him that I had just heard Ngũgĩ himself, we marveled together at his achievement and at the happy coincidence of our Ngũgĩ encounters in writing and in person. Ben indicated that he would love Ngũgĩ to appear in *Paintbrush* and asked if I might even interview him for the journal. I said I would ask him, and Ben further suggested that an entire issue of *Paintbrush* might be devoted to his work. The rich contents collected in this twentieth anniversary edition of *Paintbrush* are the results of Ngũgĩ's "yes" on both accounts.

To turn to the contents in particular:

The images by Lawrence F. Sykes of Ngũgĩ's world speak for themselves. The tyranny of words and even a detention order are no bars to the constant interface in one profile of this writer and his never disembodied world: from the stars to the streets, on or off the map, with not one center but many, never far from the ancient dancers' feet and the life rhythm, and the names that children want to know for *torrent, mountain, flower* and *forest* of buildings or shanties and trees.

If literature, as Ngũgĩ writes, "more than all the fleeting images brought about by the screen or newsprint, is one of the more enduring multinational cultural processes which have been building the basis of a shared common tradition" (13), the essays of this collection distinguish the liberty and authority of Ngũgĩ's writing within such "processes." In "(Re)turn to the People: Ngũgĩ wa Thiong'o and the Crisis of Postcolonial African Intellectualism," Neil Lazarus sees Ngũgĩ in the mid-1960s uniquely insisting, not on behalf of but in terms of "the people," "that the responsibility of African writers cannot be assessed separately from that of other categories of intellectuals; and that the responsibility of intellectuals cannot be assessed without addressing the larger and more embracing questions of national culture and political justice." In "Murdering the Sleep of Dictators: Corruption, Betrayal, and the Call to Revolution in the World of Ngũgĩ wa Thiong'o," Kathleen Greenfield finds that Ngũgĩ's revisions of *A Grain of Wheat* (1967) during the 1980s shift the book to an emphasis on political rather than personal, psychological motivations. "The center of moral struggle is no longer within the souls of Ngũgĩ's characters, but in the struggle of the 'little people'." In "Mugo and the Silence of Oppression," James Decker studies the gaps in "a book about gaps." "Silence ... has a tangible presence in *A Grain of Wheat.*" As "a document of the uncertainty and fear that arises from the brutal domination of one 'interpretative community' over another," the novel anticipates in its portrayal of Mugo what Ngũgĩ would write sixteen years later in *Barrel of a Pen*—"silence before the crimes of the neocolonial regime in Kenya is collusion with social evil"—as well as much postmodern literary theory. In "Moments of Melancholy: Ngũgĩ and the Discourse of Emotions," Simon Gikandi confronts much of the negative criticism of Ngũgĩ's ideological and polemical writing, particularly in his fiction, with the emotional power of his work. A critical awareness of the personal and political circumstances of both the reader and the author can interrogate the explicitly political content of Ngũgĩ's writing without depending on aesthetic criteria deemed to be transcendent. In "Ideology and Form: The Critical Reception of *Petals of Blood*," Joseph McLaren charts the dynamics of writing about *Petals of Blood* since its publication in 1977 to the present. Since it is a major transition in Ngũgĩ's career, a chapter of contemporary literary history derives from Ngũgĩ's "extensive use of ideology of the left in conjunction with novelistic form which derived from Western aesthetics but which contained strong elements of the African oral tradition." In "'Rainbow Memories of Gain and Loss': *Petals of Blood* and the New Resistance," Craig Smith sees Ngũgĩ juxtaposing "both the lost pre-colonial era and the postcolonial present alongside the foundational, mythic moment of the colonial period, Mau Mau." Typically employing incongruent multiple narratives, Ngũgĩ's fiction considers class more than race and the African more than the foreign reader. In "Recuperating a 'Disappearing' Art Form: Resonances of "Gĩcaandĩ" in Ngũgĩ wa Thiong'o's *Devil on the Cross*," Gĩtahi Gĩtĩtĩ finds in Ngũgĩ's first Gĩkũyũ-language novel and his subsequent fiction a variety of motifs associated with the traditional Gĩkũyũ art form of "gĩcaandĩ." It is a comprehensive term, including oral performance in a variety genres: riddles, proverbs, epigrams, biography, history, commentary, fictional narrative, satire, poetry, and song. "Gĩcaandĩ" can also be the name for the musical instrument of a calabash with picture writing on it, a kind of dance, and the site of performance. In "Decolonizing the Child," Kimani wa Njogu finds that Ngũgĩ's effort to decolonize the mind does not exclude his writing for children. The issues of the *Njamba Nene* series are not substantially different, although they are presented less complexly, from what Ngũgĩ considers in his other texts. Problems of educational theory and practice, the use of English and/or African language, and the wild unbalance of economic and cultural relations between Africa and the West figure prominently in all of Ngũgĩ's works. Furthermore, children themselves play important roles in Ngũgĩ's "adult fiction," too.

Four of the essays deal exclusively with *Matigari*, and each sees it as a new stage and a different performance in Ngũgĩ's writing. In "*Matigari ma Njirũũngi:*

What Grows from Leftover Seeds of 'Chat' Trees?," Ann Biersteker reads the novel as a profound act of naming, most notably in Gīkūyū and in the interstices between it and the translation into English. In the process, she finds that Ngūgī presents a variety of connections between modernist and postmodernist novelistic forms and contemporary orature and literature in African and other languages, a capsulized history of his own writing, and a challenge to readers to be revolutionary in their interpretations. The essays on *Matigari* by Alamin Mazrui and Lupenga Mphande, Lewis Nkosi, and F. Odun Balogun answer this challenge. In "Orality and the Literature of Combat: Ngūgī and the Legacy of Fanon," Mazrui and Mphande provide a critical narrative to support Ngūgī's contention in *Moving the Centre* that for him the literature of the 1960s, "the age of independence" in Africa, "was really a series of imaginative footnotes to Fanon" (66). Ngūgī himself escapes such a fate through his political radicalization and the simultaneous redefinition of his audience while he cultivates the oral tradition—by default as well as by design—and its wide variety of techniques and forms. "Ngūgī's development of an oral narrative style is crucial to his own auctorial identity as a committed writer activist." In his later works, "orality emerges as an organic development"—neither a "borrowed aesthetics" (Fanon) nor a "museum" conception—"through his political involvement." In "Ngūgī's *Matigari* and the Refiguration of the Novel as Genre," F. Odun Balogun sees *Matigari* as a new kind of novel that is simultaneously a new kind of oral performance. Although its fiction and satiric exaggeration are based on fact and realities when viewed in the context of contemporary political conditions in much of Africa, the novel and oral performance are also epic, hagiography, myth, yet traditionally novelistic and deconstructive. "Reading *Matigari*: The New Novel of Post-Independence," after reading "too many novels of post-indepen-dence decline and inevitable disillusionment," Lewis Nkosi reads a new kind of novel—for both Ngūgī and African literature in general. "A homeless tale" (exiled), orphaned yet at home everywhere in Africa, *Matigari* may be "a thinly veiled allegory about post-independent Kenya"; yet the story performs like a folk or a fairy tale. Moreover, the storyteller seems to revel in irony and satire while producing a contemporary, self-reflexive narrative on decolonization and self knowledge that can be tragic, comic, and farcical. Ngūgī's linguistic powers—and the novel's English translation—fuse the polemical and the mystical, the political and the allegorical. The resulting style might have been thought not only to be outdated for now, but outdated forever. In *Matigari* Ngūgī has brought it back. As a result, Ngūgī knows at the end of *Moving the Centre* "in a sense more deep than words can tell, that Matigari shall one day return to Kenya" (175) and "Africa will come back."

This new style, spirit, and indestructibly ambiguous and fabular body of a character like Matigari are at the root of the poetry by Frank Chipasula and Tanure Ojaide.

"Ngũgĩ by Telephone" suggests that an honest, holistic, and spontaneous exchange of ideas allows the greatest liberty and authority in the student/teacher relationship. Ngũgĩ writes:

> students with their passionate debates, quarrels, shoutings, and arguments make me feel at home .... But of course I am daily struck by the absurdity of the situation. In my own country I was banned from teaching .... I tell the students this, and they look amazed since what we are saying is nothing particularly revolutionary. (*Moving* 157)

He remembers his own days as a student: "What a time it was, those days at Makerere, in East Africa! It was a replica of the Wordsworthian bliss at being alive at the birth of a revolution and the possibilities of a new future. Africa, Our Africa, was coming back" (166). Ngũgĩ also writes that in exile "He is haunted by a tremendous longing for a connection" (106); and "Writing has always been my way of reconnecting myself to the landscape of my birth and upbringing" (156). Only reconnect. It is the common purpose of this collection of work, too.

Charles Cantalupo
Penn State University, Schuylkill

Neil Lazarus

(Re)turn to the People: Ngũgĩ wa Thiong'o and the Crisis of Postcolonial African Intellectualism*

NGũGĩ WA THIONG'O is of course best known to the world as a novelist, a writer of extraordinary accomplishment and vision whose current reputation fully matches those of such modern African giants as Naguib Mahfouz, Wole Soyinka, Chinua Achebe, and Nadine Gordimer. Students of African and "postcolonial" literatures also know him as the central and indefatigable spokes-person for an "Afro-centric" position in the so-called "language debate." For more than fifteen years now—most notably in his influential book, *Decolonizing the Mind: The Politics of Language in African Literature* (1986)—Ngũgĩ has been calling for African literature to be written in African languages, and arguing that, no matter what their content, the writings produced by Africans in the metropolitan languages of the former colonial powers—English, Portuguese, French—cannot but serve to perpetuate "on the cultural level" the "neo-colonial ... relationship to Euro-America" that structures contemporary African social existence on the levels of politics and economics (*Decolonizing* 26).

> *Well in advance of nearly all of his fellow African writers, Ngũgĩ had diagnosed the crisis of consciousness in progressive African thought for what it was and moved to take the measure of unfolding liberation struggles in the Lusophone African colonies and elsewhere in the world ...*

In this paper, however, I would like to refer only indirectly to Ngũgĩ's achievements as novelist and champion of African-language literatures. Instead, I would like to focus upon the decisive role played by Ngũgĩ as a radical critic of African intellectualism in the late 1960s and early 1970s. This was an era marked by the general collapse of the hopes and dreams that, barely a decade earlier, had attended the attainment of political independence in such states as Ghana, Nigeria, Senegal, Kenya, and Zaire. Over the course of the 1960s and early 1970s, as the setbacks of the immediate postcolonial period began to loom not as temporary reverses but as fixtures in the landscape of nominally autonomous African states, African cultural and intellectual discourse tended to succumb to a wholesale disillusionment. Writing in the midst of these unpromising circumstances, it was then Ngũgĩ's substantial theoretical achievement to find a way out of the impasse, to contribute to the reanimation of radical African intellectualism by restoring its connection—beyond the single "lost" moment of political independence—to the ongoing project of anti-imperialist struggle.

In order to assess Ngũgĩ's achievement in this respect, it is necessary to evoke once again the structure of feeling of late 1960s African intellectualism. I shall do so here with primary reference to literature, although it should be borne in mind that, ideologically and structurally, writers typically breathe the same air as other members of their general class fraction. Certainly, if we examine the literature of the immediate postcolonial period, we see that it did not take long, after independence, for avowedly radical African writers to realize that something had gone terribly wrong. They had experienced decolonization as a time of massive transformation. Yet, looking around them at the aftermath, they quickly perceived that their "revolution" had been derailed. Working for the most part as urban professionals, they came to see that the "liberation" they had celebrated at independence was cruelly limited in its effects. It was a liberation to suit the narrow class interests they deplored: a liberation for bankers and lawyers and big landowners and, they realized, intellectuals, not for the population at large. What they saw made them painfully conscious of the savage irony of their situation: they were writers in communities in which the overwhelming majority of their fellow countrymen were nonliterate; and they were comfortable, even wealthy, in the midst of squalor and abject poverty.

There could be no tranquility in the face of such recognitions. Some writers responded to the harsh truths of independent society with a weary, "post-political" cynicism. Others managed to steer clear of maudlin self-righteousness but still felt themselves crippled by their isolation and lack of social utility. In Chinua Achebe's A Man of the People (1966), for instance, a very bleak vision of Nigeria as leaderless and, more than this, as unleadable, is offered. The novel represents much more than a satirical indictment of the grotesque self-interest of the Nigerian political class, for it is saturated by its author's confusion and frustration. Patently, Achebe, writing in the mid-1960s, can imagine no solution to the growing lawlessness of civil society in postcolonial Nigeria. At the end of the novel, he is able only to sound a highly dubious call to moral decency. On pain of death, it seems, integrity cannot enter the arena of the political.

In nearly all of the literature of the 1960s, writers as different in other respects as Achebe, Soyinka, Ayi Kwei Armah, Kofi Awoonor, Gabriel Okara, Okot p'Bitek, and Lenrie Peters tended, in seeking to account for the defeats of the immediate postcolonial era, to focus on the parasitism of the African political class. In work after work, we find the members of this class exposed in all their ruthlessness and vulgarity: there is their ethic of conspicuous consumption, their corruption, their greed and crass materialism, and above all there is their atrocious lack of vision. The political class is portrayed as a murderously hypocritical social fraction, living not only beyond its own means but beyond the means of society as a whole. The representation is of a kleptocracy, the continuing prosperity of whose members implies the continuing poverty and powerlessness of the peasants, proletarians, and marginals toiling below them.

What then unifies Anglophone African literature of the 1960s is that it tends to be concerned, to the point of obsession, with independence as failure, with what independence did *not* bring, with the unraveling of the social unity that writers themselves confidently if uncritically assumed had existed at the moment of decolonization. Throughout the decade, as the gains of the decolonizing years increasingly gave way to fragmentation, social violence, depredation, and the intensifying structural dependence of Africa upon the imperial Western powers, there is a discernable, dramatic heightening of the intensity and the introspection of the work produced by African writers. Writers began to belabor themselves with questions: What had gone wrong? Why? How? How had "the revolution" been subverted? How had "the masses" been demobilized? How could activists have allowed themselves to be so easily coopted? It is this radical introspection that, today, serves to render such novels as *This Earth, My Brother* (1971), *The Interpreters* (1965), *Return to the Shadows* (1969), *The Beautyful Ones Are Not Yet Born* (1968), and *The Second Round* (1965) instantly recognizable as works of the first decade of independence in Africa. In one such work after another, African writers moved in expressive and sympathetic fashion to identify and deplore social injustices in postcolonial societies, and even, on occasion, to call for the revolutionary transformation of these societies. Achebe and Soyinka, the most "visible" of the Anglophone African writers during the 1960s, also wrote extensively *about* African literature and society, calling explicitly for a literature of social engagement.

For all the manifest progressivism of this writing of the 1960s, however, it remained caught up, in ideological terms, with the class project of the national bourgeoisies of the various postcolonial societies. It was not only that, in spite of its patent commitment to questions of intellectual accountability and social regeneration, the writing tended to focus centrally (and often exclusively) on the situation of intellectuals and other members of the political class in the postcolonial universe. It was also that, in the literary and critical works even of authors like Soyinka, Achebe and Awoonor, no matter how admirable or ideologically progressive, it remained possible always to discern a residual strain of elitism. This elitism—a function of their colonially and neocolonially induced alienation from the working classes of their own society—rendered African writers of the late 1960s incapable of imagining, except in the most abstract and ungrounded terms, a cogent or coherent alternative to the clientist nationalism of the entrenched political class.

The clearest example of this is provided by the career of the Ghanaian novelist Ayi Kwei Armah. Armah's political standpoint is from the beginning altogether more uncompromisingly radical than that of such writers as Achebe or Awoonor. Ironically, however, and symptomatically, Armah's three novels of postcolonialism—*The Beautyful Ones Are Not Yet Born* (1968), *Fragments* (1970), and *Why Are We So Blest?* (1972)—are, for all their militancy, among the bleakest and most disenabling texts to be produced during the first decade of independence in Africa. It is noteworthy, moreover, that while room to maneuver is severely restricted in all three of these novels, it becomes increasingly so as the 1960s "drag ... themselves into the 1970s"(6), so that by the time of *Why Are We So Blest?*, there is none. In this latter novel, radical intellectualism is phrased as an impossibility. Any attempt to justify it constitutes a cynical lie, or, at best, a "justificatory hallucination" (*Blest* 230). Revolution is similarly an impossibility, although only revolution is seen to have the potential to remedy Africa's problems. In short, everything is necessary but nothing can be done. An obvious paradox reveals itself here: the world is "dying for change" (*Education* 1753); Solo and Modin, the central protagonists of *Why Are We So Blest?*, are "dying" to change it (literally in Modin's case); and yet the novel ends as it had begun, with the world entirely unchanged—Modin's death is merely "a waste ... useless, unregenerative destruction" (*Blest* 263). The more urgently radical Armah's thinking becomes in the passage from *The Beautyful Ones Are Not Yet Born* to *Why Are We So Blest?*, the more defeated and defeating; and the more defeated, the more it tends to represent the world as unalterable.

Contemplating the alienation of radical intellectuals from the working classes that accompanied the rise of fascism in Europe during the 1930s, Bertolt Brecht once wrote that "[t]here is only one ally against growing barbarism—the people, who suffer so greatly from it. It is only from them that one can expect anything. Therefore it is obvious that one must turn to the people, and now more necessary than ever to speak their language" (80). Ultimately, it proved to be through a similar "(re)turn to the people" that the crisis of radical intellectualism in African society at the end of the 1960s came to be resolved.

Significantly, however, the resolution was achieved not initially through literary-theoretical but through political practice. Exactly at the same time as writers like Armah and Achebe were demonstrating in their work that they saw no feasible alternative to the entrenched political orders of dictatorship and neocolonial class domination, struggles for national liberation elsewhere in Africa—and, crucially, in the most viciously policed and administered territories, those of Zimbabwe and of Lusophone Guinea-Bissau, Angola, and Mozambique—were gathering momentum. In these latter struggles, it was not only the political superstructures of colonialism that were under attack, but, very clearly and self-consciously, the economic basis upon which the "political kingdom" rested. In the anti-imperialist movements that developed in Zimbabwe and in the Lusophone African colonies, as Emmanuel Ngara has written,

> [t]he question ... was not just "independence" but "what form of independence?" This was the question posed by those countries which gained their freedom through protracted armed struggles in the seventies and eighties ... When they acquired their freedom, these countries had a different concept of independence from the countries which had acceded to sovereignty in the previous two decades. Their long struggle for independence, and the experience of independent African countries now under the grip of neo-colonialism taught them to look at national independence from a radical ideological point of view, and they consequently chose the socialist path to development. (36)

The successes of these militantly anti-imperialist movements in Guinea-Bissau, Angola, Mozambique, and Zimbabwe exploded the defeatist rhetoric that had come to characterize the discourse of radical intellectuals elsewhere in Africa. The leaders of the various liberation movements in the Portuguese colonies—such as Amilcar Cabral, Agostinho Neto, Eduardo Mondlane, and Samora Machel—were *assimilados* like Solo in Armah's *Why Are We So Blest?* but they were altogether without his paralyzingly (anti-) intellectualist self-consciousness. Their practice demonstrated to their would-be counterparts elsewhere in Africa that it was necessary for them to commit themselves to *producing* the conditions of possibility of revolution, even under the most daunting and seemingly hopeless of situations. Where in *Why Are We So Blest?* Armah had addressed the alienation of intellectuals from the majority of their compatriots as not only a structural but also an insurmountable barrier, and had moved from this assumption to characterize revolution as an impossibility, the examples of Cabral and others like him now revealed this to be an unacceptably theoreticist formulation.

Throughout Africa, the remarkable success enjoyed by such liberation movements as PAIGC (*Partido Africano da Independencia da Guine e Cabo Verde*), FRELIMO (*Frente de Libertaçao de Mocambique*) and ZANU (Zimbabwe African National Union), beginning in the late 1960s and leading to independence in the 1970s, decisively undermined the prevailing defeatism of radical thought about decolonization and postcolonialism, overturning extremism and disillusion alike. Attention shifted from totalistic considerations of collaboration and resistance, continuity and change, to more subtle and nuanced inquiries into, in the words of Ben Obumselu, "the teeming and refractory particulars" of everyday life in specific and concretely defined African communities (111). Of crucial importance here was the deflection of attention away from the urban elites and onto different categories of social actor: the peasantry, the proletariat, the unemployed, the hungry, the uprooted and dispossessed, the subaltern.

This questioning of dominant paradigms and modes of thinking also proved decisive within the field of culture, where it eventually prompted a wholesale and fundamental reconceptualization, on the part of established and new writers alike, of artistic goals and effects, methods and priorities. The questions that had been at the heart of African literature during the 1960s had, as we have seen, concerned betrayal and disillusionment, intellectual responsibility, and mass political demobilization. Starting in the mid-1960s, however, the elitist address of this writing began to be subjected to radical critique. It is here that Ngũgĩ wa Thiong'o came into his own: not as a writer—for he had already made a name for himself with the publication of *Weep Not, Child* and *The River Between*, and was poised to publish *A Grain of Wheat*—but as a critic. In an important article of 1966, for instance, entitled "Wole Soyinka, T.M. Aluko and the Satiric Voice," Ngũgĩ argued that in spite of the breadth of Soyinka's social canvas, the Nigerian author's work was marred by stasis and abstraction—

defects, Ngũgĩ maintained, that derived from the marginalization of "ordinary people" in Soyinka's drama and in his novel, *The Interpreters*:

> Confronted with the impotence of the elite, the corruption of those steering the ship of State and those looking after its organs of justice, Wole Soyinka does not know where to turn ... Soyinka's good man is the uncorrupted individual: his liberal humanism leads him to admire an individual's lone act of courage, and thus often he ignores the creative struggle of the masses. The ordinary people, workers and peasants, in his plays remain passive watchers on the shore or pitiful comedians on the road.
>
> Although Soyinka exposes his society in breadth, the picture he draws is static, for he fails to see the present in the historical perspective of conflict and struggle. It is not enough for the African artist, standing aloof, to view society and highlight its weaknesses. He must try to go beyond this, to seek out the sources, the causes and the trends of a revolutionary struggle ... which, though suffering temporary reaction, is continuous and is changing the face of the twentieth century. (Soyinka 65–66)

The central problem with the type of postcolonial writing of which *The Interpreters* was such a sympathetic example, Ngũgĩ suggested (the same arguments could have been made with respect to almost any of the texts mentioned to this point), was that it was only able to pose the question of the failures of the postcolonial regimes. It was not able to suggest plausible ways of reversing these failures.

Of great importance, in Ngũgĩ's critique, was his identification of a class distance between Soyinka as intellectual and the "ordinary people" represented not only marginally but *as marginal* in his work. In all of Soyinka's writing of the 1960s, fictional and nonfictional, we encounter what, following Ngũgĩ's lead, we might describe as an elitist and self-justifying conceptualization of intellectualism. Such a conceptualization received manifest formulation in 1967, when, in a celebrated address delivered at a conference in Sweden, Soyinka spoke of the historic role of the African artist as "the record of the mores and experience of his society *and* as the voice of vision in his own time" (21). Soyinka was immediately and appropriately criticized, at this conference, for rather grandiosely overestimating the significance of writers in society. Lewis Nkosi argued that it was quixotic in the context of postcolonial Africa to attempt to retrieve or refunction an essentially Romantic conception of artists as the "unacknowledged legislators" of the world. Writers, Nkosi mused drily, "can have a fantastic capacity both for self-deception and for sheer inability to understand what is very clear" (56). To Nkosi, it seemed merely tautological to urge writers to be the bearers of a vision: "Every writer has a vision. Otherwise I do not see what he is doing writing" (57).

Beneath the ultimately secondary matter of Soyinka's hypostatization of cultural creation, however, lay the more weighty question of the social assumptions borne by African writers in social situations similar to Soyinka's own during the 1960s. For Soyinka was by no means alone in retaining throughout the decade an elitist presumption as to the uniquely privileged, hence uniquely portentous and significant, role of intellectuals in the postcolonial social process. Consider, for instance, the following passage, from Chinua Achebe's essay "The Novelist as Teacher," written in 1965:

> Here then is an adequate revolution for me to espouse—to help my society regain belief in itself and put away the complexes of the years of denigration and self-abasement. And it is essentially a question of education, in the best sense of that word. Here, I think, my aims and the deepest aspirations of my society meet. For no thinking African can escape the pain of the wound in our soul ... The writer cannot expect to be excused from the task of re-education and regeneration that must be done. In fact he should march right in front. For he is after all ... the sensitive point of his community. (44–45)

This is an extremely well-known passage, whose fame is at least partially a testament to its effectiveness. In it, Achebe economically and eloquently espouses a literature of commitment, one devoted to the progressive transformation of African society. Yet we should look closely at what is revealed in Achebe's rationalization of "teaching" as a fit vocation for the African novelist. The reader will have noticed that Achebe himself declares that there is a need for such "teachers"; that *he* determines that what is "taught" should relate to cultural retrieval; that *he* stipulates who stands to gain from his "lessons"; that *he* finds himself qualified to "teach." His stance here is presumptuous and uncritical, even if it is not necessarily authoritarian—even, as a matter of fact, if it is actually progressive. Too much rests on his mere *presumption* that in what he outlines, "my aims and the deepest aspirations of my society meet." When we sound these words today, it is impossible for us not to hear in them the echo of that bourgeois nationalist discourse which Frantz Fanon had criticized in *The Wretched of the Earth* as falsely maintaining its identity with "the innermost hopes of the whole people" (148). The critical point here is not only that there is a separation between Achebe as socially conscious intellectual and "the whole people." Also of fundamental importance is that Achebe does not seem to see this separation as an *alienation*, reflecting the divergence between his social aspirations and those of "the whole people," but only as a distance, something that, with the right training, "the people" could reduce and ultimately make disappear. Achebe's assumption here, it seems, is that the substance of his progressivism does not stand in need of verification at the hands of "the people." And it is in this assumption, ultimately, that the strain of elitism in his thought inheres.

It was precisely against such representations that Ngũgĩ moved to take up a revolutionary position on the place of the writer in postcolonial society. Responding to Soyinka's Swedish address, thus, Ngũgĩ insisted that it was necessary for African writers not merely to speak *on behalf of* "the people," but, more concretely and decisively, "in the terms of" "the people." As he put it:

> When we, the black intellectuals, the black bourgeoisie, got the power, we never tried to bring about those policies which would be in harmony with the needs of the peasants and workers. I think that it is time that the African writers also started to talk in the terms of these workers and peasants. (*Response* 25)

This declaration proved to be of epochal significance in the development of a radical aesthetic in African literature. As Ngara has commented,

> By 1967 Ngũgĩ felt that the African writer had failed. The failure referred to here was in fact not that of the African writer alone. It resulted from the failure of the African bourgeoisie to give meaningful freedom and independence to

the broad masses of the people ... In less than a decade of their rule, many African leaders proved that they were incapable of shaking off the shackles of neo-colonialism ... The essence of Ngũgĩ's complaint, therefore, was that by failing to challenge this new state of affairs, the African writer was guilty of neglecting his duty to society in general and to the African masses in particular ... [I]t was now incumbent upon [the writer] to throw in his lot with the masses once more by confronting the ideology of the new ruling elite. A new rift had surfaced in independent Africa, not between Blacks and Whites, but between the haves and have-nots, what Ngũgĩ has called a "horizontal rift dividing the elite from the mass of the people." (34-35)

Well in advance of nearly all of his fellow African writers, Ngũgĩ had diagnosed the crisis of consciousness in progressive African thought for what it was and moved to take the measure of unfolding liberation struggles in the Lusophone African colonies and elsewhere in the world—Southeast Asia, Latin America, the Caribbean—by advocating a "(re)turn to the people" on the part of radical writers. Such a (re)turn, Ngũgĩ theorized, could not possibly be grounded on the terrain of the prevailing radical way of thinking about postcolonialism. Its radicalism notwithstanding, the latter was a terrain within the larger universe of African middle-class ideology. Instead, Ngũgĩ moved to advocate a decisive break with middle-class intellectualism. Where Chinua Achebe, thus, had spoken of the committed writer as an educator, whose task it was to guide "the people," Ngũgĩ now took a leaf out of Cabral's notebook and called upon writers not only to act in solidarity with "the people's" interests but to position themselves directly among these "people"—and not, as though that were an entitlement, at their head. For he argued that African writers could only truly hope to serve their greater communities if they first "unclassed" or—Cabral's term—"reconverted" themselves. The conscious repudiation by writers of their class of ascription was an indispensable precondition of their legitimacy as representatives of "the people's" interest; only through means of such a repudiation could the forging of "a regenerative link with the people" be consolidated (*Detained* 160).

Following Ngũgĩ's lead, African writers began in the early 1970s to appreciate that they needed to change their tactics if they wanted to combat their growing social ineffectualness. It began to seem to them that whatever they were doing, it was not enough. Several leading writers began to ask fundamental questions about the nature and purpose of radical intellectualism in postcolonial societies. The questions they asked touched on every aspect of their practice as writers: For whom were they writing? Who was reading their work? Who was publishing and distributing it? Was it possible to broaden the base of their readership by establishing alternative channels of production and distribution? Did they possess the means to tap these channels, and what exactly would it take for them to do so? Would they need to write in different languages, in different ways, about different things? Should they experiment with new media, such as film, video and television? All of these questions had to do with the potential democratization of African culture. A literature written by the elite, about the elite, and for the consumption of the elite simply could not, in the end, bear the burden of social activism. Writers began to cast around for new forms and styles of writing that would enable them to escape the hidebound implications of their elitism.

As we might expect, given what has already been said, it was in Ngũgĩ's work that these changes in the fields of vision of African writing in the 1960s and the 1970s were most readily apparent. In some respects, it is useful to compare Ngũgĩ with Ousmane Sembene, the Senegalese writer and filmmaker, at least to the extent that of all the African novelists writing in English during the 1960s, Ngũgĩ from the beginning showed the greatest sensitivity to and awareness of the plight of the peasantry and the laboring classes. Even in his early work, he focused not on the activity of urban elites but on local, rural responses to colonialism in Kenya. In his third novel, *A Grain of Wheat*, published in 1967, he painted an unforgettable picture of the depredations and hardships endured by the rural population during the years of the Emergency in Kenya, between 1952 and 1956, when thousands of Kenyan men and women took to the forests to join the "Land and Freedom" armies fighting against the forces of the British colonial government.

Yet although in *A Grain of Wheat* Ngũgĩ was writing about the Kenyan peasantry and about peasant experience during the Emergency, it can be seen in retrospect that the novel was very much a transitional work, poised between two different ways of thinking about decolonization. *A Grain of Wheat* is situated on the border between an intellectualist field of vision, concerned above all to interrogate the collapse of the great expectations of independence, and representing this collapse in rather messianic terms as catastrophe, and a more soberly materialist, long-historical socialist internationalism. The novel leaves the reader with an image of hope, embodied (in rather stereotypically masculinist terms) in Gikonyo's carving of a stool in the shape of a pregnant woman, but also with the fear that, as represented, the victory over British colonialism will prove to have been a Pyrrhic one. It would only be in his fourth novel, *Petals of Blood* (1977)— a novel that it would take him seven full years to write—that Ngũgĩ would be able to find a less intellectualist register for his new political sensitivity. And even here, in the formulaic quality of the final pages, in which the specter of proletarian internationalism is rather unconvincingly seen to be arising in the collective political imagination of Kenyan workers and peasants, there is the suggestion of a residual intellectualism.

Nevertheless, in several respects, *Petals of Blood* is definitive of the new politically committed Anglophone writing that has emerged in Africa since 1970. Set mostly in the countryside, it portrays a community struggling against an environment that a combination of factors have contrived to render sterile and harsh: drought and desertification, colonial neglect and despoilation, postcolonial mismanagement and venality. To the members of this community, independence is only a word: its substantive impact on their lives has been virtually nonexistent. Between these villagers and an authentic independence there stand daunting obstacles—economic, historical, political, psychological. Yet through the whole novel there is Ngũgĩ's insistence upon the *transformability* of existing conditions. Meaningful social change will come, he suggests: perhaps not tomorrow nor the next day, nor even the day after that, but still it will come, for "the peasants, aided by the workers, small traders and small landown-ers ... ha[ve] mapped out the path" for themselves to follow (*Petals* 344).

Ngũgĩ has, of course, not only declared his commitment to a revolutionary conception of intellectualism; he has attempted to put it into practice. Increas-ingly convinced of the need to address the failures of postcolonial government in Kenya in terms of a class struggle between an indigenous bourgeoisie buttressed by and representing the interests of metropolitan capitalism, on the one hand, and the masses of the peasant and working classes, on the other, he has sought to forge and institutionalize alliances between workers, peasants, and radical intellectuals in the general cause of anti-imperialism. While still teaching at the University of Nairobi in the early 1970s, he helped to found the Kamĩrĩĩthũ Educational, Cultural and Community Centre, which devoted itself to pro-grams of community development, adult literacy, cultural action, and the like. Gearing his literary production to the needs of the Centre's membership, Ngũgĩ resolved to write not in English but in Gĩkũyũ, and to turn his hand from the form of the novel to that of workshop theater.

Since this move was designed precisely to demolish the ideologically constructed gaps, not only between "critical" and "creative" labor, but, even more ambitiously, between mental and manual labor, it is perhaps not surprising that Ngũgĩ should have incurred the wrath of the postcolonial authorities in Kenya. Ngũgĩ was imprisoned *without charge* for almost a year in 1978, stripped of his position as Chair of the Department of Literature at the University of Nairobi, and has subsequently been obliged to seek exile in the West. With grim irony, he has pointed out that it is today dangerous for African writers to attempt to represent the realities they daily encounter. From the point of view of officialdom, it would seem that what is required of African writers is that they continue to hurl abuse at colonialism while euphemizing the thuggery of different postcolonial regimes under the rubric of "nation building":

> When I myself used to write plays and novels that were only critical of the racism in the colonial system, I was praised. I was awarded prizes, and my novels were in the syllabus. But when toward the seventies I started writing in a language understood by peasants, and in an idiom understood by them and I started questioning the very foundations of imperialism and of foreign domination of Kenyan economy and culture, I was sent to Kamĩtĩ Maximum Security Prison. (*Barrel* 65)

Since the late 1960s, Ngũgĩ has moved to redefine the situation of writers along the axis of class solidarity rather than, romantically, through references to the mysteries of "imagination." He insists that the responsibility of African writers cannot be assessed separately from that of other categories of intellectual; and that the responsibility of intellectuals cannot be assessed without addressing the larger and more embracing questions of national culture and political justice.

In these terms it seems obvious that the attempt to silence such writers as Ngũgĩ must be understood as one strand within a wider crisis of legitimacy in the era of postcolonialism, and that, in spite of the brutal tactics employed by such rulers as Daniel arap Moi or Hastings Banda or Mobutu Sese Seko, this crisis not only cannot be "done away with" through repressive state measures, no matter how terroristic, but is actually intensifying through every resort to such measures. As Ngũgĩ himself noted in the early 1980s,

Today questioning the presence of foreign military bases and personnel ... on Kenyan soil is disloyalty. Questioning colonialism is sedition. Teaching the history of the Kenyan people's resistance to colonialism is sedition. Theatrical exposure of colonial culture is sedition. Questioning the exploitation and oppression of peasants and workers is Marxism and hence treason. Questioning corruption in high places is sedition. (*Barrel* 2)

Ngũgĩ is exemplary of the new outlook among African writers because he has, characteristically, been able to draw defiant lessons from his persecution at the hands of the Kenyan state. It is not, as he has repeatedly pointed out since his detention, that he would "wish the experience of prison" on any other writer. And yet, "[t]o be arrested for the power of your writing is one of the highest compliments an author can be paid" (Moorsom 334). The point is that, in a neocolonial state such as Kenya, it is often only through persecution or imprisonment that a writer can indeed forge a "regenerative link with the people." In his prison memoir, *Detained*, Ngũgĩ recalls that in the first week of his incarceration in 1978, he encountered Wasonga Sijeyo, a fellow inmate at Kamĩtĩ Prison, who told him: "It may sound a strange thing to say to you, but in a sense I am glad they brought you here. The other day ... we were saying that it would be a good thing for Kenya if more intellectuals were imprisoned. First, it would wake most of them from their illusions. And some of them might outlive jail to tell the world" (8-9). Certainly, Ngũgĩ has lived to "tell the world." And, as he would be the first to acknowledge, he is less and less alone.

Works Cited

Achebe, Chinua. "The Novelist as Teacher." *Morning Yet on Creation Day*. London: Heinemann, 1977.

Armah, Ayi Kwei. *Why Are We so Blest?* London: Heinemann, 1974.

—. "One Writer's Education." *West Africa* 26. August 1985.

Brecht, Bertolt. "Popularity and Realism." Tr. Stuart Hood. *Aesthetics and Politics*. London: Verso, 1986.

Fanon, Frantz. *The Wretched of the Earth*. Trans. Constance Farrington. New York: Grove Press, 1968.

Fraser, Robert. *The Novels of Ayi Kwei Armah*. London: Heinemann, 1980.

Moorsom, Sasha. "No Bars to Expression." *New Society*, February 1981.

Ngara, Emmanuel. *Art and Ideology in the African Novel: A Study of the Influence of Marxism on African Writing*. London: Heinemann, 1985.

Ngũgĩ, James (Ngũgĩ wa Thiong'o). Response to Wole Soyinka's "The Writer in a Modern African State." *The Writer in Modern Africa*. Ed. Per Wastberg. New York: Africana Publishing Corporation, 1969.

Ngũgĩ wa Thiong'o. "Wole Soyinka, T. M. Aluko and the Satiric Voice." *Homecoming: Essays on African and Caribbean Literature, Culture and Politics*. London: Heinemann, 1978.

—. *Petals of Blood*. London: Heinemann, 1977.

—. *Detained: A Writer's Prison Diary*. London: Heinemann, 1981.

—. *Barrel of a Pen: Resistance to Repression in Neo-Colonial Kenya*. Trenton, New Jersey: Africa World Press, 1983.

—. *Decolonizing the Mind: The Politics of Language in African Literature*. (London: James Currey; Nairobi and Portsmouth, New Hampshire: Heinemann; Harare: Zimbabwe Publishing House, 1986.

Nkosi, Lewis. Response to Wole Soyinka's "The Writer in a Modern African State." *The Writer in Modern Africa*. Ed. Per Wastberg. New York: Africana Publishing Corporation, 1969.

Obumselu, Ben. "Marx, Politics and the African Novel." *Twentieth Century Studies* 10. December, 1973.

Soyinka, Wole. "The Writer in a Modern African State." *The Writer in Modern Africa*. Ed. Per Wastberg. New York: Africana Publishing Corporation, 1969.

*An earlier, different version first appeared in *Resistance in Postcolonial African Fiction*, Yale University Press, 1990.

Kathleen Greenfield

Murdering the Sleep of Dictators: Corruption, Betrayal, and the Call to Revolution in the Work of Ngũgĩ wa Thiong'o

> Our pens should be used to increase the anxieties of all oppressive regimes. At the very least the pen should be used to "murder their sleep" by constantly reminding them of their crimes against the people, and making them know that they are being seen. The pen may not always be mightier than the sword, but used in the service of truth, it can be a mighty force.

THUS, IN *BARREL of a Pen*, Ngũgĩ proclaims his intention to use his art "in the service of the masses engaged in a fierce struggle against human degradation and oppression" and against the "exploiting oppressing classes" (69). By the time of the publication of *Petals of Blood* in 1977, Ngũgĩ's writing had become what Fanon in *The Wretched of the Earth* calls a "literature of combat," his targets the forces of neocolonialism and their agents in Kenya (240). African writers and critics, Ngũgĩ says, "should form an essential intellectual part of the anti-imperialist cultural army of African peoples political liberation from domination" (*Writers in Politics* 31). His subsequent novels, *Devil on the Cross*, and *Matigari*, can be seen as attempts to create, in the language and oral traditions familiar to workers and peasants, a fictional modeling of the motives and techniques leading to a revolutionary transformation of Kenyan society.

> *African writers and critics, Ngũgĩ says, "should form an essential intellectual part of the anti-imperialist cultural army of African peoples for total economic and political liberation from imperialism and foreign domination"*

Seen in terms of his sense of mission as a writer, the critical juncture in Ngũgĩ's work comes between the 1967 publication of *A Grain of Wheat*, which is written in a critical realist mode, and the writing in the early 1970s of *Petals of Blood* (Sicherman 9), which retains elements of critical realism, but has a different moral focus than the earlier novel. *A Grain of Wheat* explores the moral conflicts which occur within the characters of a village reacting to colonial oppression during a revolution. In the later novel the moral center of struggle has shifted; Ilmorog and its inhabitants struggle against overwhelming external forces of exploitation and corruption. This shift in the center of moral conflict corresponds to a change in enterprise: from explaining the past, Ngũgĩ has shifted to justifying the demand for social change and creating models for taking the first steps toward it.

The nature of this shift in moral focus is illustrated in changes Ngũgĩ has made in *A Grain of Wheat* in revisions during the 1980s. In its original version, *A Grain of Wheat* is a profound study of the personal experience of revolution. The historic events in the conflict being played out on a national stage form the backdrop to the struggles of the inhabitants of the Rungei area whose private lives become part of the national drama. Some, like Kihika and John Thompson, have already come to see their own lives in the broader context of the struggle of their people for freedom. Others, like Mugo, try to live private lives until they are drawn into the maw of revolution.

Most, like Gikonyo and Mumbi, who are explicitly cast as archetypes of the Gĩkũyũ village family, are called to play their roles in the national struggle by feelings of solidarity with the people, but remain fundamentally committed to their private lives. Gikonyo the carpenter exemplifies the values of community. His work—creating with wood—is a labor of love carried out with traditional African subordination of economic to social considerations. He does the needed work whether he will be paid or not and gets personal fulfillment from his role as the village carpenter as much as from the income produced by his labor. His marriage to Mumbi is a true love-bond. In spite of this "Gikonyo walked toward detention with a brisk step" planning to "come back and take the thread of life, but this time in a land of glory and plenty" (*A Grain of Wheat*, 1980 printing, 90).

Gikonyo's detention in the revolutionary cause comes at great personal cost which he bears out of loyalty to the community and commitment to the ideal of achieving freedom. In detention he labors in the quarry while day-dreaming of the stool he will carve for Mumbi and the life he will have in the new Kenya. When, after six years, he hears that Kenyatta has lost his case at Kapenguria, Gikonyo, along with other detainees, sees that "the day of deliverance had receded into a distant future" (93).

The essential conflict within Gikonyo is articulated by Gatu, whose wisdom and humor sustain the spirits and determination of the other prisoners. In a moment of self-revelation, Gatu and Gikonyo speak of the private lives they have left behind. Gatu tells a parable:

> A certain man, the only son of his parents, once wanted a woman. And the woman also wanted to marry him and have children. But the man kept on putting off the marriage because he wanted to build a new hut so that children would be born in a different hut. 'We can build it together' she often told him. In the end, she was tired of waiting and letting life dry in her. She married another man. The first man went on trying to build the hut. It was never finished. (96)

As Gatu walks away, Gikonyo concludes, "weak, weak like any of us" (96). The next day, Gatu, who had been one of the most stalwart advocates of the national struggle for freedom, is found hanging in his cell. "Gloom fell on Yala. They never discussed him. His name, he who had taken godhead into his hands and ended his life, was never mentioned in Yala detention camp" (96).

After this episode, Gikonyo suffers a nervous breakdown, during which he injures himself by deliberately piercing his hand on the barbed wire which surrounds the camp. In a period of unconsciousness he dreams of Mumbi's "angel's smile" (98) and of her purity. When he awakes, he confesses the oath (although he does not betray others) and begins the long process of returning to the village. Gikonyo's betrayal of the revolution is thus perceived by Ngũgĩ as a psychological and moral event: torn by the conflict between building his own hut and risking that personal goal for the elusive objectives of the community, Gikonyo lacks the strength to sustain indefinitely his commitment to the public good. When he returns home to "build his hut" and discovers Mumbi's betrayal (she has had a child by the traitor Karanja after a single moment of weakness), his rage is fueled by his own guilt as well as hers. His rejection of her (and of the community values of his former life) finally leads to her abandonment of their hut.

In addition to Gikonyo and Mumbi the other major characters—Mugo, Karanja, Kihika, John Thompso—and many other more minor characters have been wounded or destroyed in one sense or another by the revolution, their blood or ruined lives the seed which will bring forth a new Kenya. Each of them carries a measure of guilt. Mugo has betrayed Kihika to the white man after trying to remain a man alone, not a traitor to the revolution, but a nonparticipant. Karanja has remained behind and become a traitor to the people in order to remain near Mumbi. Kihika has left behind the woman he pledged never to leave, abandoned any possibility of building his own "hut" and willingly sacrificed his own life that the nation might be born. John Thompson has stripped away his own illusions about his commitment to the "civilizing mission" and laid bare the brutal white man within himself. In each case, the central focus of the novel is on the interior development of characters whose daily lives are swept into the struggle for the nation. It is the sacrifices made by these people (and many like them), the fundamental moral decisions they have individually made, their collective sacrifice symbolized by the death and rebirth of the seed which has fallen to the ground, which has brought forth the new nation.

In his 1986 revision of the novel, Ngũgĩ has altered the setting and significance of the parable of the hut to reflect a new way of seeing the struggle he has described. In the revised version of the novel, Gatu's story follows Gikonyo's revelations about his longing to see Mumbi; now, however, Gatu's revelation implies that he has no woman to whom he will return. Furthermore, Gatu no longer has "watery eyes," nor does he have increasingly wild fantasies and gaze beyond the barbed wire (1986 printing 109; 1980 printing 95). Now family and home are not forbidden subjects (110; 96). The significance of Gatu's parable has been reinterpreted for the reader: "He then rested his eyes on Gikonyo and continued as if he was talking straight into Gikonyo's heart. 'So, you see, we all have our separate losses ... for the cause. We have to, we must remain strong together'" (110; 96). Gikonyo's emotional response is also different. He reflects on Gatu's weakness, then concludes: "'So that's why he's so strong. He has no woman like Mumbi. How dare he talk to me about collective strength ?'" (111)

The new inferences Gikonyo draws provide more explicit explanation for his alienation from the Movement and characterize his impending confession of the oath as an isolated act of betrayal, not a collapse of moral strength made understandable by the general circumstances they all face. However, these inferences are not well-grounded in the preceding dialogue. Gatu has not, in fact, talked about "collective strength."

The circumstances of Gatu's death are entirely different than in the earlier version. Now Gatu's leadership of the detainees has singled him out for torture, and he is threatened by the camp commandant: "'We shall get you!'" Gatu never breaks down under the stress of an indefinite future of detention and torture. Instead of taking the "godhead into his hands" (1980; 96), Gatu is murdered by the authorities: "The soldiers came for Gatu in the quarry. That very evening the others found his body hanging against the wall of his cell. 'Hanged himself ... ' the commandant told them, laughing. 'Guilt, you see! Unless you confess, you'll end up like him'" (1986; 111). It is hopelessness born of brutality and torture, not of the moral conflict between loyalty to home and nation, which sets the stage in the new version for Gikonyo's nervous breakdown and subsequent betrayal of the revolution. "The event shook Gikonyo. 'I should have known it was coming,' he told himself, scared of his own weakness" (111). He than proceeds to suffer a nervous breakdown and confess the oath as in the earlier version. The effect of Ngūgī's revisions is to reduce the emphasis on the moral conflict between loyalty to home and family and faithfulness to the revolutionary cause. It accentuates the conflict between the detainees and their colonial masters. The revision also introduces an act—the hanging of Gatu by camp authorities and subsequent flimsy story about suicide—which raises the ruthless brutality of camp authorities to a new level (although, here, as elsewhere, Ngūgī's description of British and settler brutality is not exaggerated when compared to actual events, even in the new version).

The other major revision in the 1986 version of the novel also simplifies the moral complexity of the revolutionary situation. In the first version of the novel a minor character, Lt. Koinandu, helps two men gain access to his boss, the spinster Dr. Lynd, so they can rape her:

> There came one night, it was so dark outside, when the boy called her to open the door rather urgently. On opening the door, two men rushed at her and dragged her back to the sitting-room, the houseboy following. She looked to him for help, but he was smiling. She waited for them to kill her, for after the initial shock she had resigned herself to death. But when she saw what they wanted with her, she felt terribly cold all over. People say that women faint on such occasions or else struggle. She wished she could faint or die there and then. But that was the terrible part, she saw everything, was fully conscious .... (1980; 41)

This incident is part of a minor subplot which lays bare the hostility underlying the master-servant relationship between whites and blacks in Kenya. Dr. Lynd admits she often scolded her "boy" (who had served as a cook in the army in

World War II), but the fact that she has never "harmed anybody" and the generally decent treatment she feels she has accorded him lead her to assume his loyalty. The action of the African men and Koinandu's part in it is their response to her presumption. Ngũgĩ does not moralize upon this event. It stands as the most heinous deed committed by Africans in the book, implicitly explained by the underlying hostilities between the races and the stresses of the colonial situation.

It depicts an aspect of the Mau Mau rebellion prominent in the extravagant fears of white Kenyans. However, Edgerton notes that "not one of the 'debased creatures' of Mau Mau was accused of raping a white woman at any time during the entire period of the rebellion" (112). In Ngũgĩ's novel the incident has only minor significance, explaining the hatred of Dr. Lynd and her dog for all Africans, and the depression and fear of Koinandu. It expresses the lingering hostility and distrust which will divide black and white Kenyans after years of mutual terror. However, this moral conflict, like others in the book, is seated within the psyches of the participants as well as in their external relationships. Koinandu and Dr. Lynd both have their own personal guilt to live with in the new Kenya (although Dr. Lynd probably does not realize it).

In the revised version of the novel, Ngũgĩ has removed the rape. Koinandu, renamed Lt. Koina, gains entrance to Dr. Lynd's house looking for arms and kills her dog in the process. The houseboy, now resistance fighter, no longer reacts to his chance meeting with Dr. Lynd at Githima by looking "debauched" and "haunted," but by looking "weary, a little pained" (1986; 152). He admits on questioning that at Githima he saw "ghosts" that make him "wonder about what we are really celebrating!" (153) Recollection of the incident merely hardens Dr. Lynd's resolve not to leave her property to the Africans she hates (165). Dr. Lynd thus becomes an example of whites who remain behind when former colonists such as John Thompson leave or, as in the case of Dr. Van Dyke, commit suicide. She remains in the new Kenya, consumed by hatred and fear of Africans and determined to hang on to the property which supports her elevated status. When John Thompson comments that she will need more homeguards, she takes the remark as serious advice and starts "talking about the qualities of the most loyal and the most ferocious guard dogs" (165).

The effect of Ngũgĩ's revision of this minor subplot is to simplify and clarify motivations and events while reducing the level of inner moral conflict of the Africans (in the case of the rape, making the story a more accurate account of events as they actually happened) and accentuating the hostility and fear of the colonial type represented by Dr. Lynd. Not the moral complexity of the events of the Emergency, but the stark moral conflict between African and European oppressor is emphasized in the new version. In all fairness, it must be noted that even in this form the book presents an understatement of European brutality and terror against both insurgents in the forest and peasants who remained in the villages. The focus of the work remains on the souls of the villagers, not on the issues or tactics of the conflict which engulfs their lives.

Asked in 1990 about his reasons for the revisions described above, Ngũgĩ cited his growing familiarity with the history of the period covered by A Grain of Wheat. (For example, there was an incident in which a white man shot an African for raising—not throwing—a stone against his dog.) With regard to the parable of the hut, Ngũgĩ explained that he wanted to shift from psychological to political motivations. "The question is whether the personal, psychological, or the political motives receive first emphasis—which comes out of the other" (personal conversation, Penn State University, State College, Pennsylvania, March 30, 1990).

These revisions, although they do not change the fundamental character of A Grain of Wheat, move the novel in the direction Ngũgĩ had already taken in Petals of Blood, which is structurally similar to A Grain of Wheat but approaches moral conflict in a different way. Both novels brilliantly bring to life a village community and place the lives of the citizens on the stage of national history. As we have seen, the people of Thaibai are inevitably swept into the revolution which leads to independence. The citizens of Ilmorog are similarly victims and participants in the impoverishment of the village produced by the deforestation of the area to feed the railway and then are dispossessed as their village is swept into the modern world of highways, factories, churches, policemen, and money, all serving the ends of foreign and native exploiters and opportunists. (It is interesting that none of the major characters in Petals of Blood are really peasants of Ilmorog. All have come to Ilmorog with identities forged in modern neocolonial Kenya, have rejected that world for one reason or another, but in the school, their trek to the city, and their enterprises, are the agency which brings a passive and largely invisible Ilmorog to the attention of bureaucrats and capitalists.)

As is the case in A Grain of Wheat, none of the characters in Petals of Blood is drawn in heroic proportions or presented as a paragon of perfect virtue. All have their flaws and blind spots and all operate within the scale of local life. However, Ngũgĩ has switched the lense through which he sees local life. In A

Grain of Wheat, the colonial system is a distant cause of the struggle which engulfs the lives of the inhabitants of Thaibai. As Peter Nazareth says, "not only does he [Ngũgĩ] want to show how Kenya gained its independence but also he wants to find out what happened in the process to the souls of the people" (Killam 245; *Petals of Blood* 297). In *Petals of Blood*, the focus is on the intrusive system of neocolonial relationships which frame the action. Ngũgĩ "names" the social relationships he describes and offers a "precise diagnosis" of the social ills which result from those relationships (Onoge 37).

This shift of focus is at the heart of a fundamental change in Ngũgĩ's artistic enterprise. *A Grain of Wheat* is fundamentally an historical novel describing relationships which independence has ended. It was written soon after independence and could only forecast in a general way the emergence of a neocolonial state and economy. By the 1970s, the neocolonial state had taken shape and Ngũgĩ was addressing not the past, but the present and future of Kenya. Unlike *A Grain of Wheat*, *Petals of Blood* is a direct challenge to existing economic, social, and political relationships. In *Petals of Blood*, Ngũgĩ remains a socialist realist (Onoge 38), but a socialist realist whose writing has become an act of combat (Fanon 240).

To achieve this, Ngũgĩ has shifted his moral focus. Although Munira, Wanja, Abdullah, and Karega, remain all too human, blinded and maimed by their own wounded lives, they are the victims of a system external to themselves and their own community, a system whose exploitation and corruption are the central evils to be overcome. The center of moral struggle is no longer within the souls of Ngũgĩ's characters, but in the struggle of the "little people" to fend off the intrusion of a rapacious and corrupt system which undermines a peasant economy and consigns the tillers and their children to the bottom ranks of urban society (*Writers in Politics* 94). Only her emergence from the peasantry and her own victimization by the system, for example, distinguish the wealthy owner of a brothel (Wanja) from the moral depravity of the rich capitalists who are her major customers. Wanja must sell her body and those of her employees in order to gain wealth and enough power to survive; Kimeria, Chui, and Mzigo use their wealth and power to buy the bodies of powerless women.

Munira gains the reader's initial sympathy as he struggles to overcome the psychically-shattering experience of failure brought on by his refusal to cooperate with the European-dominated education at Siriana and with the opportunities to take his place in the neocolonial elite with his family. His attempts to carve out a small space for constructive action are thwarted by his own weaknesses and by the sweep of the forces which transform Ilmorog.

Wanja is personally stronger than Munira. She returns to Ilmorog a wounded soul, the victim of the sexual depravity and exploitation of one of Kenya's neocolonial opportunists. She is more resiliant than Munira, bringing what life she can to the soil and to Abdullah's place, even though unable to bring forth life within herself. When Ilmorog is overwhelmed with changes she sells out, salvaging what she can of traditional Ilmorog in the form of her land and hut and selling herself—the only commodity she has—for a high price in the market economy of New Ilmorog. At the end, Wanja recognizes that she has chosen her life, even though her range of choices has been constrained. "She could not now return to a previous state of innocence. But she could do something about her present circumstances" (328). She resolves to break off her relationship with Kimeria—"on her own terms" (328). She will strike a blow against the oppression that has crippled her life.

Abdullah, literally maimed by the struggle for independence, stands as its most noble victim, enduring the loss of his leg and his donkey, and then his shop. Even though he winds up a drunken peddler, his integrity makes him the logical father to the next generation. He is on his way to eliminate Kimeria when Munira preempts his plan. The actions planned both by Wanja and Abdullah at the end of the novel correspond to what Fanon identifies as the prerevolutionary stage in which the task of the revolutionary writer is to envision for the people and sanction by the rationale he provides "all revolts, all desperate actions, all those abortive attempts drowned in rivers of blood" which lead eventually "to more widespread, organized, and effective forms of revolt" (Fanon 207).

When Karega, previously eschewing alcohol, is found in a drunken stupor, he later explains: "I don't know how I succumbed to it. I think I just wanted to lose myself. So many things hitting at you on every side. You just want to forget" (*Petals of Blood* 126). Karega alone among the citizens of the old Ilmorog has come to understand the system which has transformed the physical and moral landscape. He is already building the base within the union movement which will ripen into revolution on a broader scale, enabling the mass of the people to overwhelm their oppressors: He says to Wanja:

> Can't you see: we, the workers, the poor peasants, ordinary people, the masses are now too awake to be deceived about tribal loyalties, regional assemblies, glorious pasts ... when we are starving and we are jobless, or else living on miserable pay.

Do you think we shall let foreign companies, banks, insur-
ances—all that—and the local rich ... , the new black landlords ... do
you think people will let a combination of these two classes
and their spokesmen in parliament, at universities, in schools,
in churches and with all their armies and police to guard their
interests—do you think that we shall let these owners of stolen
property continue lording it over us for ever? No ... it is too
late ... we shall no longer let others reap where they never
planted, harvest where they never cultivated, take to their
banks from where they never sweated .... (326)

Karega the labor organizer has comprehended the global and national context
of the woes of Ilmorog and understood the need for mass organization which will
move the revolution against neocolonial oppression to a new stage.

The targets of that revolution are depicted on the broad canvas of *Petals of
Blood*, first during the journey of the citizens of Ilmorog to Nairobi, then in the
invasion of New Ilmorog by the institutions of modern Kenya. The forces of
neocolonialism are caricatures, almost cartoon-like characters who are multidi-
mensional only in their vices, a depiction which Ngũgĩ explicitly defends (*Barrel
of a Pen* 20). Hawkins Kimeria is perhaps the most fully drawn of the villains in
this novel. He has seduced, impregnated, and abandoned Wanja, then, on the
journey to Nairobi, extorted sex from her in exchange for freedom. Before that,
he betrayed Abdullah and by extension the independence movement. He lives
in the Blue Hills, home of the former colonial oppressors of Kenya. In large
measure he has simply stepped into the shoes of those oppressors, but with the
added guilt produced by hypocrisy—the pretense of being one of the people while
preying on the unsuspecting like a hyena and of indulging his basest appetites
under the cover of propriety and respectability. Kimeria and others thus
represent not only economic oppression, but moral depravity as well.

This dual theme forms the central focus of Ngũgĩ's next novel, written
largely in detention in 1977, *Devil on the Cross*. *Devil on the Cross* was written
during another period of transition. Written in Gĩkũyũ as *Caitaani Mũtharaba-
inĩ* and published in 1980, the novel echoes the message of the play, *Ngaahika
Ndeenda* (*I Will Marry When I Want*), published with Ngũgĩ wa Mĩriĩ in the same
year. The play was written as part of a community theater project in Limuru in
1976, at about the same time Ngũgĩ began working on the novel which he
continued to write on toilet paper in detention (*Detained* 11). Both works exhibit

a consistent theme and technique: they rip the veil of normalcy, respectability, and justice from the existing political order in Kenya and proclaim the duty of revolution. For Ngũgĩ the artist, they represent the transition from the proclamation of revolutionary truths to the production of a literature of action, in which the act of creation is part of the process of organization for revolution.

Devil on the Cross is, like all of Ngũgĩ's works, fundamentally concerned with moral choices. In this work, perhaps distilled from the resolve of a man not intimidated but steeled in his purposes by a year in jail, the reader is offered a stark moral choice:

> Our lives are a battlefield on which is fought a continuous war between the forces that are pledged to confirm our humanity and those determined to dismantle it; ... those whose aim is to open our eyes, to make us see the light and look to tomorrow, asking ourselves about the future of our children, and those who wish to lull us into closing our eyes, encouraging us to care only for our stomachs today, without thinking about the tomorrow of our country.
>
> It is a war without spectators. For each man is part of the forces that have been recruited for creating, building, making our humanity grow and blossom in order to nurture our human nature and create our own Heaven, thus taking on the nature of God—these are the forces of the clan of producers; or he is part of the forces of destruction, of dismantling, of harassing and oppressing the builders and the creators, the forces that seek to suppress our humanity, turning us into beasts in order that we should create our own Hell, thus taking on the nature of Satan—these are the forces of the clan of parasites. (53)

In this war, "Our actions are the bricks that we use to construct either a good or an evil heart" (54). In contrast to *Petals of Blood* and earlier works, Ngũgĩ has here constructed a novel which pays little homage to the usual European constraints. Using parables, elements of fable, and a variety of devices which connect the work with conventions of orature (Cook and Okenimkpe 121-2). The use of italics to indicate words which were given in English in the Gĩkũyũ original emphasizes for the reader of the English version the invasion of Gĩkũyũ culture by European things, customs, and ideas, and provides a means by which the experience of a Gĩkũyũ reader may be imagined. We follow Warĩĩnga, the central character, from her near suicide at the beginning to her execution of the Rich Old Man at the end, but even she is not a fully drawn character. Above all, she is a victim of corrupt men and the corrupt system they represent and, with her, we learn the lessons which lead her to comprehend the nature of the system which has oppressed her and to strike out against its most heinous human agent.

It is the lesson which is central to the work, not Warĩĩnga or what happens to her or the place where it happens. The lesson is conveyed by Warĩĩnga's conversation with an earnest intellectual, with a fellow passenger on the matatu to Ilmorog (who speaks the lines quoted above),and in the counter arguments of Mwara that money is his God (56). The parable of the talent—familiar to Christians and thus to Kenyans of many ethnic backgrounds—is transformed into an explication of the value of labor, with the servant who is given 500,000 shillings doubling the money entrusted to him by buying cheaply from rural peasants and selling dear to urban workers, while the servant given 200,000 shillings "bought cheaply from producers, and sold dearly to consumers" thus also doubling his investment (83). The servant who received 100,000 shillings, however, buried his and demonstrated that money would not increase in value "without being watered with the sweat of the worker" (84).

In the devil's cave (the "finest of houses?" 92), Warĩĩnga witnesses the competition to see who will be hired by foreign companies. Contestants vie to prove their prowess as robbers and thieves: not petty thieves, but on an "international" scale, "those who steal because their bellies are full" (95). The competition among thieves is full of bitter satire as they reveal themselves to be rapacious exploiters, cunning and unrepentent. They are also buffoons—ludicrous, affected black "Europeans" given to gluttony and lust thinly veiled by a pretended respectability. They measure their worth in houses, cars, mistresses, and conspicuous consumption of food and alcohol. Their rise to wealth has been smoothed by the maneuvering of their fathers before and after independence. They have used the methods of the whites and sold themselves as front men for white businesses who need black faces to continue to exploit the people of Kenya. Cunning slaves, they willingly sell to foreigners the resources of their country and the best interests of its people. They specialize in the fruitless profiteering of land speculation and the cunning of the con artist who works on a grand scale, eschewing all forms of investment which would bring genuine benefit or profit to the land and people. As a group, they cooperate in sharing insider information, bribery, and favors, all of which are necessary to lubricate the wheels of commerce and justice in Kenya. They are the personification of evil and the agents of neocolonial exploitation.

In the end, Wariinga strikes down the Rich Old Man and delivers a blow for justice. As a model for all the workers of Kenya who are cornered by powerlessness and poverty, his striking back identifies in unmistakable and unforgettable terms who the enemy is and what he deserves.

The comprador bourgeoisie is the primary subject of *Devil on the Cross*, presented in satirical caricatures against the backdrop of the struggle of one of their innocent victims for some measure of human dignity. In his analysis of neocolonial society in Kenya, Ngũgĩ lubricates a starkly Marxist analysis of the relations between workers and the national bourgeoisie with a metaphorical language rich in Christian imagery. Consistent with his other novels, in this work Ngũgĩ views organized Christianity as a curtain of hypocrisy and a mechanism for encouraging passive acceptance of oppression. He uses Christian imagery, however, as a major medium of his message since it provides a literary language universally understood among his Kenyan audience. At the same time, however, Ngũgĩ remains a moralist, if not a specifically Christian moralist. The evil of exploitation is embodied in men and women who are morally depraved in every sense of the word. The same appetite which maximizes profits through bribes and strike breaking uses its power to consume food, drink, and the sexual favors of young women without restraint, kills its enemies when they raise obstacles, and sells its soul to the highest bidder. Such men will not be reformed; they are proud of their crimes. They must be exterminated.

This realization is the theme of Ngũgĩ's latest novel, *Matigari*, in which the return of a savior-figure from the Mau Mau era first tests the possibility of finding truth and justice through peaceful means, then signals the resumption of armed struggle, fortified with words of truth and justice. Clearly, Ngũgĩ intends in this work "to depict reality in its revolutionary transformation" (*Moving the Centre* 73). The spare and tightly-woven structure uses elaborate Christian millenarian symbolism to imbue a simple plot with profound meaning and to create a call to revolution which appeals simultaneously to the intellect and to the emotions of his reader. As in *Devil on the Cross*, many of the literary devices in this work depend on the conventions of African orature and not those of European fiction.

Against realistic snapshots of the great farms of rich black and white "parasites," factories of the comprador bourgeoisie, bars and scrap heaps which collect the leavings of the neocolonial economy, Ngũgĩ paints a myth of return of "the patriots who survived the bullets" (*matigari ma njirũũngi*) (*Matigari* 20). Matigari is the champion of the tillers and tailors and builders who are deprived of the fruits of their labor by "those-who-reap-where-they-never-sowed" (75). Matigari, who cannot be hit by bullets, is not seen to eat, and escapes miraculously from a burning house which is surrounded by police, is richly endowed with messianic symbols drawn primarily from the Bible. The satirical interludes show the increasingly frantic and farcical efforts of the neocolonial state—particularly the attempts of the Minister of Truth and Justice—to apprehend and silence this true bearer of truth and justice. This permits a juxtaposition of the forces of good and evil in a kind of cat-and-mouse progress through the venues of Kenyan neocolonial society. This conflict is simultaneously extravagantly fictional and grounded in the historical and present realities which led to the round-up of the original "*matigari*"–freedom fighters who would not put down their arms until hunted down by the Kenyatta government—and now produce the untimely deaths of political activists and even the actual search by police for Ngũgĩ's fictional Matigari (Edgerton 221-3; Gikandi 162;*Matigari viii*).

The use of Christian imagery seems to provide a vehicle for Ngũgĩ's millennarian message rather than an appeal to any church-based Christian establishment—which is always attacked in this work as in the novels described above, although some writers argue otherwise (Brown 179). However, in this work as in all of the novels discussed above, Ngũgĩ imbues the carefully-delineated structure of neocolonial domination with rampant moral corruption. Lies, theft, adultery, extortion of sexual favors and money, brutality, and bestial self-indulgence, all thinly painted with the respectability of cocktail parties and church meetings, are inherent in the opportunistic exploiters of Kenyan peasants and workers. Thus, while Ngũgĩ does not advocate Christianity and condemns Christian teachings as lies designed to produce passive acquiescence in an unjust and destructive system, He continually condemns the behavior of his villains on moral as well as economic grounds.

This aspect of Ngũgĩ's later work presents a fascinating paradox: as we have noted, *Petals of Blood*, *Devil on the Cross*, and *Matigari* all end with individual acts of violence which represent the desperate acts of the oppressed against their oppressors. (In *Petals of Blood* the fact that Kimeria, Mzigo, and Chui are executed by the religious fanatic, Munira, is merely an accident, since both Abdullah and Wanja had similar acts in mind.) In each case the act is personalized. Wanja and

Abdullah, Wanjiiku, and Matigari all have personal reasons for striking out against specific individuals whose personal moral depravity justifies the action as much as political motives do. In fact, Ngũgĩ entangles his carefully constructed analysis of the place of peasants and workers in the economic, political, and social framework of neocolonial relations in an elaborate web of personal acts of oppression, exploitation, and domination. Only Karega and Matigari act out of generalized political motives not personal revenge. This emphasis on personal revenge which coincides with truth and justice gives such acts significance beyond the merely personal, but still places the motivation for revolution in the wounded "souls" of his protagonists.

On one level, this seems to be an implementation of Fanon's exhortation "to sanction all revolts, all desparate actions, all those abortive attempts drowned in rivers of blood" (207) which lay the groundwork for broader, more carefully organized, and more successful mass revolutionary movements. On another level, the intertwining webs of corruption and betrayal provide the medium for an emotional connection between Ngũgĩ's intended peasant/worker audience and the abstract Marxist analysis to which Karega gives voice and which Warĩĩnga and Matigari "discover." In other words, melodramatic stories of the seduction of schoolgirls and bloated moral depravity are the spice which makes palatable arid economic analysis. The focus on personal corruption and betrayal may well be a literary device akin to Ngũgĩ's abundant use of Christian imagery. Both devices tap into the existing culture of Ngũgĩ's audience and provide avenues of communication richer and more effective than pure economic analysis. Furthermore, Ngũgĩ points out in *Barrel of a Pen* that his image of the national bourgeoisie is accurate. They are "happy, content really, to be only the agents for international tractors, motor vehicles, pharmaceuticals, textiles, boots, canned foods and fruits, videos, television sets, bottled water, every little thing manufactured abroad ....Their laziness, inefficiency, corruption, nepotism, ethnic chauvinism, does not make them play their messenger role efficiently" (20). Thus, Ngũgĩ's satirical portraits will ring true with his intended audience. They will be able to place both themselves and their oppressors into the roles provided in Ngũgĩ's novels.

There is a more profound issue raised by portraying economic oppression intertwined with moral depravity, however. The abiding theme of Ngũgĩ's novels is a call to moral responsibility, to take up the spade of national duty and put aside the knife of "eat or be eaten" (*Petals of Blood* 291). He calls upon his readers to be willing to share the single bean which has dropped to the ground.

To what extent, however, do his readers equate corruption with betrayal of themselves and the nation? How many, like Wanja's and the corrupted teacher in *Devil on the Cross*, seeing the system and its power, opt instead to play the game according to the rule of "eat or be eaten"? For example, in his study of the Bukusu, Jan De Wolf found that "One votes for a councillor or an MP because one expects tangible benefits from their performance, and not because they have a good reputation for honesty or sociability" (203). To what extent do the peasants and workers of contemporary Kenya see themselves, like the working class of Robert Roberts' Salford, as competing with each other and looking about for a big fish to swim behind? The Kenyan audience of Ngũgĩ's fiction could not help but see themselves caught in the jaws of international capitalism. It remains to be seen, however, whether they find his call to the defense of truth and justice against the agents of that system as compelling as the nationalist call to freedom from white colonialism.

Works Cited

Brown, David Maughan. "Matigari and the Rehabilitation of Religion." *Research in African Literatures* 22 (1991):177-8.

Cook, David and Michael Okenimkpe. *Ngũgĩ wa Thiong'o, an Exploration of His Writings*. London: Heinemann, 1983.

DeWolf, Jan J. *Differentiation and Integration in Western Kenya. A Study of Religious Innovation and Social Change among the Bukusu*. The Hague, Paris: Mouton, 1977.

Edgerton, Robert B. *Mau Mau, an African Crucible*. New York: The Free Press and London: Collier Macmillan, 1989.

Fanon, Frantz. *The Wretched of the Earth*. New York: Grove Press, 1963.

Gikandi, Simon. "The Epistemology of Translation: Ngũgĩ, Matigari, and the Politics of Language." *Research in African Literatures* 22:4 (Winter, 1991): 162-7.

Killam, G. D. *Critical Perspectives on Ngũgĩ wa Thiong'o*. Washington, D. C.: Three Continents Press, 1984.

Ngũgĩ wa Thiong'o. *Barrel of a Pen: Resistance to Oppression in Neo-Colonial Kenya*. London: New Beacon Books, 1983.

—. *Decolonizing the Mind: the Politics of Language in African Literature*. London: James Currey, 1986.

—. *Devil on the Cross*. London: Heinemann, 1982 (orig. in Gĩkũyũ, 1980).

—. *A Grain of Wheat*. London: Heinemann, 1967 (rev. ed. 1986).

—. *Matigari*. Oxford: Heinemann, 1989.

—. *Moving the Centre: The Struggle for Cultural Freedoms*. London: Heinemann, 1993.

—. *Petals of Blood.* New York: E. P. Dutton, 1977.

—. *Writers in Politics.* London: Heinemann, 1981.

— and Ngũgĩ wa Mĩriĩ. *I Will Marry When I Want.* London: Heinemann, 1982 (pub. in Gĩkũyũ, 1980).

Roberts, Robert. *The Classic Slum: Salford Life in the First Quarter of the Century.* Harmondsworth: Penguin, 1973 (1971).

Sicherman, Carol. *Ngũgĩ wa Thiong'o: The Making of a Rebel: A Source Book in Kenyan Literature and Resistance.* London: Zell, 1990.

THE PUBLIC SECURITY (DETAINED AND
RESTRICTED PERSONS (REGULATIONS 1966

DETENTION ORDER

regulation
IN EXERCISE of the powers c   sons)
(Detained and   ed
(1) of the Public S   on or
Regulations 1966, the
that it is necessary
exercise control, b

over

HEREBY ORDERS

(hereinafter re
that the detai

1977.

Date this

(D. T. Arap Moi)

MINISTER FOR HOME AFFAIRS.

44

James Decker

Mugo and the Silence of Oppression

BOTH TEMPORALLY DISJOINTED and polyphonous, Ngũgĩ wa Thiong'o's *A Grain of Wheat* displays many features in common with postmodern novels from the West[1]. The novel's lack of a monistic narrative perspective, as well as its deferral of meaning, align it with texts like *V* or *If on a Winter's Night a Traveler*, and it seems quite tempting to apply poststructuralist theory to *Grain*. To do so, however, would severely underestimate the political and historical significance of Ngũgĩ's text. *Grain's* disruptive narrative, while having obvious resemblances to the postmodern, reflects the struggle between the colonial discourse and that of the colonized on the eve of political independence. Mugo, a character who appears quite reluctant to speak, functions as an emblem for this linguistic tension, even as Ngũgĩ's sophisticated manipulation of flashback and memory decenters the reader; the security of a linear narrative gone, the reader first struggles to decode the mystery of Mugo's silence, but ultimately s/he realizes that no easy answer will be forthcoming.

Ngũgĩ continuously presents the reader with characters who "want" to speak, who have a "catch" in their throats, whose voices are "broken," who cannot find the "right" words.

Even Mugo's eventual confession fails to explain his reticence fully, for the character has ample opportunities to tell others of his betrayal. Why, the reader asks, does not Mugo speak? Indeed, Mugo often seems as though he cannot physically articulate even the crudest of sounds. The lacunae evident in the narrative seem paralleled by those in Mugo's silence, and would thus suggest that Ngũgĩ means to employ Mugo as a metaphor for the novel's stylistic concerns. Mugo, then, equals text.

All texts, regardless of their degree of ostensible "explicitness," ultimately fail to communicate a uniform message to their audience. The singularity of each reader, coupled with the continual flux of language, renders the concept of an "authoritative" (objective, definitive, etc.) reading of a passage—much less an entire book—into nothing more than a delightful chimera. Somewhere during the process in which writers attempt to transfer their private thoughts into public language, and then again as readers translate writing into thought, gaps in understanding develop. One may tentatively define "gap" (or lacuna, to adopt linguistic parlance) as any point within the text, author, or reader that requires a hermeneutical investigation. If one accepts de Saussure's contention that "the bond between signifier and signified is arbitrary," then it would therefore appear as though the text itself—and Mugo—constitutes a lacuna (67). Taking this proposal to its most radical extreme (as Derrida does in *Of Grammatology* and elsewhere) would necessitate the formulation of a construct in which language proves indeterminate. Why, however, should one defer to the theories of de Saussure or Derrida?

Katherine Williams proposes a much more fruitful avenue of inquiry for Ngũgĩ's texts with her contention that "deprived of a native language, the African writer is deracinated and decultured" (54). Williams (among many others, including Ngũgĩ)[2] argues that the very choice of language represents the central political issue for African writers, for it raises the question of cultural primacy and its corollary question of whether culture produces language or vice versa. While Williams contains herself for the most part to Ngũgĩ's later novels (and his decision to write in Gĩkũyũ), I would like to assert that Ngũgĩ concerns himself with the disruptive influence of the colonial tongue to an extraordinary degree in *Grain*. The novel, while undoubtedly engaged in portraying the circumstances leading to Kenyan independence, employs a complex pattern of communicative breakdowns that function to underscore the potential for neocolonialism in the fledgling free nation.

Overt examples of lacunae appear on almost every page of the novel. Ngũgĩ continuously presents the reader with characters who "want" to speak, who have a "catch" in their throats, whose voices are "broken," who cannot find the "right" words. Additionally, Ngũgĩ almost completely defines characters such as Gitogo and Mugo by their inability to speak. As mentioned above, Ngũgĩ also employs more subtle techniques to illustrate Kenya's dysfunctional communication. The narrative withholds crucial information from the reader, and shifts perspective quite abruptly. Silence pervades the text. As Kenneth Harrow points out, this silence "is rarely heroic ... rather it ... is the manifestation of missed or failed communication" (257). Commentators should note the ramifications of such an "unheroic" silence since it plays such a crucial role in the novel, and it foreshadows Ngũgĩ's more recent theories on language.

Before explicating *Grain*, Stanley Fish's concept of "interpretive communities" and Edward Said's notion of the critic merit some investigation. Fish asserts that

> if the self is conceived of not as an independent entity but as
> a social construct whose operations are delimited by the
> systems of intelligibility that inform it, then the meanings it
> confers on texts are not its own but have their source in the
> interpretive community (or communities) of which it is a
> function. (335)

Fish's insightful remarks displace the ultimate authority for an interpretation
from individuals to the society (and its concomitant philosophies) that informs
them. I agree for the most part with Fish's hypothesis, for people seldom exist
in isolation; their experience is usually at least partially defined by others. As any
sociologist realizes, individuals generally formulate their intellectual, religious,
and interpersonal ideas (among many others) by accepting or rejecting social
mores (including those that have created the immediate physical conditions
surrounding the individual). Introspection is the process of assimilating or
repudiating—in essence, interpreting—these signals. This means, paradoxically,
that difference, even to the point of violent revolution, stems from the same
signals that produce conformity. Most societies, however, generally view
difference in pejorative terms.

The preceding argument obviously has limitations in scope. For instance,
it treats "society" as a closed system; it neatly differentiates cultures and assumes
autonomy. This thesis does not account for those societies dominated by
imperialist powers, nor does it acknowledge positive interchanges between
cultures. Interpretive communities, however theoretically complex, appear
marked by extreme provincialism. In their very efforts to label and categorize—
even if the meanings of such signifiers are deemed "indeterminate"—interpretive
communities tend to alienate one another. A closed system, no matter how
ostensibly dynamic and all-encompassing, proves essentially incomplete and
naive. Hermeneutical strategies that fail to embrace the "Other" automatically,
albeit implicitly, create a hierarchy in which the strategy itself has a privileged
position.

The role of the Western critic has shifted from interpreter of texts for the
public to interpreter of texts for other interpreters of texts—a closed system.
Notice that the "dialogues" over books generally take place in journals with
extremely low circulations; hence the average individual finds her/himself

excluded from the process (or scholars ignore her/his input as "uninformed"). Paul de Man writes of theoretical movements (i.e., interpretive communities) that "they are, at times, centered on a single, dominating personality and take on all the exalted exclusiveness of a secret society, with its rituals of initiation and hero-worship" (54). Irony notwithstanding, de Man's notion that the supercritic approximates a religious figure finds a parallel in Said:

> We have reached the stage at which specialization and professionalization, allied with cultural dogma, barely subli-mated ethnocentrism and nationalism, as well as a surpris-ingly insistent quasi-religious quietism, have transported the professional and academic critic of literature—the most fo-cused and intensely trained interpreter of texts produced by the culture—into another world altogether. (25)

Academia no longer views texts as processes that change individuals or provide impetuses for action; instead, many critics clinically analyze them, claiming that communication proves impossible because words cannot capture essence. Rand Bishop asserts that the "overriding concern for extra-aesthetic considerations is perhaps, for the Westerner, the single most troublesome aspect of ... African literary criticism" (176). For many Western critics, history is taboo, because, in the words of Derrida, "the written signifier is always technical and representa-tive. It has no constitutive meaning" (11).

What, however, does this argument have to do with Ngũgĩ, the text, Mugo? Regardless of the fact that many commentators separate representations from their historical moment(s), certain theorists do have goals that align them with the non-academic public. In the West, feminists, Marxists, and minority critics (among others) do not want to interpret merely for interpretation's sake. They desire to change the world by raising public consciousness. Although even these critics contribute to elitist journals, their articles challenge the academic institution and attempt to change it. In this regard, these "radical" critics have much in common with postcolonial theorists. Many postcolonial critics have agendas other than tenure or upward mobility. They desire to function as a social force and eliminate neocolonial oppression. Mutiso writes that "in African societies art has traditionally been highly functional" (9). The critic/artist does not merely have a concern for aesthetics; s/he has a concern for politics (of which aesthetics merely constitutes one element). This concept makes Ngũgĩ cry out,

"Let our pens be the voices of the people. Let our pens give voices to the silent" (*Barrel* 69). Similarly, Chineweizu declares, "*literary criticism* is ultimately a branch of *social criticism*" (303). Despite claims to the contrary, written language *does* have meaning for most people. It reinforces, destroys, or creates belief, and belief manifests itself in *action*. We should stress the human element in literature once more. Emmanuel Ngara concurs:

> The Meaning of a work of art is ... not purely cognitive, it is emotive, it is affective; it is not subject to a purely rational analysis. A purely rational analysis of literature cannot do justice to literature, for literature is not scientific, and so a purely scientific approach to literature can only kill the writer's creative effort. (11)

This is why I shall read *Grain* not as an affirmation of the indeterminate nature of language, but as a document of the fear and uncertainty that arises from the brutal domination of one "interpretive community" over another.

If one decides to eschew poststructural theory, how can one interpret the novel's textual gaps? Before one may answer this question, the critic must first attempt to convince the reader that these abstract lacunae actually exist, and that they indeed prove central to the experience of reading the book. In *Barrel of a Pen*, a collection of essays from 1983, Ngũgĩ, though properly horrified and outraged at neocolonial injustice, seems indignant not so much at the perpetrators of evil deeds as at those who remain silent in the face of inequity. "The sad truth," Ngũgĩ muses,

> is that the neocolonial regime (under Kenyatta and Moi) has arrogantly betrayed everything for which our people have struggled for because it has been able to count on the silence of us Kenyans. (3)

Ngũgĩ chastises those who collaborate with the oppressor not with their actions, but with their inaction; the government uses the voicelessness of the public as a means of oppression. One major source of power, therefore, lies in the exclusiveness of government discourse. It disseminates information with little opposition; hence an illusion of unquestioned authority arises (the government interprets silence as tacit approval). Sensing a mandate, the government continues its ways without fear of retaliation. Ngũgĩ thus claims, "silence before the crimes of the neocolonial regime in Kenya is collusion with social evil" (1). Suppressing one's voice is tantamount to treason.

Ngũgĩ published *Grain* in 1967, well before the essays in *Barrel*. One may detect, however, an almost uncanny similarity between the two texts, for silence and communication serve as the crux for both books. While Ngũgĩ overtly mentions silence as an abettor of neocolonial injustice in *Barrel*, its presence seems more covert in the novel. Ngũgĩ pays extremely close attention to the modulation of his characters' voices. The author tells the reader on virtually every page that "the appeal in her eyes and voice belied the calm face" (*Grain* 29) or that Gikonyo spoke "almost in a whisper" (69). Additionally, the characters constantly appear on the *verge* of saying something. Ultimately, however, they say nothing: "They were on the brink of change, she reflected, and still he would not talk" (52) or "She opened her mouth as if to shout" (30). Gitogo, a deaf and dumb character, dies because he cannot declare his innocence. Furthermore, as previously stated, the novel's fragmented form itself serves as an impediment to communication, forcing the reader to develop opinions about characters before the novel reveals key information. Most readers, for example, will initially empathize with Mugo, even though later evidence establishes him as a traitor. Silence and lack of silence also play a role in regards to the oath. The concept of the oath provides a framework for Ngũgĩ's concerns:

> The detainees had agreed not to confess the oath, or give any details about Mau Mau: how could anybody reveal the binding force of the Agĩkũyũ in their call for African freedom? (105)

Most, of course, eventually confess the oath, causing the freedom fighters to doubt themselves and their worth; Mugo gains his exalted reputation because he did not "confess" the oath. Silence, therefore, definitely has a tangible presence in *Grain*.

The question of how to interpret this silence remains. I believe that the breakdowns in communication in *Grain* have their sources in colonization. By violently imposing their "interpretive community" (with its accompanying value, language, and religious systems) over those of the villages that now constitute Kenya, the British imperialists have rendered interpersonal communication dysfunctional. Three of the manifestations of this impaired social intercourse are a fragmented community, mental anguish/fear, and a hesitancy to hope. Each of these phenomena contributes to a deafening silence, for as Ngara states, "there is so much suffering, so much pain, that reticence and not shouting is the only way to express what one feels deep down" (83). Rather than launch into a prolonged jeremiad, Ngūgī's characters emphasize the extent of their torment by remaining mute. In analyzing the three rubrics, one can begin to glean the source of this and why it should be overcome.

It is self-evident that the colonizing force destroys the existing communal state of the colonized. Even if the imperialist powers employ a "laissez-faire" system of colonization—allowing autonomy in domestic affairs—the social system of the colonized nonetheless still finds itself drastically altered. The authority of the previous rulers seems hollow when juxtaposed with that of the new rulers; hence the people might begin to look toward the colonizers for answers to particularly difficult problems (witness, for example, how characters seek out Thompson for advice). The situation also psychologically affects the subalterns, because although the imperialists *appear* peaceful, the community cannot overlook the threat of violence. The people must constantly "look over their shoulders" to see if the mood of the oppressors has changed. Other affected areas—for example, freedom of movement, foreign policy, and freedom of expression—would further distort the pre-colonial social structure.

If a relatively peaceful colonization process has such far-reaching repercussions, imagine, then, what ravaging effects a violent implementation of imperialism (the norm, of course) inflicts on a society. At the most basic level, the authority of the village becomes displaced. Power is no longer distributed collectively; it now manifests itself centrally, individually. Whenever power rests within a specific individual, some people obsequiously try to earn the favor of that authority. This propensity increases dramatically when this bureaucrat controls one's very existence. Colonization, therefore, pits neighbor against neighbor in the struggle to survive: lackey versus rebel. A further effect is that the "master discourse" demeans the native language and negates its authority. The discourse of power, the colonial tongue, forces people to begin to doubt the effectiveness of their own language. The rhetoric of colonial schools, where teachers establish the "superiority" of the imperialist language as empirical fact, reinforces this doubt. Ngūgī elaborates:

> To control a people's culture is to control their tools of self-
> definition in relationship to others. For colonialism this

involved two aspects of the same process: the destruction or the deliberate undervaluing of a people's culture, their art, dances, religions, history, geography, education, orature and literature, and the conscious elevation of the language of the coloniser. (*Decolonising* 16)

In essence, the colonizers maintain an enforced silence through the privileging of their own aesthetic and moral codes. While Ngũgĩ wrote the preceding passage in 1986, one may easily recognize its tenets in *Grain* when the Teacher Muniu (acting as an agent of colonialism), faced with irrefutable evidence brought forth by young Kihika, must establish his imperialist interpretation of the Bible with corporal punishment. The whipping quite "convinces" those members of the class without Kihika's resolve that the reading is indeed correct, and the British interpretive community establishes its dominance once more, as most of the students are afraid to speak. Communication based on doubt and fear hardly communicates anything at all. Rather, such an intercourse usually seems hesitant and weak. Often it simply cannot exist: silence reigns. Ngũgĩ illustrates the consequences of these upheavals in community and language in *Grain*.

Rather than attempt to analyze each character's silence and failure to communicate—and to some degree each character *does* fail at communication—I will concentrate on Mugo. Ngũgĩ immediately brings Mugo's fragile mental state to the reader's attention: "Mugo felt nervous" (1). In many ways Mugo remains nervous throughout the entire book. Ngũgĩ develops Mugo through a series of negatives: he will not speak at the rally; he will not confess at the camp; he will not admit that he betrayed Kihika (until his confession to Mumbi); he will not talk. Mugo's reticence does not represent the self-control or inner peace of the sage (although the village interprets it as such). Rather, it functions as a manifestation of deep-rooted mental anguish. Most readers cannot fail to develop the opinion that something emotionally torments Mugo, as Ngũgĩ's descriptions leave little room for doubt: "Mugo's throat was choked; if he spoke he would cry" (23) and "[Mugo's] mouth was dry; thoughts and words refused to form" (123). Mugo appears incapable of communicating to the villagers; other people must practically force him to speak (and even this does not always work). Ngũgĩ, moreover, parallels Mugo with both Gitogo, the deaf mute, and Moses, who had doubts about his capacity for speech. In essence, Mugo has lost his voice, and with it his confidence.

Mugo's verbal paralysis echoes his physical paralysis. The initial dream sequence foreshadows this impotence: "He tried to move his head: it was firmly chained to the bed-frame" (1). The mental pain that plagues Mugo has other ramifications than silence. Later one sees Mugo attempting to speak with his aunt, but, lacking the courage, he fails:

> ... he again felt another desire to see her. There was a bond between her and him, perhaps because she, like him, lived alone. At the door he faltered, his resolution wavered, broke, and he found himself hurrying away, fearing that she would call him back.... (6)

Despite his intentions, something within Mugo prevents him from acting; village life seems alien to him, and he retreats into a self-imposed exile. Although he no longer must reside in a prison camp, he creates a cell from out of his own unuttered desires. Mugo's paralysis manifests itself in other ways as well. Mugo's shamba seems poorly run; he lacks the drive to make his land productive, even though as a young man he dreamt of getting ahead. He seems economically isolated from the rest of the people. Furthermore, Mugo has no intimate relationships. Much of *Grain* centers on the tensions—both sexual and emotional—that arise from personal interaction. Mugo does not respond well to efforts at intimacy. Even Mumbi's overtures are in vain. Finally, even Mugo's important status in the revolutionary cause finds its basis in inaction. Mugo did not confess (at one point he stutters meekly to Kihika that "I–I have never taken the oath" [192]); therefore the people lionize him as a "hero" and a "leader," composing songs and tales about Mugo's supposed virtues. Ironically, Mugo does nothing tangible for the struggle (in the manner of General R., for example), but instead unwittingly assumes a figurehead position. Mugo's inaction equals his silence, a fact Mugo himself recognizes when he listens to Kihika's speech:

> Mugo felt a constriction in his throat. He could not clap for words that did not touch him. What right had such a boy, probably younger than Mugo, to talk like that? What arrogance? Kihika had spoken of blood as easily as if he was talking of drawing water in a river.... I hate him.... (15)

Mugo's rage seems targeted not so much at Kihika's politics than at his eloquence. Kihika has a remarkable gift for oration, something that Mugo lacks. Kihika's self-confidence enables him to speak fluidly, whereas Mugo's confusion and self-doubt render him mute and politically impotent.

It is no wonder, then, that Mugo betrays Kihika, although even Mugo's collaboration with the imperialists displays a marked lack of speech and commitment:

> "I know—" he gulped down saliva. Panic seized him. He
> feared that the voice would fail him. "I know," he said quietly,
> "I know where Kihika can be found tonight." (199)

Mugo stutters, repeats himself, and finds himself almost paralyzed before he can utter his fateful message. Mugo's language fails him within the community of the oppressor as well as in his own community. His tentative steps toward speech reveal a pattern in which communication is constantly aborted. Even years later, when Mugo could serve the cause of Uhuru, he questions his ability to communicate, and assumes that the elders desire to trick him:

> Yes ... they want me ... me ... to make a speech ... praise Kihika
> and ... all that ... God ... I have never made a speech ... oh,
> yes! ... I have ... they said so ... said it was a good one ... Ha! ha!
> ha! ... told them lies upon lies ... they believed ... Anybody ... why
> me ... me ... me ... want to trap me .... (64; Ngũgĩ's ellipsis)

Notice that even Mugo's thoughts and memories display an extreme fragmentation. Mugo appears quite bewildered in remembering a time when his language could affect others. In fact, he transfers authority to "them," not even believing his own powers of recall. In sum, Mugo cannot talk with even himself, much less interact with the village's people.

Many societies would ostracize a man such as Mugo. Communities often perceive an inability or unwillingness to communicate as rudeness or conceit. Similarly, they also generally view a person who lacks the drive to work or reproduce as socially useless (witness Unoka in *Things Fall Apart*). In *Grain*, however, society neither shuns nor ridicules Mugo: it reveres and loves him as a legend. Further complicating this paradox is the fact that the people later discover Mugo to have betrayed the village's greatest martyr—Kihika. Why has this silent individual assumed such a level of importance in the village?

I contend that Ngũgĩ did not fail to recognize the irony of placing an alienated individual in a position of central importance and that Mugo personifies the village itself. Michael Vaughan states that "Mugo's consciousness contains the truth of the individual lives of the community" (31). I believe that Vaughan's statement is essentially correct, for all three elements of impaired social intercourse (fragmented community, mental anguish, and hesitancy to hope) appear present to an extreme degree in Mugo. Thaibai has become disjointed due to the presence of the British colonizers. Authority is centralized in figures such as Thompson, a man who views the Africans as little more than animals. Others, like Dr. Lynd, humiliate the villagers and destroy their confidence. Many people are impotent against these imperialists because the specter of the gun looms behind their rhetoric. Some, like Kihika, have the courage to die proudly for the freedom of the collective, but many, like Mugo and Karanja, value individual survival above all else, including loyalty to their people. Neighbor betrays neighbor, wife betrays husband, friend betrays friend, all in an effort to maintain personal welfare. Karanja becomes a toady not out of malice, but out of fear. The threat of physical violence leads to suppressed language or attempts to learn the "master" discourse. People cannot talk openly for fear of retribution or betrayal. The torture that occurs before the mass confessions of the oath illustrates the utter futility of resisting: the will is "silenced" as the prisoners are forced to speak.

Thaibai thus seems a parody of its past glory. No longer do people gather in the center of the village to talk; they now go to the railroad station, the very heart of imperialism. Mugo, too, functions as a caricature. The fear and alienation that mark the village manifest themselves in Mugo in exaggerated proportions. Like Karanja, Mugo has become an imperialist lackey. Mugo's betrayal, however, seems far greater than Karanja's, because Kihika in many ways symbolizes the hope of the village (i.e. Mugo attempts to destroy much more than an individual in betraying Kihika). Mumbi and Gikonyo's failure to communicate is also represented in Mugo; both characters open up to Mugo, but the silent man cannot help them with the healing process, and, indeed, only serves as a reminder that relationships are extremely fragile in an atmosphere of fear and suspicion. Similarly, General R.'s doubt at the worth of his contributions to the cause finds an echo in Mugo's assertion that "I am not a fit man to lead them" (154). Mugo thus embodies all of the village's problems.

By placing the village's hope in Mugo, Ngũgĩ ultimately makes it clear that the system created by the imperialists is but an illusion of a society. Fear and loathing can create nothing positive in the long run. R.L. Townsend asserts, "Mugo's desired isolation" is "destructive in terms of the corporate struggle" (51). While this certainly seems a valid reading, one may also posit that Mugo's negative characteristics ultimately function in a positive fashion. After they discover that Mugo has committed treason, the villagers must look within themselves. Mugo serves as a mirror in which one may find the worst traits of Thaibai's people, as well as the emotional wounds that the imperialists have inflicted upon the community. Gikonyo, for example, asks of himself, "what difference is there between [me] and Karanja or Mugo or those who had openly betrayed people and worked with the whiteman to save themselves?" (245). By destroying Mugo, however, the village can shatter the mirror and survive. Mugo becomes a target against which the community can unite, a reluctant healer. Interestingly, a communal voice narrates much of the final portions of the text— including the reader's first explanation of Mugo's treason. The unity that eludes the village for much of the novel starts to surface toward the end. Even Gikonyo and Mumbi make overtures at a dialogue: "What has passed between us is too much to be passed over in a sentence. We need to talk, to open our hearts to one another ... " (247). Ultimately, Ngũgĩ has the villagers reify Mugo—first as pure beneficence then finally as pure evil—so that the village itself does not have to suffer total annihilation. Mugo will also live on as a symbol of that which may arise out of imperialism, a reminder for those who would betray their country for the sake of neocolonial avarice. Silence in the face of oppression can rarely succeed. By destroying the silent qualities that Mugo represents, the village can prosper once more. In essence, Mugo symbolizes the "grain of wheat" that must die in order to create. Gikonyo's stool carved with a "woman big—big with child" proves that Mugo's death is indeed regenerative (247).

Notes

[1] I would like to extend my thanks to Harveen Mann and Kenneth Womack for reading early drafts of this essay.

[2] Ngũgĩ writes, "The choice of language and the use to which language is put is central to a people's definition of themselves in relation to their natural and social environment, indeed in relation to the entire universe" (*Decolonising* 4).

Works Cited

Bishop, Rand. *African Literature, African Critics*. New York: Greenwood, 1988.

Chinweizu, et al. *Toward the Decolonization of African Literature*. Washington, D.C.: Howard UP, 1983.

de Man, Paul. *The Resistance to Theory*. Minneapolis: U of Minnesota P, 1986.

de Saussure, Ferdinand. *Course in General Linguistics*. New York: McGraw-Hill, 1966.

Derrida, Jacques. *Of Grammatology*. Baltimore: Johns Hopkins UP, 1976.

Fish, Stanley. *Is There a Text in This Class?*. Cambridge: Harvard UP, 1980.

Harrow, Kenneth. "Ngũgĩ wa Thiong'o's A Grain of Wheat." *Research in African Literatures* 16 (1985): 243-63.

Mutiso, G-C. *Socio-Political Thought in African Literature*. London: Macmillan, 1974.

Ngara, Emmanuel. *Stylistic Criticism and the African Novel*. London: Heinemann, 1982.

Ngũgĩ wa Thiong'o. *Barrel of a Pen*. Trenton: Africa World P, 1983.

—. *Decolonizing the Mind*. London: James Currey, 1986.

—. *A Grain of Wheat*. London: Heinemann, 1967.

Said, Edward. *The World, the Text, and the Critic*. Cambridge: Harvard UP, 1983.

Townsend, R.L. "The Heroism of Mugo." *Fort Hare Papers* 8.2 (1987): 46-53.

Vaughan, Michael. "African Fiction and Popular Struggle." *English in Africa* 8.2 (1981): 23-52.

Williams, Katherine. "Decolonising the World: Language, Culture, and Self in the Works of Ngũgĩ wa Thiong'o and Gabriel Okara." *Research in African Literatures* 22.4 (1991): 53-61.

I thiomi cia kiiriu, thiomi cia uthitarabu na uthii na mbere ta King'enu, Giitariani, Kiibaranja, na Kiinjeremaani? ... One ningi njiongirabi! Wee ndwendaga kumenya njuui cia ruraaya; irima cia ruraaya; ndia cia ruraaya; miti ya ruraaya! Wendaga ati wambe umenye uhoro wa njuui na irima na ndia na miti na miumbire yoothe ya guku kwanyu. Ugakiuhinga ri? Njiira.
(Ngugi 1982 a: 3)

[... when will you learn to speak civilized languages like English, French, or German?... Now come to geography, you are not interested in knowing the rivers, mountains, lakes, and trees of Europe .... You say that you want to first know those rivers, mountains and animals in your own country. When will you ever learn?]

Simon Gikandi

Moments of Melancholy: Ngũgĩ and the Discourse of Emotions

> I came back after the first term and confidently walked back to my old village. My home was now only a pile of dry mudstones, bits of grass, charcoal and ashes. Nothing remained, not even the crops, except for a lone pear tree that slightly swayed in sun and wind. I stood there bewildered. Not only my home, but the old village with its culture, its memories and its warmth had been razed to the ground. (*Detained: A Writer's Prison Diary*)

I T IS DIFFICULT to forget the intense moments of melancholy—and the emotion of loss—that permeate the life and works of Ngũgĩ wa Thiong'o. It is even more difficult to forget the numerous ways in which the discourse of emotions generates his most powerful narratives of self and nation, of culture and tradition, of place and exile. We are, of course, familiar with this discourse because we have encountered it in the romance of the landscape and the sentiment of contested histories in Ngũgĩ's early novels (*The River Between* and *Weep Not, Child*), whose very titles denote the hiatus that positions historical loss and nationalist desire in an ambivalent narratorical relationship. We have also encountered the discourse of loss in many of Ngũgĩ's germinal artistic moments, at crucial junctions of ideological change and artistic transfiguration. We have often heard how the novelist's moments of loss have provided him with sites of self-reflection and knowledge: we know from reading *Decolonizing the Mind* and *Detained*, for example, that Ngũgĩ's decision to write a novel in Gĩkũyũ was an act of defiance against his imprisonment.

In reading Ngũgĩ's works, then, we are abound to encounter an important confluence of emotion and range in which the novelist, in an attempt to analyze and mediate his imprisonment in colonial culture and the postcolonial dictatorship, falls back on the emotions generated by his experiential situation.

We cannot, in short, forget the melancholy that marks key autobiographical moments in Ngũgĩ's works as he struggles to account for his own emplacement in the colonial tradition and his displacement from his ancestral culture. In reading Ngũgĩ's works, then, we are abound to encounter an important confluence of emotion and range in which the novelist, in an attempt to analyze and mediate his imprisonment in colonial culture and the postcolonial dictatorship, falls back on the emotions generated by his experiential situation.

So why is it that in reading Ngũgĩ's novels—and more specifically his narrative strategies—we rarely reflect on the ideological and narrative implications of this discourse of emotions? Why are we so eager to read his novels according to the positivist schema he has assiduously promoted in his later essays at the expense of the emotive moments that have generated such works? Why is it that even when we try to understand the function of emotions in Ngũgĩ's works we are still prisoners of an epistemology of reading which considers the analysis of subjectivity to be an unwelcome corruption of the ideological? Why are we so resistant to any mode of reading that positions the moment of melancholy as the enabling condition of Ngũgĩ's ideological and narrative practices? I want to begin this essay on the relation of ideology and the discourse of emotions in Ngũgĩ's work by reading a very localized moment of melancholy and rage in the author's own experiences.

1

Readers of Ngũgĩ's prison notes will recall that innocuous—and clearly oxymoronic instance—when the figure of Lazarus intrudes and deflates a highly-charged denunciation of the politics of neo-colonialism in Kenya:

> Colonial Lazarus raised from the dead: this putrid spectre of our recent history haunted us daily at Kamĩtĩ Prison. It hovered over us, its shadow looming larger and larger in our consciousness as days and nights rolled away without discernible end to our suffering. We discussed its various shades and aspects, drawing on our personal experiences, often arriving at clashing interpretations and conclusions. Who raised colonial Lazarus from the dead to once again foul the fresh air of Kenya's dawn? (63)

Lazarus appears in *Detained* as a figuration of a comprador bourgeoisie trying to resurrect "the imagined grandeur and dubious dignity of colonial culture"; for this African ruling class, "Arise colonial Lazarus" is the "celebratory call to divine worship at the holy shrines of imperialism" (62). For Ngũgĩ, then, a "Colonial Lazarus" raised from the dead becomes the symbol of what he denounces as the corrupt history of the postcolony.

But there is something missing in Ngũgĩ's symbolic economy: in spite of the obvious connection he makes between a common biblical figure and the cultural ideologies of the postcolony, the deployment of Lazarus appears revisionist in a very arbitrary way; the symbol of suffering and death seems out of place in a discourse on power and domination. For irrespective of the iconographic schema we adopt, it is difficult to associate Lazarus with power and oppression; his very name resonates with forms of ennoblement and melancholy that would seem to contradict Ngũgĩ's satirical intentions. In Christian doctrine, as most readers will recall, Lazarus of Bethany is one of the most prominent symbols of the possibility of hope, of resurrection and renewal: his name (Eleazor, in Hebrew) means "God has helped"; his tomb functions, in the Western iconographic tradition, as the site of affirmation and homage, not grief.

Ngũgĩ's deployment of Lazarus as the icon of power and corruption appears even more arbitrary if we recall that since the 1920s, the Africanized Christian Churches of Central Kenya have used the figure of Lazarus (Lazaro in the Gĩkũyũ bible), as a symbolic—and quite dramatic—site for representing the emotions of loss and the possibility of redemption. In the hermeneutics of both mainstream (Protestant) and Karĩng'a (independent) churches in Central Kenya, Lazarus of Bethany is both the man of sorrows and of hope; he is valorized (more than even Job) as the symbol of the people's suffering under the yoke of colonialism and of their inevitable emancipation from the strictures of empire.

And yet, there is a sense in which what appears to be Ngũgĩ's vulgarization of Lazarus, when read in terms of the emotions it generates, does not deviate from earlier deployments of this figure in cultural discourse in Central Kenya. For no sooner has he associated Lazarus with the resurrection of imperial culture, than Ngũgĩ falls back on the melancholia of loss, displacement and betrayal which connects him, from his spot in a maximum security prison, to earlier generations of cultural nationalists. "Who raised Lazarus from the dead to once again foul the fresh air of Kenya's dawn?" The question is not important because of the apparent misuse of Lazarus, but the emotion behind it and the sentiments it provokes. For as Ngũgĩ and his fellow detainees struggle to answer this question, they discover that while it may provoke different ideological responses and diverse rationalizations of the political situation in Kenya, it eventually crystallizes around a common feeling of "historical betrayal," "mounting despair," and "bitter reflections" (63).

And so, despite his new robe of identity as the symbol of colonial reversion, Lazarus still remains in the reader's mind as the man of sorrows and of hope. Indeed, as Ngũgĩ's readers become engaged with these emotions, the value of the Lazarus figure is secured, in a subliminal way, by a more traditional iconography: as the voices of suffering prisoners foreground the dual images of oppression and resurrection, the colonial Lazarus seems to fade in the background. In the process, the reader is forced—almost subconsciously—to sublimate the imperial Lazarus to a more familiar symbol of suffering. A touching melancholic moment is superimposed on the allegory of a resurrected colonial culture.

More profoundly, Ngũgĩ does not rationalize his radical revision of Christian iconography, nor does he seem to connect the somatics of Lazarus to the semantics of cultural imperialism: he proceeds, instead, to develop a rhetorical program in which the emotions of sorrow and hope contextualize his cultural and historical imprisonment. Emotions become a string that allows Ngũgĩ to connect his cultural imprisonment to a previous historical moment defined by similar sentiments: he sees his situation mirrored in the experiences of cultural nationalists from the 1930s who, like Ngũgĩ in the 1970s, had their songs and dances banned, and yet continued to chant "their patriotic songs of protest and commitment to freedom" (65).

Now, emotions are by their very nature abstract, but here they enable the author to recover and concretize historical memories: Ngũgĩ recalls authors of "Mau Mau" songs who were banished to "detention camps, prisons and cruel deaths" in the 1950s, but who "even behind the barbed wire and stone walls of the colonial Jericho" went on composing new songs and "singing out a collective patriotic defiance that finally brought those walls tumbling down" (66). Imprisoned in his own cell in Kamĩtĩ prison, Ngũgĩ recalls—and reads—these earlier moments of cultural imprisonment in order to convert his melancholia into a gesture of defiance:

> We are not afraid of detention
> Or of being sent to prison
> Or of being sent to remote islands
> For we shall never give up
> Our struggle for Land/Freedom

Kenya is an African people's country (66)

For Ngũgĩ, this "Mau Mau" song generates the cultural defiance he needs to counter the threat that the prison—the most visible symbol of perverse power in the postcolony—poses to his body and mind.

And yet, as anyone who has heard this famous song sung by old nationalists will attest, its overt rhetoric—a rhetoric of defiance and empowerment—always seems to be at variance with its melancholic tone. I cannot forget the strange feelings evoked by this song when I first it heard as a little boy: it was in 1962, the year of self-government and hence nationalist arrival; Kenyatta had become prime minister and we had gone to witness the return of a group of nationalist activists from guerrilla camps and detention centers; we were certainly struck by the words of defiance and resistance in their song, but we were also overwhelmed by the feelings of sadness and loss carried by those voices in what should have been a moment of celebration. I was to hear the song sung on many occasions and contexts (including important state occasions), but I never heard it—or any other "Mau Mau" song, for that matter—sung without a note of melancholy even when the lyrics advocated resistance.

Ngũgĩ is certainly right to argue that such songs generate courage and defiance and pride, but they also seem to raise a troublesome question: why is the discourse of resistance and national restitution in Central Kenya—like Ngũgĩ's own fictional discourse—generated by what Julia Kristeva has called a "melancholy moment"—"an actual or imaginary loss of meaning, an actual and imaginary despair, an actual or imaginary razing of symbolic values including the value of life"? (128).

2

I want to call attention to the place of such melancholy moments in Ngũgĩ's works—and the emotions they proffer—for two reasons: First we need to question the efficacy of some of the most dominant paradigms for reading these works. We need to break out of the empirical schema in which Ngũgĩ's works are often read, sometimes with the author's encouragement, as vehicles for explicit ideological intentions: this mode of reading assumes that these works are produced under an explicit theoretical and social program (Marxism) in which the modes of cultural production (materialism) are expressed in a synchronic form (realism). What Renalto Rosado has called the "cultural force of emotions" would seem to have no place in this schema. Secondly, Ngũgĩ's theory of literature seems suspicious of subjectivity, the emotional idiom, and affect. Because his most powerful essays privilege historicity, objectivity, and externalize representation, he would be wary of the premise that underlines most studies of emotion as a "form of social action that creates effects in the world, effects that are read in a culturally informed way by the audience for emotion talk" (Abu-Lughod and Lutz 12).

But as my iconoclastic reading of the Lazarus episode in *Detained* suggests, the discourse of emotions constitutes an important subtext in Ngũgĩ's works masked by an overt rhetoric that promotes an authorial *theoria* which is, nevertheless, sustained by emotive figures and melancholy moments. It is when we pay attention to this subtext that we realize the extent to which Ngũgĩ uses emotive figures not merely for affect, but also to position the writing self in its cultural bearings while accounting for the textualization of the historical and autobiographical event. In addition, if the emotion of loss seems dominant in Ngũgĩ's early works, it is because of the condition from which these texts simultaneously arise from and refer to: these are texts seeking to account for their liminal emplacement between colonial and postcolonial culture, striving for a language and strategy in which they can express, as de Certeau would say, the subject's foreignness in its natal landscape (320).

In Ngũgĩ's early novels, as numerous readers have noted, the landscape is more than the signature of colonial dispossession; it is also a fundamental mode for generating the melancholy that summons historicity and displays it in gestures of defiance and affirmation. As the case of Njoroge in *Weep Not, Child* illustrates so well, it is when the colonial subject engages with the emotions generated by its historical condition that it begins to grasp the gravity of its alienation and the necessity of an alternative narrative. It is only when the exigencies of history have forced him to confront his contingent situation—when his experiences come to him "as shocks that showed him a different world from what he had believed" (120)—that Njoroge gains insight into his true displacement by colonialism.

In addition, narrative knowledge in Ngũgĩ's works is realized through a dramatic rendering of the gap that separates the ideals that define colonial subjects and their actual fate in the theater of history. At the beginning of *The River Between*, for example, Waiyaki is taken to the top of the hill by his father; from here he surveys the landscape with a mixture of awe and bewilderment; he listens to his father's voice—"charged with strong feelings"—as the old man claims possession of the land, but the landscape seems to contain meanings the little boy cannot grasp:

> Chege was standing beside his son, but a few steps behind. He
> looked across the ridges, across the hills, gazing still into
> space, like a man in a vision. Perhaps he was looking at
> something hidden from Waiyaki. Waiyaki strained his eyes
> but could not see anything. Although he feared for his father,
> he was becoming overpowered by the words flowing from the
> old man. And his father spoke on, not really talking to
> Waiyaki, but rather talking to himself, speaking his feelings
> and thoughts aloud. As his voice vibrated, Chege seemed to
> gain in stature and appearance so that Waiyaki thought him
> transfigured. (17-18)

This scene contains important clues to the discourse of emotions in Ngūgī's
works: words in themselves are not vehicles of meanings; rather, it is the emotions
behind such words, and the conjunction of feelings and thoughts inherent in
such emotions, that promise the kind of transfiguration Waiyaki seeks in the
novel. Emotions are crucial to the constitution of knowledge and its narration
in another sense: it is only when characters like Waiyaki have become enchanted
by the beauty of the land from which they have been alienated that they can begin
to understand the meaning of colonialism. In such circumstances, it is the
emotion that Ngūgī invests in the land that creates the performative desire to
commemorate and historize its loss.

But the emotional force, as Renalto Rosaldo has reminded us, "derives less
from an abstract brute fact than from a particular intimate relation's intimate
rupture" (2). Such intimate ruptures occur frequently in Ngūgī's novels, but they
are most revealing when they are shown, in his own mode of analysis, to generate
his aesthetic. We find a quite explicit link between biographical rupture and
Ngūgī's aesthetic in the touching account of the transformation of his home
village under the state of emergency, the scene of return which I use as my
epigraph. Here, it is the violent rupture of the schoolboy from his natal
landscape—and the resulting feeling of loss and displacement—that generate the
theme of return in Ngūgī's fictional works: "Many critics have noted the
dominance of the theme of return in my novels, plays and short stories... . But
none has known the origins of the emotion behind the theme. It is deeply rooted
in my return to Kamīrīīthū in 1955. The return of Mau Mau political detainees

was to come later" (74).

To read the trope of return in Ngũgĩ's novels as simply the thematization of historical loss is to succumb to the seduction of the objective; for the historical event in a novel such as *A Grain of Wheat* cannot be conceptualized except within the emotions the history of colonialism generates in those who have lived. Those who read the historical event outside the emotions it generates fail to understand how history itself remains what Tom Conley would call an unmarked space, "an absence on which the visible evidence of the truth is based" (xix). Those who read the multiple gaps in this novel—the gap between the promise of Kĩhĩka and the mystery of his death, of Mũmbi's romantic aspirations and the brutality of life, and the promise of independence and its betrayal—as simple effects of history fail to realize how the narrative itself tries to mediate the gap between a repressed history and its ironic moment of return.

Let us consider, for example, the emotions behind some of the most famous scenes of return in *A Grain of Wheat*: On his release from detention, Gĩkonyo returns home eager to see Mũmbi and "take up the thread of his life where he had left it," but he walks into a landscape he can longer recognize; when he eventually finds his wife, he is shocked to discover that she has a child with Karanja, his childhood friend and ideological rival: "The years of waiting, the pious hopes, the steps on the pavement, all came rushing into his heart ... Life had no colour. It was one endless blank sheet, so flat" (114-115). It is on the moment of return—of the self's ostensible reconciliation with its landscape—that it becomes acutely aware of the repressed histories that govern its life, or the abyss that marks the site of historical desire.

Gĩkonyo tries to write Mũmbi's history into this abyss: he recreates her scene of seduction by Karanja "in its sordid details: the creaking bed; Karanja's fingers touching Mũmbi everywhere; their heavy breath merging into one—and, oh, Lord, the sighs, those sighs" (120). But as the reader soon finds out, the actual scene of seduction is quite different: Mũmbi gave in to Karanja only when she got news of Gĩkonyo's inevitable return; because her seduction arose out of her utter devotion to her husband, it cannot be considered an act of betrayal. The important point though is that Gĩkonyo's motives are triggered by what he thinks he knows about this absent history: without access to the real event, the carpenter allows his life to be governed by his imaginary inscription of the act of betrayal.

It hence seems that a repressed history cannot be recovered or be made visible except at that site in which "the repressed resurges as something seen as other, and recognizably different from what conveys it", at that moment in which history is "rewritten in the abyss between the idea of the repressed and the fear of its continuous return" (Conley xix). One could assume, for example, that the moment of independence marks the closure of the nationalist's eschatological plot, but at that moment when the truth of history should become explicit and its conflicts should be resolved, what strikes us is the absence of meaning and closure:

> In our village and despite the drizzling rain, men and women and children, it seemed, had emptied themselves into the streets where they sang and danced in the mud.... . Everybody waited for something to happen. This "waiting" and the uncertainty that went with it—like a woman torn between fear and joy during birth-motions—was a taut cord beneath the screams and the shouts and the laughter (203).

3

There is an even more profound connection between the emotion of loss and the ideas that dominate Ngũgĩ's narratives of the postcolonial condition; as he notes in his preface to *Secret Lives*, his creative autobiography is marked by the confluence of ideas and moods affecting the writer as he reflects on his historical situation: "My writing is really an attempt to understand myself and my situation in society and history. As I write I remember the nights of fighting in my father's house; my mother's struggle with the soil so that we might eat, have decent clothes and get some schooling.... . I remember the fears, the betrayals, Rachel's tears, the moments of despair and love and kinship in struggle and I try to find the meaning of it all through my pen." It is when the personal and the historical have been recalled, through the topography of emotions, that narration becomes possible; at the same time, however, it is the narration of "the memories of beauty and terror" that realizes the emotions that underwrite Ngũgĩ's conceptualization of the past. In both cases, however, there is no doubt that the discourse of emotions in Ngũgĩ's works seems to be the primary condition for recovering a history foreclosed from the self by the culture of empire and neo-colonialism.

As an undergraduate at Makerere University in 1960, for example, Ngũgĩ began to read African and West Indian writers, and to realize that "the song they sang, was different from what I had heard from the British writers who had been crammed down my throat in schools and at the University"; the African writers "spoke to me, they spoke about my situation. What was my situation?" (*Homecoming* 47-8). It is significant that African writers speak to Ngũgĩ through songs, for it is the shared community of feelings between the author and the texts he reads that gives such texts emotive and ideological value; by gesturing toward a common experience of loss, such texts clear a space in which the young writer can understand himself. The space of loss is also the space of memory and commemoration:

> One day I heard a song. I remember the scene so vividly: the women who sang it are now before me—their sad faces and their plaintive melody. I was then ten or eleven. They were being forcibly ejected from the land they occupied and sent to another part of the country so barren that people called it the land of black rocks. This was the gist of their song:
>
> > And there will be great great joy
> > When our land comes back to us
> > For Kenya is the country of black people.
> >
> > And you our children
> > Tighten belts around your waist
> > So you will one day drive away from this land
> > The race of white people
> > For truly, Kenya is a black man's country
>
> They were in a convoy of lorries, caged, but they had one voice. They sang of a common loss and hope and I felt their voice rock the earth where I stood literally unable to move. (48)

But this melancholy moment does not, in itself, constitute knowledge: "That song I heard as a child then spoke of things past and things to come. I was living in a colonial situation but I did not know it. Not even when I went to school" (49).

It is only when Ngũgĩ sees this emotion represented in the writings of other colonized writers that they become endowed with an epistemic value. It is, moreover, in the act of writing about the past that such emotive moments become both empathetic and epiphanic: the author, alienated from his peasant roots by his colonial education and culture, reproduces the voices of the subaltern by regenerating emotions from his past in his narratives; such acts of regeneration become, in turn, moments of intense self-realization which enable him to conceptualize the crisis of culture in colonial Kenya.

My argument here can be put in simpler terms: in trying to understand the colonial situation, Ngũgĩ does not deploy the rational discourse of a materialist historiography that we will later find in his novels and essays; instead, he falls back on his own phenomenal experiences to mediate the colonial situation of his childhood. Does this mean that the discourse of emotions is distinct from the modes of ideological analysis that Ngũgĩ would prefer as models for reading his novels and plays? What happens to the discourse of emotions when he explicitly adopts materialist forms of cultural analysis in his later works?

We can respond to these questions by recalling the traditional opposition between ideology and the discourse of emotions in social analysis:

> Tied to tropes of interiority and granted ultimate facticity by being located in the natural body, emotions stubbornly retain their place, even in all but the most recent anthropological discussions, as the aspect of human experience least subject to control, least constructed or learned (hence most universal), least public, and therefore least amendable to sociocultural analysis. (Abu-Lughod and Lutz 1)

In Ngũgĩ's later works, however, subjects are not capable of social analysis or even proper understanding until they are able to reconcile facticity (historical experience) with their own subjectivity. We find an excellent example of this reconciliation in a moving scene in *Petals of Blood* where Mũnira, having struggled to analyze the facts of his life without much success, recalls Wanfa's autobiographical narrative: "What struck him most, listening to her the other night, was the way her experiences took the form of stories, a kind of ballad of woes with a voice that demanded and compelled a hearing, and which ended by binding the listener even more to her life and fate" (139). It is through the utterance of the emotions concealed in the body that knowledge of the other is effected.

In addition, it is precisely because the discourse of emotions is not subject to censorship and control that it functions as an important instrument of cultural nationalism. And while this discourse has appeared least amendable to ideological analysis, it is, in its performative function, an important vehicle of social articulation. For how can we read Ngũgĩ's later plays except as powerful performances of history and ideology through emotions? After every performance of *The Trial of Dedan Kĩmathi* in Nairobi (1976-77), as I can attest from personal experience, the audience was not fixated by Kĩmathi's denunciation of colonialism as much as it was transfixed by an unforgettable melancholy moment in the play when a group of forest fighters sang the "Song of Kĩmathi":

> When our Kĩmathi ascended
> Into the mountain alone
> He asked for strength and courage
> To defeat the white man
>
> He said that we should tread
> The paths that he had trodden
> That we should follow his steps
> And drink from his cup of courage
>
> If you drink from this cup of courage
> The cup that I have drunk from myself
> It is a cup of pain and sorrow
> A cup of tears and death and freedom... (62-63)

This song connects the audience with Kĩmathi's drama and quest in ways his speeches cannot do: for while Ngũgĩ may conceive the nationalist hero as a figure of insurgency, his song deploys a Christian discourse already legitimized in the audience's mind; and while the performative moment is intended to prepare us for the hero's final gesture of defiance, the emotions of the song, the emotions of loneliness, of pain and sorrow, of death and freedom, momentarily fill the abyss between a repressed historicity and the fear of its return.

5

I want to conclude with a confession: I have always been attracted to Ngũgĩ's discourse of emotions more than his analysis of the economy of power in the postcolony; it is through reading his writing of suffering and sorrow that I was first able to fill the gaps between my own repressed historical moment (a colonial childhood) with the culture of my adolescence, a postcolonial culture whose most dominant emotion was the fear that the founding father might die and that the past of "trouble and grief" (*hingo ya thĩĩna*) might return.

I was born in the middle of the state of emergency in Kenya, and like many other families in the country, mine was marked by the facticity of the "Mau Mau" war: my maternal grandfather and great uncle had been killed in the conflict, most of my age-mates did not survive their first years in colonial encampments, otherwise known as villages. And yet when I was growing up, now in the full glow of independence and national restoration, nobody talked about these events from the past. It was not until I first read *Weep Not, Child* at the age of ten, that I could begin to pose questions about the repressed, now that it had made its way into a book, which, in my parent's Presbyterian culture, was the ultimate object of legitimation. I rarely got straight answers to my questions, but reading Njoroge's travails became an imaginary way of recovering the period that no one spoke about and the emotions that made it hard for those who had lived the immediate past to utter it.

From that moment on, emotive moments in Ngũgĩ's works could always provide a launching pad into forbidden areas of our culture and history: reading *The River Between* as an assigned text in junior high school made it possible for me to know more about the war between cultural nationalists and the church over the issue of "female circumcision," a war which nobody had mentioned to me although it was launched from my family's church, the Church of Scotland Mission at Tũmũtũmũ. As a child growing up in postcolonial Kenya, I had found it difficult to understand the sense of melancholy that surrounded the lives of former freedom fighters and political detainees, including prominent ones in my own extended family such as the Gĩkũyũ writer Gakaara wa Wanjaũ.

It was difficult for me to comprehend the contradictory moments of colonialism and postcolonialism, of its conflicting moments of "despair and love and kinship": Gakaara's father, the Reverend Wanjaũ, a prominent Presbyterian cleric had been killed by the "Mau Mau," but his son was to spend years in detention for his nationalist activities. It was by reading *A Grain of Wheat* and *Petals of Blood* that I began to mediate such contradictory moments. By the time I got to the University of Nairobi in 1976, I knew I wanted to be an intellectual because I had come to realize, through reading Ngũgĩ's works, that the politics of knowledge could ultimately determine the future of our society.

I was anticipating my second and third year at the university: I could finally take Ngũgĩ's popular course in the European Novel and partake of the debates that flowed from his seminars on materialism and cultural criticism. Alas! It was not to be: I woke up one morning to be confronted by newspaper headlines announcing that Ngũgĩ had been imprisoned. And so I shall never forgive "The Public Security (Detained and Restricted Persons Regulations 1966)" for having denied me my own epiphanic moment and for having burdened me with a year of melancholy and pain!

Works Cited

Abu-Lughod, Lila and Catherine A. Lutz. "Introduction: Emotion, Discourse, and the Politics of Everyday Life." *Language and the Politics of Emotion.* Ed. Catherine A. Lutz and Lila Abu-Lughod. Cambridge: Cambridge UP, 1990.

Certeau, Michel de. *The Writing of History.* Trans. Tom Conley. New York: Columbia UP, 1988.

Conley, Tom, "Translator's Introduction: *For A Literary Historiography.*" *The Writing of History:* vi-xxviii.

Kristeva, Julia. *Black Sun: Depression and Melancholia.* Trans. Leon S. Roudiez. New York: Columbia UP, 1989.

Ngũgĩ wa Thiong'o. *Detained: A Writer's Prison Diary.* London: Heinemann, 1981.

—. *Petals of Blood.* London: Heinemann, 1986 [1977].

—. *Homecoming: Essays on African and Caribbean Literature Culture and Politics.* Westport: Lawrence Hill, 1972.

—. *Secret Lives.* London: Heinemann, 1975.

—. *A Grain of Wheat.* London: Heinemann, 1986 [1977].

—. *The River Between.* London: Heinemann, 1965.

—. *Weep Not, Child.* London: Heinemann, 1987 [1964].

—. and Micere Mũgo. *The Trial of Dedan Kĩmathi.* London: Heinemann, 1976.

Rosaldo, Renato. *Culture and Truth: The Remaking of Cultural Analysis.* Boston: Beacon Press, 1989.

Joseph McLaren

Ideology and Form: The Critical Reception of *Petals of Blood*

THE LITERARY CONTRIBUTION of Ngũgĩ wa Thiong'o is substantially represented in his large body of fiction. As a successful and controversial author, Ngũgĩ has generated a considerable amount of critical commentary. His six novels have been particularly suited to critical analysis because of the strong political and historical dimensions which they present. Literary critics in the West and Africa have produced a counter-text, a body of interpretations which attempt to explain, evaluate and judge *The variety of critical re-* the merits of Ngũgĩ's fictional corpus.[1] This *sponses by critics in Eu-* large body of critical commentary is a sign *rope, the United States,* of the "preeminence of Ngũgĩ wa Thiong'o as *Canada, and Africa point* a writer articulating central issues for Afri- *to the far reaching effects* can literary culture" (Sicherman iv). *of Ngũgĩ's forceful politi-* From the onset of *cal assertions.* its publication in 1977 to the early 1990s, crit- ics have approached *Petals of Blood* with par- ticular attention to its ideological message, which reflects Ngũgĩ's support of a Marxist interpretation of history. Critics of the novel have addressed narrative perspective, presentation of characters, and plot techniques in relation to the novel's ideological framework. The immediate international reaction to the novel considered the viability of characterization in conjunction with authorial political intention. Although the bulk of support for the novel came from African critics, there was no uniform acceptance by African reviewers and literary scholars of Ngũgĩ's politicizing of certain characters. The essential criteria of assessment concerned the devices of "realistic" fiction and their validity in voicing political imperatives.

The variety of critical responses by critics in Europe, the United States, Canada, and Africa point to the far reaching effects of Ngũgĩ's forceful political assertions. The responses of Kenyan critics show both support and disapproval, revealing the controversial nature of the political novel and the continued debate regarding art as ideology.

Petals of Blood, one of the more complex and extended works of post-

Independence African fiction, provoked a much stronger critical reaction than did earlier novels by Ngũgĩ, such as *Weep Not, Child* (1964), *The River Between* (1965) and *A Grain of Wheat* (1967). As Ngũgĩ's fourth novel, *Petals of Blood* was a turning point in his conception of novelistic form and his presentation of political ideology of the left. The publication of the novel preceded Ngũgĩ's year-long detention, which began with his arrest on December 30, 1977, and, along with the staging of his play *Ngaahika Ndeenda* (*I Will Marry When I Want To*) in Limuru, was part of the literary-political background of his incarceration. After *Petals of Blood*, Ngũgĩ's works of fiction were written in Gĩkũyũ and were based more explicitly on devices of orature.

Petals of Blood showed Ngũgĩ's interest in historical memory through his retelling the interrelated stories of four main characters, Munira, Karega, Wanja and Abdulla, who, at the beginning of the novel, are suspected of having committed the murder of a number of wealthy businessmen. Using flashbacks and multiple narrative perspectives, Ngũgĩ details the metamorphosis of Ilmorog, a fictional village, as it is transformed by influences of neo-colonialism and the seduction of Western capital to the New Ilmorog in which the masses of the population are marginalized. The novel closes with the possibility of political organization by the working classes.

The European and North American Reception:

With the release of *Petals of Blood*, critics in the West began to review the work with particular attention to political ideology and novelistic form, often raising questions regarding the role of literary art. One of the first reviews to appear was Christopher Ricks's "Power Without Glory in Kenya," published in the June 26, 1977, issue of the London *Sunday Times*. Ricks was complimentary of Ngũgĩ's achievement and used the metaphor of power to explain the literary effects of the novel. *Petals* was hailed as a "remarkable" and "compelling" novel which was successful because of the way in which it presented political issues within the context of "other things" (Ricks 41). In using the metaphor of power, Ricks suggested the inherent power of art to transform: "art at work upon the old and the new to create something which is at once new and old ... " (41). Furthermore, *Petals of Blood* was innovative in its use of language despite its being written in traditional English prose.

Another response in the British press was offered by Homi Bhabha in the August 1977 issue of the *Times Literary Supplement*. The main critique was that traditional novelistic form was not an appropriate vehicle for a political message.

Bhabha suggested that Ngũgĩ "seems not to be embarrassed by the very sound of his most potent political message" (Bhabha 989). Bhabha investigated the principal conflict of the novel, the transformation of Ilmorog from a primarily agricultural village to an industrialized one. He also recognized the use of traditional story telling modes of African orature. It was, however, the question of literary form which most troubled Bhabha. Ngũgĩ's stylistic form, identified as the social realistic, was seen as contrary to the revolutionary socialism which was inherent in the novel's development (Bhabha 989). This critique related ideology to novelistic form, one of the overriding critical issues surrounding the novel.

In January of 1978, Hugh Dinwiddy in *African Affairs* connected Ngũgĩ's political ideas to those of Sekou Touré and Frantz Fanon (Dinwiddy 127). For Dinwiddy, Ngũgĩ was able to achieve a successful marriage of artistic form and political content. "It is a masterly book of long gestation: the tone is messianic" (128). Dinwiddy, however, suggested that in the ending of the novel, the "message, delivered with conviction, comes across: the points made for the detached observer, perhaps too simplistically" (129).

Françoise Albrecht's contribution to *Échos du Commonwealth* (1980-81), a French journal, explored the development of imagery. "Blood and Fire in *Petals of Blood*" traced the use of "blood" as image and metaphor, "the blood of life, the blood of the men and women who are the life-force of a village, the blood that flows away towards the town, putting the village in jeopardy." "Fire" is also a traceable motif in the novel, presented as an "ambivalent image" because it is sometimes a destroyer and other times "illuminates and purifies" (85-86).

Reviews in American publications also addressed the issue of political ideology. In the February 1978 *New York Times Book Review*, Charles Larson, who had published *The Emergence of African Fiction* (1971), commented sympathetically on Ngũgĩ's detention but saw *Petals* as weakened by the introduction of what he called "the author's somewhat dated Marxism: revolt of the masses; elimination of the black bourgeois; capitalism to be replaced by African socialism" (Larson, "Afric. Diss." 22). Nevertheless, Larson was especially praiseworthy regarding Ngũgĩ's treatment of Wanja and her relationships with her lovers.

Larson also reviewed *Petals* for *World Literature Today*. He complimented Ngũgĩ on certain aspects of the novel but again negatively viewed the use of political ideology (Larson, "Anglophone" 245-47). Unlike Homi Bhabha's review, Larson's did not comment on the use of form generated from a Western realistic tradition which had influenced Ngũgĩ's fictional style.

Later in 1978, *World Literature Today* continued its discussion of *Petals of Blood* in Andrew Salkey's review, which was essentially positive, acknowledging that the novel "satisfies both the novelist's political intent" as well as his artistic "obligation" (Salkey 681). However, Salkey did suggest that the story line was somewhat "crudely" presented and ironically "too compact." Other critics had commented on what they thought was the rambling nature of the novel. By January of 1979, shortly after Ngũgĩ's release from detention on December 12, 1978, the *New Republic* presented its review written by Paul Berman. Similar to the form of other reviews, it offered some explication of the text, suggesting that the plot "leans heavily on coincidence," the "Zola-esque" qualities viewed as positive. Ironically, this review ended with the comment, "This is an anti-imperialist novel, but it is not, properly speaking, anti-American" (40).

Well-known American novelist and short story writer John Updike reviewed *Petals* for *New Yorker* magazine in July of 1979. In a satirical manner, Updike suggested that Ngũgĩ's use of political issues detracted from his writing style. Updike remarked, "Whatever else political fervor has done for Ngũgĩ, it has not helped his ear for English; the fine calm style of 'A Grain of Wheat' ... has here come unhinged" (92). Was Updike suggesting that the novel was totally flawed stylistically or just the particular passage he chose to cite? Updike must certainly have been aware that Ngũgĩ's "political fervor" had resulted in Ngũgĩ's detention and that his own comment would ring with a facetious tone. Updike's remarks reflected a critical position which was insensitive to the larger political context surrounding Ngũgĩ's conscious ideological statements. The allusion to the "calm style" of Ngũgĩ's earlier fiction implied that strident narrative perspectives somehow weakened the fictional work.

Critical interest in *Petals of Blood* continued to be expressed into the mid-1980s by American journals.[2] *Research in African Literatures* devoted its Summer 1985 issue solely to Ngũgĩ. The issue contained Christine Pagnoulle "Ngũgĩ wa Thiong'o's 'Journey of the Magi': Part 2 of *Petals of Blood*," which pursued a close reading of the journey of the Ilmorog villagers to the "Big City," Nairobi, in search of social justice. Pagnoulle offered parallels to the Yeatsian theme inherent in the larger title of the section, "Toward Bethlehem." A mostly formalist reading, Pagnoulle's piece did contribute to the explication of *Petals* (Pagnoulle 264).

After 1985, the importance of *Petals of Blood* as a political novel resulted in its inclusion in works dealing specifically with ideological issues. George M.

Gugelberger's *Marxism and African Literature* (1986), an edited collection, offered a variety of perspectives on a range of African writings. Included in the collection was "The Second Homecoming: Multiple Ngūgīs in *Petals of Blood*," contributed by the Ugandan writer and critic Peter Nazareth. Nazareth's article summarized the essential structure of the novel and critiqued its form by posing a theory of authorial voices. For Nazareth, Ngūgī had presented three differing voices: the Ngūgī of "the village," who is "in pursuit of a deeper Christianity," the Ngūgī of secular "radical political ideas," (122) and the Ngūgī who is "struggling to be born but being resisted by the first two" (124). These "multiple Ngūgīs" often rivaled one another within the narrative structure. Nazareth also questioned Ngūgī's political intentions, accusing him of using cliches, especially in the closing of the novel. Ngūgī's plotting was also critiqued by Nazareth who suggested that the original plot intention of the novel, to discover the killer of Mzigo, Chui, and Kimeria, was not fulfilled. Nazareth cited examples which he thought showed a "failure of organic technique, an arbitrariness in the movement through time" (126). On the other hand, Nazareth recognized the effectiveness of the novel in conveying the results of colonialism and neocolonialism despite Ngūgī's lack of recognition of his multiple selves.

Published the same year as Gugelberger's work, Carol Boyce Davies and Anne Adams Graves's *Ngambika: Studies of Women in African Literature* (1986) also considered a specific critical issue, the presentation of women by African writers and the parameters of African feminist theory. A collaborative work by a Caribbean and an African-American critic, *Ngambika* included remarks on the broader issue of Ngūgī's treatment of female characters. Davies suggested that Ngūgī saw the "woman's struggle as inextricably intertwined with the total struggle" (Davies and Graves 11).

Ngūgī's commitment to political struggle in *Petals of Blood* continued to be a concern for Western critics of the 1980s. In 1986, in "The Politics of the Signifier: Ngūgī wa Thiong'o's *Petals of Blood*," which appeared in *World Literature Written in English*, a Canadian journal which published other commentaries on the novel, Stewart Crehan questioned the role of the literary critic who avoided considering the literary merits of *Petals of Blood*. He remarked, "Could it be that the moralistic urgency of *Petals of Blood* is so infectious that the resultant spiritual heat has led otherwise level-headed critics to throw certain critical criteria out of the window?" Crehan also suggested that Ngūgī's political status might have influenced critics to avoid negative appraisals of certain issues so as not to be labeled "agents of neo-colonialism" (Crehan 2). Crehan's comments indicated a critical perspective which challenged a reading of the novel that placed its political correctness above its literary accomplishments.

In contrast, one evaluative critique after 1985 contained little mention of political positions and was primarily a reader's guide to the novel. The appearance of K.B. Rao's "*Petals of Blood*" summary in *Masterplots II: British and Commonwealth Series* (1987) is an example of a critical context which offered a non-judgmental analysis, explicating the narrative as evidence of its standing in the canon of Commonwealth literature (Rao 1320-1324).

The interest in *Petals of Blood* by Commonwealth journals such as *World Literature Written in English* has been reflected in a variety of critical statements. In 1988, Joyce Johnson's "A Note on 'Theng'eta' in Ngũgĩ wa Thiong'o's *Petals of Blood*" emphasized the symbolic significance of "Theng'eta," the drink which is consumed by the four main characters, and its multiple effects of both unity and fragmentation, serving as a representation of "the revolutionary impulse" (Johnson 15) but also as an indicator of the abuses of commercialism.

Ngũgĩ's use of indigenous symbols such as "Theng'eta" interestingly contrasted with his employing of Christian symbolism, a theme which Hugh Dinwiddy developed in "Biblical Usage and Abusage in Kenyan Writing," which appeared in the *Journal of Religion in Africa* in 1989. Dinwiddy, who had reviewed the novel in 1978, thought that *Petals of Blood* was to a great extent "structured on Biblical associations" (Dinwiddy 42).

By 1990, Western critics had begun to link the work to other texts which bore ideological similarities. In "The Untruths of the Nation: *Petals of Blood* and Fuentes's *The Death of Artemio Cruz*," published in *Research in African Literatures*, Edna Aizenberg approached both novels in terms of the colonial struggle and independence movements. She considered *Petals of Blood* as part of a "shift" in "novelistic discourse" which paralleled historical time. *Petals of Blood* reflected this transition in its "anguished vision" (Aizenberg 85-86). Aizenberg observed that both novels were received with mixed appreciation by their respective critics. She emphasized that the critical responses pointed to the characteristics of modernism in fiction which included the "breakup of the straight line of narrative, splintering of the authorial voice, fissuring of time and character," all of which reflected "the crisis of language" (Aizenberg 95).

The comparative interpretation of *Petals of Blood* in relation to other works of literature was also addressed in a 1991 article in the *Journal of Black Studies*, the African-American publication edited by Molefi Asante. In the issue edited by Abu Shardow Abarry, Leonard A. Podis and Yakubu Saaka argued in "*Anthills of the Savannah* and *Petals of Blood:* The Creation of a Usable Past" that Achebe's 1987 novel had "narrowed" the "ideological gap" between Achebe and Ngūgī. Just as *Petals of Blood* had been viewed as a major turning point in the ideological and literary direction of Ngūgī, Podis and Saaka suggested that *Anthills of the Savannah* represented a similar decisive "watershed" (Podis and Saaka 105-106). In assessing the differences in characterization, they noted that Ngūgī's more expansive work contained characters who were often "drawn more one-dimensionally" as opposed to the portrayal of characters in Achebe's novel in which the government officials were "generally not the absolute incarnations of evil that their counterparts tend to be in *Petals*" (106-107). Further parallels were drawn between the novels in terms of plot development and characterization as well as in the common theme of "the regeneration of community based indigenous roots" (110).

The African Reception

The novel's reception in Africa also revealed patterns of critical assessment involving ideology, form and characterization. Certain Western critics had been concerned with Ngūgī's presentation of Marxist ideological themes; a good number of African critics were equally interested in this issue from the onset of their responses to *Petals*. Kenya's the *Weekly Review* of June 27, 1977, provided a thorough review titled "Ngūgī's Bombshell." Focusing on the complex of characters, the anonymous reviewer discussed Ngūgī's interweaving of plot and characters to produce a novel which would have a particular impact on Kenyan readers. Described as Ngūgī's "crowning literary achievement," the novel was presented as a pinnacle in Ngūgī's fictional technique. It was also noted that a Kenyan reader might get the effect that Ngūgī has been "walking all over your soul" because of the way the novel questioned the results of independence. Another issue was the absence of humor in the text which was thought to be a shortcoming: " ... laughter is totally lacking and it seems to take laughter out of an African's life is to misread him" ("Ngūgī's Bombshell" 40). For the reviewer, Ngūgī "overestimates the secularism of the people" and their absorption of Marxist philosophy.

> People don't walk into the Hilton Hotel from their cardboard dwellings in Kawangare and turn into roaring Trotskytes. Neither is it possible that the workers of Ilmorog could shout the slogans of Che Guevera! (40)

Ngũgĩ's politicizing of his characters was brought to question, echoing the remarks of Bhabha and Larson regarding Ngũgĩ's movement to the left.

A few weeks after the *Weekly Review* assessed *Petals*, another Kenyan publication, the *Daily Nation*, reviewed the novel. Joe Kadhi recognized the impact of the work in terms of its political assault. The novel was "without doubt, the most hard-hitting novel criticising contemporary Kenyan society written since independence" (Kadhi 14). Similar to the previous review, Kadhi's remarks considered the reactions of the insider, of the Kenyan citizen who might read the novel as a historical and political assessment of his country's transformation from colonialism to independence. Among the Kenyan writers who have criticized the "system," Ngũgĩ had achieved the most successful rendering of the issues in fiction. According to Kadhi, "No writer has yet been able to expose the evils of such a system in as bold and fearless a manner as Ngũgĩ has done in his present book" (14). One irony observed by Kadhi was that the novel was published by Heinemann, a company based in London and which could be seen as a "foreign company." *Petals of Blood* often focused on the negative influences of foreign investment; the novel's discussion of an "Anglo-American international combine" would be evidence of this concern (Ngũgĩ 281). Furthermore, those Kenyans who were painted in a negative light could possibly accuse Ngũgĩ of "committing a sin of omission" by "failing to portray the good society of contemporary Kenyan society" (14). Kadhi did not consider the difference between Ngũgĩ's status as a writer as opposed to the entrepreneurial governing class presented in the novel.

Another popular Kenyan publication, the *Standard*, reviewed *Petals* in its July 15, 1977 issue. Chris Wanjala, a prominent Kenyan literary scholar, recognized the ground breaking nature of *Petals* and Ngũgĩ's departure from previous novelistic issues.

> Ngũgĩ has written a novel which at once rates him very highly amongst writers of the Third World and marks a welcome *tour de force* from the narrow concerns of Gĩkũyũ nationalism of his early novels. (Wanjala 12)

In Wanjala's view, Ngũgĩ had also achieved a level of literary critique which surpassed popular Kenyan writers of the "post-Mangua" period in Kenya. Many of these writers had focused on "cheap sex, prostitution, brothel life, wanton lust for intoxicating liquor" without making connections to the "materiality of life in Africa." Ngũgĩ's novel, on the other hand, was a critique of various segments of the Kenyan population which had "betrayed the masses." Wanjala saw the central focus of the work in the portrayal of Karega, a Dedan Kimathi figure and "the embodiment of every Kenyan critical force against the *status quo*." Another observation underscored the visual portrayals and the possibility of Ngũgĩ's having conceived the novel in cinematic terms because of the "vivid manner that would be even more lucid on the screen." Despite Wanjala's mostly praiseworthy remarks, he did fault Ngũgĩ's use of doctrinaire Marxism, a view held by certain critics in the Western press as well. Wanjala's projection that the novel would be widely read in the West was prophetic.

Petals of Blood and Ngũgĩ's earlier novels were given continued critical attention as a result of his detention and support by various international organizations. Often African writers expressed their views of the novel in magazines and journals published in the West but which were focused primarily on African concerns. *West Africa*, published in London, is a prime example of this kind of publication. Less than two months after Ngũgĩ's detention, Lewis Nkosi, the well-known South African writer and critic, assessed *Petals of Blood* in the February 20, 1978 issue of *West Africa*. Aptly titled "A Voice from Detention," Nkosi's article raised a number of issues concerning Ngũgĩ's prior novels and Ngũgĩ's ideological shift in *Petals*.[3]

Nkosi's interpretation of *Petals of Blood* began with the recognition that the novel's thematic content would offend those in "higher places" in Kenyan society. From a formal perspective, the work suggested characteristics of the fable rather than a novel and was evidence of Ngũgĩ's "attempt to think aloud about the problems of modern Kenya" (334). Nkosi saw the elements of satire, parody and especially fable as contradictory in terms of the conventional fictional goals and Ngũgĩ's translation of socialist thought to novelistic structures.

> I think Ngũgĩ's latest fiction fails because the author is so conscious of not having written a "socialist novel" before that he gives up concrete observation, which is the correct starting point of all true materialists, in favor of a fable-cum-satire-cum-realist fiction in order to illustrate class formations in modern Kenya. (Nkosi 335)

Ngũgĩ's ability to portray the contrasting and often conflicting emotions of

Wanja were, for Nkosi, the measure of his literary skill. Certain segments of dialogue spoken by Wanja to Karega revealed "how well Ngũgĩ can dramatise these contradictions." The essence of fictional success might rest in the "concrete" depiction of characters and the writer's willingness to "delve into his characters" (335). This argument for depth of portrayal and concreteness is the measure of the traditional realistic novel. As many critics such as Nkosi observed, Ngũgĩ had clearly departed from the requirements of this tradition.

During Ngũgĩ's detention in 1978, other evaluations of *Petals* were published by African writers. The recognition of Ngũgĩ's ideological movement to the left was addressed by Marxist critics. Ngethe Kamau's "'Petals of Blood' as a Mirror of the African Revolution," published in *African Communist*, a London-based journal, in 1978, was an example a straightforward Marxist interpretation of the novel.[4] Kamau's approach to the novel linked the ideological intentions of *Petals* with Leninist philosophy. Kamau asserted, "Ngũgĩ's novel is a demonstration of the truth and validity of Lenin's penetrating analysis as applied to the post-independence state, not only in Kenya but in Africa as a whole" (74). By quoting various passages from the novel, Kamau demonstrated Ngũgĩ's similarity of intention to specific ideological statements of Lenin. In a close example, Kamau demonstrated the way Lenin's remarks on infrastructure and road building could be paralleled to Ngũgĩ's portrayal of the Trans-African highway in *Petals*. Kamau saw the relationships between Leninist views and *Petals* as a positive representation of political ideology in fiction. Unlike those who saw Ngũgĩ's politicizing of the masses as unrealistic, Kamau discussed this element of the novel as the "proletarianization of the African peasantry and the rest of the working masses" without attention to its feasibility within the "realistic" context.

Critics continued to offer a variety of interpretations of *Petals* in 1978. In *Ufahamu*, Ntongela Masilela approached *Petals* with a summary of Marxist interpretations of the relationship between literature and history. Using the ideas of Walter Benjamin and Lukács, Masilela suggested that "Ngũgĩ's profound understanding of the complex relation between history and literature" could best be understood after a grounding in literary historical relationships from the Marxist perspective. The connection between realism and history was also addressed through the use of numerous references which punctuated the general discussion of Ngũgĩ's historical schematic design. The essential meaning of realism, so important to the critical assessment of Ngũgĩ's novel, was also addressed when Masilela used Brecht's definition as the "most succinct and lucid": "'revealing causal connections in society, unmasking dominant points of view as the points of view of the dominators, writing from the point of view of the class which is ready with the widest solutions to the most pressing difficulties in which human society is enmeshed'" (Masilela 16). Of equal importance was the larger question of critical reception and the need to examine the way literary works have been received.

Also in 1978, Kelwyn Sole in "Art and Activism in Kenya," published in *Africa Perspective*, a South African journal, discussed the range of political and artistic issues surrounding *Petals of Blood* as well as *The Trial of Dedan Kimathi*. Acknowledging that Kenyan written literature of the day was concerned with "political, social and economic problems," Sole questioned the links between political ideology and artistic achievement. Again, Ngũgĩ's use of ideological messages was addressed in terms of the Western tradition of the novel. For Sole, both works of Ngũgĩ "fall prey at times to a doughy social realism which recalls the unhappy days of Russian literature under Zhdanov" (Sole 27). After citing a passage from *Petals* which contained clear Marxist language, Sole claimed that "form and language" were "stylized and vague" and that some of the characters in the novel were rendered in a "two-dimensional" fashion. However, Sole realized that Ngũgĩ's choice in overtly presenting political ideology was important because it revealed the dilemma of African authors in general and the stance of Western critics.

> The Western-trained critic, then, should perhaps not be too quick in condemning his [Ngũgĩ's] lack of subtlety. The fact of the matter is that a discussion Ngũgĩ's consciously chosen position as regards literature relates to the problem of the position of the African writer in his or her society and connected problems of criticism. (Sole 28)

Ultimately, Sole recognized the problems of analyzing "high art" and "political art" and the importance of measuring African literature by "fresh critical concepts" which reconsider the intentions of Eurocentric critical ideas.

The following year, F. Odun Balogun's "Ngũgĩ's *Petals of Blood*: A Novel of the People" appeared in a 1979 issue of *Ba Shiru*. Unlike certain critics who questioned the balancing of message and art, Balogun argued positively for the unity of form and ideology. He compared *Petals* to achievements attained by other African writers of the period such as Achebe in *Things Fall Apart* and *A*

Man of the People and Armah in *The Beautiful Ones Are Not Yet Born*. The importance of *Petals of Blood* was that Ngũgĩ had "gone beyond most African writers in creating a 'novel of the people'" (50).

In 1980, *Petals of Blood* was reexamined in John Chileshe's "*Petals of Blood*: Ideology and Imaginative Expression," published in the *Journal of Commonwealth Literature*. As with the majority of African critics, Chileshe grappled with the question of ideological message and the "work of art." For Chileshe, the artistic success of *A Grain of Wheat* was not duplicated in *Petals of Blood* because *Petals* was "weakened somewhat by the conflict between authorial ideology and the literary mode of expression used" (Chileshe 133). Chileshe saw Ngũgĩ as an artist involved in a "nationalistic struggle against imperialist hegemony," an activity which suggested certain contradictions because artists engaged in this struggle were often waging battle from "*within* the imperialist hegemonic structure" (134). This issue was complicated by the medium and artistic form which were "weapons" which had been "inherited from the culture at which the struggle was directed." However, Ngũgĩ had achieved a narrative structure for his multiple and collective narration by using elements of the traditional African story-telling mode which demonstrated one of the "potential strengths of the novel" (134).

Contrary to Chileshe's assertions regarding inconsistency of ideology and characterization, the review by Ugandan writer S. K. Wasswa, which appeared in a 1981 issue of *Forward*, a Ugandan journal, supported the consistency of form and ideology by suggesting the significance of Ngũgĩ's message to Ugandan society. Unlike those critics who took issue with Ngũgĩ's projection of ideology and form, Wasswa held that Ngũgĩ had "displayed a mastery of content and form" as Ngũgĩ had done in his earlier works. The political significance of *Petals* was expressed in terms of its "crucial relevance to Uganda's present situation" (Wasswa 13-14).

Angela Smith's commentary in a 1983 issue of *Outlook*, published in Malawi, showed that the critical appraisals of the work had begun to generate their own text against which critics such as Smith began to present their assessments. Smith identified four prominent critics, Gerald Moore, Eustace Palmer, G.D. Killam and Clifford Robson, all of whom had given the novel "a good deal of space in their studies" (Smith 12). Smith's contention was that the four critical appraisals had identified Munira as the central character of the work. She thought that it was a "misreading of both *A Grain of Wheat* and *Petals of Blood* to ferret about for one central character or hero" (24).

One of the last review-type appraisals of *Petals of Blood* appeared in a 1984 issue of *The Native*. Kenyan Gītahi Gītītī's "*Petals of Blood* as a Stage in Ngũgĩ wa Thiong'o's Evolving Social Perspective" examined the novel in relation to *The River Between* and Ngũgĩ's works to 1984. Gītahi Gītītī observed a crucial transition in the novels of Ngũgĩ from critical realism to social realism. In a positive view, Ngũgĩ's achievement was based on his linking of "all the major preoccupations of the anti-colonial and ideologically sound African novel from its beginning to the present day" (26-27). *Petals*, however, suggested a point of contention for Gītahi Gītītī because the novel did not "conform" to Ngũgĩ's statements concerning African literature expressed in African languages. This post-*Petals of Blood* stance of Ngũgĩ's could be used to address his work following *Petals*. If *Petals* is viewed as the transitional novel in Ngũgĩ's use of indigenous language, then one might expect to view the seeds of this new direction rather than a fully formed representation.

During the 1980s, the rise of literary criticism which focused on the portrayal of African women expanded the critical debate concerning form and ideology. Kavetsa Adagala's "Wanja of *Petals of Blood*: The Woman Question and Imperialism in Kenya," published in 1985, placed *Petals* within a historical and ideological framework. One of the goals of her critique was to "criticize Wanja from a historical standpoint employing the dialectical approach" (Adagala 1). Wanja was explored as a character who represented multiple characteristics as a result of her transformation from "schoolgirl, unwed mother, barmaid, destitute prostitute and poor peasant" to "a woman who is determined to acquire riches, never marry and prepared to sell her body to wealthy men and tourists" (Adagala 22). Wanja, then, represented the choices which were available to the symbolic Kenyan or African woman in the transitional neo-colonial state. At the same time, these choices or options were to a degree defined by the forces which led Wanja toward the negative extremes of her actions.

According to Adagala, Ngũgĩ was not offering a character who was either stereotype of the African woman—mother or prostitute. Ngũgĩ was suggesting that prostitution was not confined to women but was part of the larger issue of bartering away the promise of Independence. Wanja eventually triumphed over these forces and in the end remained an image of the reemerging consciousness which for Ngũgĩ was bound to the political ascendancy of the workers.

In 1986, a year following the publication of Adagala's critique, Peter Amuka's doctoral dissertation, "Kenyan Oral Literature, Ngũgĩ's Fiction and His Search for a Voice," examined the relationship between Ngũgĩ's use of the novel form and "the social effects of Ngũgĩ's written ideas on a predominantly oral audience" (Amuka vii). Like other Kenyan critics, Amuka's argument grew out of his first-hand contact with Kenyan cultural issues. Amuka's conclusion considered the applicability of the novel form to a coalescing of "art and action." In tracing the development of Ngũgĩ's fiction, Amuka viewed *Petals of Blood* and *Devil on the Cross* as transitional works which established a more "visible" and unsuppressed authorial voice (Amuka 160). The dilemma for Amuka was that the written mode of discourse suggested a "passive" application of art and action (217).

Most African critics of the *Petals of Blood* were willing to approach the novel as written discourse which could be discussed in terms of plot structure and narrative perspective. Ayo Mamudu's "Tracing a Winding Stair: Ngũgĩ's Narrative Methods in *Petals of Blood*," which appeared in *World Literature Written in English* in 1987, considered the narrative structure and Ngũgĩ's "revelatory approach" which involved the "interlacing of past and present" to create a kind of circular effect which has meaning in the future as well (Mamudu 18). Mamudu did not object to the political characterizations but rather saw the "integration of form and content" rather than a "cleavage" (Mamudu 25).

The debate among African critics of *Petals of Blood* continued to address political and formal issues. One of the emerging Kenyan critics of the 1980s, Simon Gikandi, had written a major critical work on the African novel, *Reading the African Novel* (1987). Gikandi, who responded to the implications of Chinweizu's approach to African literature, explored *Petals of Blood* in a chapter titled "The Political Novel," which included discussions of Ousmane's *God's Bits of Wood* and La Guma's *In the Fog of the Season's End*. Gikandi showed an appreciation of Ngũgĩ's development of his quartet of characters in *Petals of Blood*. Gikandi, who explored the novel principally in terms of Ngũgĩ's presentation of Munira, Abdullah, Wanja and especially Karega, considered the relationship between "character and consciousness." The "problem," as Gikandi viewed it, was in Ngũgĩ's using character to "reflect society"; this approach of Ngũgĩ's had flaws because of the limitations of "one man's vision" (Gikandi 134). The difficulty of balancing a realistic depiction of society with the "logical development of the interaction of characters" represented the challenge of *Petals of Blood* and other African novels with clear political intentions. Gikandi examined Ngũgĩ's portrayal of each of his central characters by focusing on the various narrative perspectives and reliability of certain personas. Gikandi was particularly concerned with the way Ngũgĩ as author served as critic of his various narrators, subjecting many of them to "authorial censure" (135). Unlike Gĩtahi Gĩtĩtĩ, Gikandi objected to the reduction of the novel to a fundamental conclusion which underscored Ngũgĩ's political intention.

Like Gikandi, Chidi Amuta also produced a substantial critical work on African literature. Amuta's *The Theory of African Literature* (1989) opened with remarks concerning Chinweizu's *Toward the Decolonization of African Literature*. Gikandi had also used Chinweizu's ideas as a starting point in *Reading the African Novel*. Amuta responded to what he called the "kind of reductionism and romantic simplification represented by the Chinweizu formation." In Amuta's substantial remarks on *Petals of Blood* in the section titled "Class Struggle and the Socialist Vision: Ngũgĩ's *Petals of Blood*," part of a larger section on "History and Dialectics of Narrative," Amuta challenged the opposing critics who objected to the ideological intentions of the novel.

> Against the timid imputations of bourgeois critics, the deci-
> sive ideological thrust of *Petals of Blood* does not weaken its
> artistic identity. On the contrary, the strength of the novel
> derives from the sheer aesthetic force of its informing and
> objectified ideology. (Amuta, *The Theory* 148)

Amuta stressed the close interrelationship of the "dialectic of content and form" which he considered central to understanding the symbolic nature of the novel's structure (*The Theory* 148). Amuta also addressed *Petals of Blood* a year following the publication of his theoretical work. In another of Amuta's writings on *Petals of Blood*, "The Revolutionary Imperative in the Contemporary African Novel: Ngũgĩ's *Petals of Blood* and Armah's *The Healers*, published in *Commonwealth Novel in English*, Amuta observed the close relationship between history and modern African writing. Both novels represented a presentation of "revolution-ary consciousness" (Amuta, "Revolutionary" 132) and, when viewed together, showed the "dynamism and rapid change which are perhaps the most dominant characteristics of modern socio-political experience." These characteristics can be observed particularly in the African novel (Amuta, "The Revolutionary" 141).

Conclusion

Because *Petals of Blood* represented a major transitional period in Ngũgĩ's literary career, its critical reception has been central to understanding Ngũgĩ's use of ideology of the left in conjunction with novelistic form which derived from Western aesthetics but which contained strong elements of the African oral tradition. As the critical discussion moved beyond the initial years of the novel's publication, observers still questioned the validity of straightforward ideology imbedded in characterization and expressed in undisguised narrative commentaries. On the whole, critics could not deny that much of what Ngũgĩ had achieved in the novel was based on his infusing the work with complexity of plot and characterization, the layering of the work with political dimensions which ultimately generated the most controversial critical attack.

The success or failure of *Petals of Blood* for a particular critic was not necessarily a function of the critic's national origin but was rather based on his or her aesthetic and political criteria. Critics of both the West and Africa who saw ideology as a weakening element were most often exponents of a kind of realism which eschewed bold political character representations. On the other hand, certain African critics supported Ngũgĩ's use of the novel form to present political issues and ideology regardless of their effects on characterization.

The critical discussion which has surrounded *Petals of Blood* not only demonstrates the potency of political issues in African literature but the complexity of literary concepts of form in modern African writing. Although African writers such as Ngũgĩ initially patterned their works on Western fiction, they were not bound to continue that particular tradition. In *Petals of Blood*, Ngũgĩ's notion of "realism" was based more on authorial purpose than on a supposed believability of action. Ngũgĩ's assumption of a narrative voice which projected historical interpretation indicated his breaking the boundaries of any proscribed notion of authorial distance. In so doing, many of the characters in *Petals of Blood* take on larger-than-life significance which might be seen as "unrealistic" within the novel's context of characterization.

Petals of Blood showed Ngũgĩ's willingness to risk a conception of novelistic form which had earned him his initial successes in order to assert political ideas which he considered crucial to the righting of Kenya's social dilemmas. Despite the often strong critique of this intention in *Petals of Blood*, Ngũgĩ continued to infuse his subsequent novels with a political imperative directed toward both revaluation and rectification.

Notes

[1] The wealth of critical materials on Ngũgĩ's works have been compiled in the very useful work of Carol Sicherman, *Ngũgĩ wa Thiong'o: A Bibliography of Primary and Secondary Sources, 1957-1987* (New York: Hans Zell, 1989). Furthermore, *Petals of Blood* has been treated in a variety of book-length studies of African literature, including Eustace Palmer's *The Growth of the African Novel* (London: Heinemann, 1979), Emmanuel Ngara's *Stylistic Criticism and the African Novel* (London: Heinemann, 1982), Chinweizu, Onwuchekwa Jemie and Ihechukwu Madubuike's *Toward the Decolonization of African Literature*, Vol. I (Washington, D.C.: Howard University Press, 1983) and Simon Gikandi's *Reading the African Novel* (Portsmouth, N.H.: Heinemann, 1987).

Sicherman served as a great help and resource in tracking down a number of the reviews in African journals and other relevant sources.

[2] Although critiques in periodical literature would continue to appear after 1980, the growth of post-Independence African literature led to the increased production of book-length studies devoted to authors such as Ngũgĩ. By 1980, Ngũgĩ's development as a novelist led to the first full-length treatment of his works. G.D. Killam's *An Introduction to the Writings of Ngũgĩ* (1980) contained a section devoted to *Petals of Blood*. Three years later, Cook and Okenimkpe's *Ngũgĩ wa Thiong'o: An Exploration of His Writings* (1983) furthered the extensive scholarly interpretation of *Petals of Blood*, followed in the subsequent year by the publication of Killam's edited collection, *Critical Perspectives on the Writings of Ngũgĩ wa Thiong'o* (1984), which included commentaries by African as well as Western critics. The collaborative work of Cook and Okenimkpe represented a fusion of Western and African critical perspectives. These book-length treatments offered extensive critical treatments of *Petals of Blood*.

[3] In February, groups such as the African Students Union of the United Kingdom, the London-based Pan African Association of Writers and Journalists, and PEN had all begun to mount protests against Ngũgĩ's imprisonment. This kind of concern for Ngũgĩ's detention was expected to achieve the end result of his release. At that time, Nkosi observed, "Unless the Kenyatta Government sees fit to free its famous novelist or at the very least to bring him to trial, it is likely that the international campaign for his release will acquire more passion and nerve" (Nkosi 334). Ngũgĩ's detention was based on his alleged violation of the Public Security Laws, but, in fact, his activities were primarily literary and creative in his involvement with the production of *Ngaahika Ndeenda*.

[4] Although credited to Ngethe Kamau, this article was later published under the name Grant Kamenju in George M. Gugelberger, ed., *Marxism and African Literature* (Trenton, NJ: Africa World Press, 1986), 130-35.

Works Cited

Adagala, Kavetsa. "Wanja of *Petals of Blood*: The Woman Question and Imperialism in Kenya." Nairobi: Derika Associates, 1985. Orig. Univ. of Nairobi Department of Literature Staff Seminar Paper. 1981.

Aizenberg, Edna. "The Untruths of the Nation: *Petals of Blood* and Fuentes's *The Death of Artemio Cruz.*" *Research in African Literatures* 21.4 (1990): 85-103.

Albrecht, Françoise. "Blood and Fire in *Petals of Blood.*" *Échos du Commonwealth* 6 (1980-81):85-97.

Amuka, Peter. "Kenyan Oral Literature: Ngũgĩ's Fiction and His Search for a Voice." Dissertation. University of California at Los Angeles, 1986.

Amuta, Chidi. "The Revolutionary Imperative in the Contemporary African Novel: Ngũgĩ's *Petals of Blood* and Armah's *The Healers.*" *Commonwealth Novel in English* 3.2 (1990):130-142.

—. *The Theory of African Literature: Implications for Practical Criticism.* London: Zed Books, 1989.

Balogun, F. Odun. "Ngũgĩ's *Petals of Blood*: A Novel of the People." *Ba Shiru* 10:2 (1979) 49-57.

Berman, Paul. Rev. of *Petals of Blood*. *New Republic* 20 Jan. 1979:40.

Bhabha, Homi. "African Praxis." Rev. of *Petals of Blood*. *Times Literary Supplement* 12 Aug. 1977: 989.

Chileshe, John. "*Petals of Blood*: Ideology and Imaginative Expression." *Journal of Commonwealth Literature* 15.1(1980): 133-137.

Crehan, Stewart. "The Politics of the Signifier: Ngũgĩ wa Thiong'o's *Petals of Blood.*" *World Literature Written in English* 26.1 (1986): 1-24.

Davies, Carol Boyce and Anne Adams Graves, eds. *Ngambika: Studies of Women in African Literature.* Trenton, N.J.: Africa World Press, 1986.

Dinwiddy, Hugh. "Biblical Usage and Abusage in Kenyan Writing." *Journal of Religion in Africa* 19.1 (1989): 27-47.

—. Rev. of *Petals of Blood*. *African Affairs* 78.1 (Jan.1978): 127-29.

Gikandi, Simon. *Reading the African Novel.* London: James Currey, Nairobi: Heinemann Kenya, 1987.

Gĩtahi Gĩtĩtĩ, [Victor L.]. "*Petals of Blood* as a Stage in Ngũgĩ wa Thiong'o's Evolving Social Perspective." *The Native* 1.1 (1984): 26-33.

Gugelberger, George M., ed. *Marxism and African Literature.* Trenton, NJ: Africa World Press, 1986.

Johnson, Joyce. "A Note on Theng'eta in Ngũgĩ wa Thiong'o's *Petals of Blood.*" *World Literature Written in English* 28.1 (1988): 12-15.

Kadhi, Joe. "'Petals' Will Land with a Thud." Rev. of *Petals of Blood*. *Daily Nation* 15 July 1977: 14.

Kamau, Ngethe. "'Petals of Blood' as a Mirror of the African Revolution." *African Communist* 80 (1978): 73-79.

Larson, Charles. "African Dissenters." Rev. of *Petals of Blood*. *New York Times Book Review* 19 Feb. 1978: 3, 22.

—. "Anglophone Writing from Africa and Asia." *World Literature Today* 52.2 (1978): 245-47.

Mamudu, Ayo. "Tracing a Winding Stair: Ngũgĩ's Narrative Methods in *Petals of Blood*." *World Literature Written in English* 28.1 (1988): 16-25.

Masilela, Ntongela. "Ngũgĩ wa Thiong'o's *Petals of Blood*." *Ufahamu* 9.2 (1978): 9-28.

Nazareth, Peter. "The Second Homecoming: Multiple Ngũgĩs in *Petals of Blood*." *Marxism and African Literature*. Ed. George M. Gugelberger. Trenton, NJ: Africa World Press, 1986: 119-129.

"Ngũgĩ's Bombshell." *Weekly Review* 27 June 1977: 39-40.

Ngũgĩ wa Thiong'o. *Petals of Blood*. 1977. New York: E.P. Dutton, 1978.

Nkosi, Lewis. "A Voice from Detention." *West Africa* 20 Feb. 1978: 334-335.

Pagnoulle, Christine. "Ngũgĩ wa Thiong'o's 'Journey of the Magi': Part 2 of *Petals of Blood*." *Research in African Literatures* 16.2 (1985): 264-75.

Podis, Leonard A. and Yakubu Saaka. "*Anthills of the Savannah* and *Petals of Blood*: The Creation of a Usable Past." *Journal of Black Studies* 22.1 (1991): 104-122.

Rao, K.B. "*Petals of Blood*." *Masterplots II: British and Commonwealth Fiction Series 3*. Ed. Frank N. Magill. Pasadena: Salem Press, 1987: 1320-1324.

Ricks, Christopher. "Power Without Glory in Kenya," *Sunday Times* 26 June 1977: 41.

Salkey, Andrew. "Kenya." Rev. of *Petals of Blood*. *World Literature Today* 52.4 (1978): 681-682.

Sicherman, Carol. *Ngũgĩ wa Thiong'o: A Bibliography of Primary and Secondary Sources, 1957-1987*. New York: Hans Zell Publishers, 1989.

Smith, Angela "*Petals of Blood*." *Outlook* 1.1 (1983):12-31.

Sole, Kelwyn. "Art and Activism in Kenya." *Africa Perspective* 8 (1978): 26-31.

Updike, John. "Books: Mixed Reports from the Interior." Rev. of *Petals of Blood*. *New Yorker* 2 July 1979: 89-94.

Wanjala, Chris. "New Novel by Ngũgĩ Keeps Him at Top." *Standard* 15 July 1977: 12.

Wasswa, S.K. "Literature: A Tool in the Struggle." Rev. of *Petals of Blood*. *Forward* 3.2 (1981): 13-16.

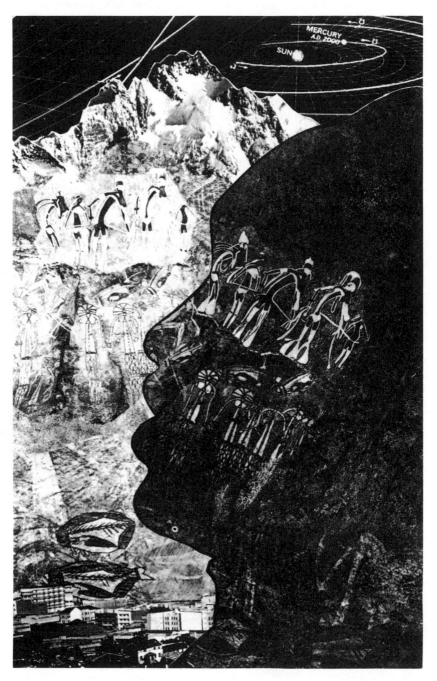

Craig V. Smith

"Rainbow Memories of Gain and Loss": *Petals of Blood* and the New Resistance

> Literature is of course primarily concerned with what any political and economic arangement does to the spirit and the values governing human relationships. (*Homecoming*, xvi)

I WANT TO READ *Petals of Blood*'s representation of one issue that calls for attention in a study of Ngũgĩ's political imagination. This is the problematic confrontation between Mau Mau as a revolutionary movement and the resurgent malaise of ethnic identification in Kenya. And I want to read it in the context of the socio-cultural changes in Kenya which Ngũgĩ maps out broadly and urgently. These changes, to summarize, involve rural decline and urban growth, American cultural influence, economic collapse and stratification, the penetration of neocolonial interests into Kenyan politics, commerce and culture, the bureaucratization of state power and its monopolization by one-party government, and the deliberate forgetting of resistance traditions. In the face of such challenges to the presence within the "New Kenya" of "the people"—peasants and workers and marginalized persons: Ngũgĩ's constituency—the text offers a broad, multifaceted exploration of

> *Typically, Ngũgĩ grounds his representation of Mau Mau, as of all socio-historical movements, in the experience of individuals: their specific involvement comes to stand for, and at the same time illuminate, their nation's involvement.*

the forces which have shaped and the events which have marked some twelve years of independent history from Uhuru, December 1963, to the mid-'70s. Throughout he is concerned to re-authorize buried stories of struggle before, during and after the colonial occupation; to investigate the impact of capitalism on citizens already losing a competition dominated by middle-aged men who rejected what *A Grain of Wheat* called "the movement"; to imagine the experience of women within this strongly gendered, greedy new world; and, in effect, to re-center Kenya, to shift its social, cultural and political desire to more worthy internal goals: an egalitarian state which will participate in a pan-African and then wholly "Third-World" struggle against economic underdevelopment, of which Kenya's Mau Mau moment was the beginning.

Published in 1977 but written over the five years from 1970-75—in, as the final citation reveals, a symbolic troika of locations: Kenya, America and the Soviet Union—*Petals of Blood* should be read against a wider backdrop of Kenyan, African and international politics. Most urgent in this background is the discourse of disillusionment which saturates African novels of the 1970s, a disillusionment usually attributed to the clear failure of many postcolonial regimes to implement the policies for which independence movements fought.[1] For someone with Ngũgĩ's radical politics it was clear by 1970 that such regimes were in too many ways merely the African successors to colonial exploiters: capitalism flourished, having "Africanized" itself by adopting black leaders. At the same time, and even as a result of Uhuru's failure, revisionist social scientists were formulating a new paradigm to explain the Third World's continued subjugation to the West. The optimistic "development theory" of the 1950s, which held that nations could be helped to the point of "take off" whereupon they could function competently on their own, gave way to the much more critical "dependency theory," which argued that mechanisms within the global capitalist system operate in order to keep underdeveloped nations in a state of dependency, willing to give their natural resources and labor, even their sovereignty, too cheaply in exchange for consumer imports they are prevented from manufacturing themselves.[2] So *Petals of Blood* is produced at a time of change, hope, failure and new, pessimistically yet critically enabling visions of postcolonial places.

More than Ngũgĩ's previous novels, *Petals of Blood* insists upon the primacy of class and the disasterous effects of social stratification upon people and polity alike. Because of this awareness of class—class within a generally if not yet completely capitalist system—the later text seems "modern" in a way its precursor did not; in it one can trace the way class consciousness, capitalism and modernity co-produce each other. A major component of this text's response to the co-production of modernity, class and capitalism within a postcolonial state is its attempt to construct, through revisionist historiography, a romantic nationalism which can cope with the trials of the present by telescoping past forms of consciousness into present viability. Mau Mau is the medium for this radical history. As a result, *Petals* offers an extended historiography that actively collapses the past into the present in order to accelerate political awakening.

A schematic account of the ways in which this novel reorients its project would suggest that it transforms its targets from foreign to local, shifts its discourse from race to class, and seeks a new area of readership. While the novel's epigraphs may still come from Blake or Whitman or Yeats, its urgent mission is to alert *Kenyan* readers to the problems it raises. The reorientation of readership appears in the text's frequent, prominent and sometimes untranslated use of African words, sayings and especially songs, though not until *Devil On The Cross* does Ngũgĩ take the radical step of writing in Gĩkũyũ. Above all the text invokes its new reader in its attempts to define the experience of these characters within the context of African independence, solidarity, rivalry and shared experiences, the "rainbow memories of gain and loss, triumph and failure, but above all of suffering and knowledge in struggle" (123). From the problematic of race to the problematic of class; from foreign to African reader: these shifts are all part of the authenticity which Ngũgĩ's young militant, Karega, tries to name: "a communal struggle ... new beginnings ... the right to define ourselves ... African populism" (173-4).

The new mode of resistance authorized by what I am calling "romantic nationalism" deploys these "rainbow memories of gain and loss" in a local, immediate struggle rather than a quietest, defeated nostalgia. Through the memories and their revisionary deployment, the text juxtaposes both the lost pre-colonial era and the postcolonial present alongside the foundational, mythic moment of the colonial period, Mau Mau. Then, through this juxtaposition, the text participates in a national project resolutely neglected by African elites and colonial bureaucrats, producing an archive of the life of the masses. Written after colonialism, the text finds security in the fact that colonialism itself can be periodized, contained: in its most virulent form it was of limited duration and not, in the end, the point of African history. In a benevolent way this offers proof of survival, validates resistance; in a malevolent way it opens up the postcolonial present for all kinds of new scrutiny.

Ngũgĩ represents independent Kenya by continuing two narrative techniques he developed in *A Grain of Wheat*. He orchestrates multiple narrators whose perspectives concatenate, and couples these with flashbacks which take the reader from the narrative present, circa 1975, back again and again to the years since independence. Rather than a linearity which would produce clear effects of logic and causality, he arranges an archaeology which unearths complicated layers of circumstance, motivation, participation and comprehension. One of the novel's many meta-fictional jokes justifies this method: "Africa, after all, did not have one but several pasts which were in perpetual struggle. Images pressed on images" (214). The imagery and the ethos of Mau Mau form one site for this "perpetual struggle," for the pursuit of popular nationalism, and for the rejection of "tribalism."

"We really were our people": Mau Mau as revolution

I want to emphasize Ngũgĩ's representation of Mau Mau for a number of reasons. First, it affords us the opportunity to study the evolution of his political vision since *A Grain of Wheat*. Second, Mau Mau provides one of this novel's key thematics: of the four central characters, one was a soldier and the other three, in various ways, wish they had been. Conversely, all of their four nemeses are anti-Mau Mau, either collaborating with the white regime or ignoring Mau Mau's goals, abusing its veterans or defaming its legacy. As it did in his previous novel, Mau Mau thus provides proof of political orientation: a character's attitude betrays his or her politics. Third, as Ngũgĩ revises the meaning of Mau Mau it becomes one vehicle of his critique of contemporary Kenya. Redefining the reason for the struggle, he can insist that it should and does continue. The acknowledgment page dedicates this text to "Many others / One in the struggle / With our people / For total liberation." In *A Grain of Wheat* Ngũgĩ inserted Mau Mau into a centuries-long tradition of African resistance to colonialism. Here he extends that tradition up to his postcolonial present by claiming for Mau Mau—and thus for the tradition of which it is part—an unfinished opposition to social stratification, class exploitation and national fragmentation.[3]

Mau Mau provides a discourse in which Ngũgĩ can begin to construct a history of colonial Kenya usable in this present. When Karega begins searching for the knowledge he needs to develop a politics, he knows only that he "hoped for a vision of the future rooted in a critical awareness of the past" (198). Much the same can be said for Ngũgĩ's project. By making Mau Mau stand for a much broader phenomenon, namely Africa's struggle for independence from all foreign rule—and within this the African popular struggle for economic and social justice—Ngũgĩ delivers both future hope and critical awareness. The question, once argued by Abdulla and Karega, is whether Mau Mau "was only for the return of the white highlands to black owners and the end of the colour bar in big buildings and in business or whether it was something more" (314). The clear answer Ngũgĩ gives to this question rests upon the revisionist historiography in *Petals of Blood*.

Typically, Ngũgĩ grounds his representation of Mau Mau, as of all socio-historical movements, in the experience of individuals: their specific involvement comes to stand for, and at the same time illuminate, their nation's involvement. Munira is the first instrument the novel uses to sound out the experience of Mau Mau: "Munira's stomach tightened a little at the revelation [that Abdulla had fought in the forests]. He always felt this generalised fear about this period of war: he also felt guilty, as if there was something he should have done but didn't do. It was the guilt of omission: other young men of his time had participated: they had taken sides: this defined them as a people who had gone through the test and either failed or passed. But he had not taken the final test" (62). His shame over his father's collaboration with the British, and the wealth that it allowed, complicates Munira's consciousness: torn by loyalty to family versus loyalty to a cause, Munira ends up ashamed of his past, longing to participate in Kenya's present but paralyzed by an alienation which results from his refusal to recognize any symbiosis between the personal and the political. The novel faults him for his quietism, revealing to us what Munira must face for himself: he has compromised. While his compromise may not equal the active collaboration of his father, never mind that of the politicians who positioned themselves for independence by playing both sides, it is punished. It costs him the friendship of the novel's valorized characters and then leads him into the fervid religious paranoia which ultimately sparks a radical action (the arson which kills Chui, Mzigo and Kimeria) for a reactionary reason (to "save" Karega from Wanja).[4]

But if Mau Mau provides all Kenyans with a test of their past political alignment, so too does it occasion a searching test of Kenya's contemporary values. As *Petals of Blood* gradually unearths Abdulla's involvement in the movement and his marginalization after independence, it indicts the present's hypocritical and apolitical memory. Recalling a Mau Mau song which warned "You black traitors, spear-bearers" for the British, that forest fighters will have their revenge—"we knew / Kenya is a black man's country"—Abdulla unfolds a veteran's vision of Uhuru:

> I waited for land reforms and redistribution ... waited for a
> job ... waited for a statue to Kimathi as a memorial to the
> fallen ... waited. ... I heard that they were giving loans for
> people to buy out European farms. I did not see why I should
> buy lands already bought by the blood of the people. Still I
> went there [to the land office]. They told me: this is New

Kenya: No free things. Without money you cannot buy land: and without land and property you cannot get a bank loan to start a business or buy land. It did not make sense. For when we were fighting, did we ask that only those with property should fight?

... The man who came to the office was the one who had betrayed me and Nding'uri [to the British]. He had, as I later gathered, a contract with the company to transport the company's goods all over. The clerks were saying after he had gone inside: Uhuru has really come. Before independence no African was allowed to touch the company's goods except as a labourer. Now Mr. Kimeria handles millions! ... I remained rooted to the ground. So Kimeria wa Kamianja was eating the fruits of Uhuru! (254-5, ellipses in text).

Abdulla's distaste for "New Kenya" signifies beyond its bitter irony. As Robert B. Edgerton notes, the slogan "Nothing is free" was coined by Kenyatta shortly after Uhuru in the pretense that hardship was universal (218).[5]

Ngũgĩ's retrospective account of Mau Mau's betrayal by Kenya's elites entails a double vision of the movement. On one level it was part and (for a moment) culmination of Kenyan resistance to foreign invaders, Arab, Portuguese, and British. This phase of Mau Mau succeeded, for despite military defeat it hastened Britain's withdrawal. On the second level, Mau Mau was a class war, of the poor and exploited against the bourgeoisie, black and white. And this phase of Mau Mau, in Ngũgĩ's representation, has only just begun. Abdulla recalls his thoughts when he was released from a detention camp on the eve of Uhuru:

The flowering of faith ... the crowning glory to a collective struggle and endurance. This would now change. No longer would I see the face of the white man laughing at our efforts. And the Indian trader with his obscenities ... Kumanyoko mwivi ... he too would go. Factories, tea and coffee estates would belong to us. Kenyan people. I remembered all those who had daily thwarted our struggle. I remembered the traitors: those who worked with Henderson.[6] Vengeance is mine, saith the Lord: but I did not care: I would not have

minded helping him a bit in the vengeance: at least weed our
the parasites ... collaborators. (253; my footnote)

And Nyankinyua, Ilmorog's spirited elder, insists she will march alone to Limuru
if need be, because "'my man fought the white man. He paid for it with his
blood ... I'll struggle against these black oppressors" (276).

Mau Mau recycles as a resistance ethic for the present; anti-colonialism
modifies into anti-neocolonial resistance, of which the most immediate component is class consciousness. Putting Ngũgĩ's representation of Mau Mau in the
Gramscian terms suggested by Raymond Williams (108-114), one could
understand British hegemony contested by the alternative hegemony of African
elites and then both contested by the counter-hegemony of the Kenyan masses.
This scheme, however, leaves in place the reality of hegemony, which Ngũgĩ's
radical position wants also to invalidate: his vision of genuine society has no
room for domination. Thus a more teleological (and utopian) scheme would see
Kenya's evolution from British rule as an incomplete dialectic. The struggle
between white rule and the nationalist movement produced a false and unstable
synthesis, a capitalist Kenya ruled by an African elite in alliance with the foreign
powers. Only the second stage, the struggle between this new elite and the
Kenyan people, will produce the revolution Ngũgĩ seeks: "Why, anyway, should
soil, any soil, which after all was what was Kenya, be owned by an individual?
Kenya, the soil, was the people's common shamba, and there was no way it could
be right for a few, or a section, or a single nationality, to inherit for their sole use
what was communal" (302). In their different ways and with their variously
preserved resources, Wanja, Karega and Abdulla understand this—and, with the
added impetus of her unique motivation, Wanja acts, killing Kimeria. But the
revolution remains a hope and a promise; as we have seen, the most subversive
act undertaken in the narrative present arises from religious zeal, not class
politics.

Once again, Abdulla delivers the text's revolutionary vision when he
remembers his early awakening to social injustice:

He was a worker at a shoe-factory near his home, where
strike after strike for higher wages and better housing had
always been broken by helmeted policemen. He had asked
himself several times: how was it that a boss who never once
lifted a load, who never once dirtied his hands in the smelly

water and air in the tannery or in any other part of the complex, could still live in a big house and own a car and employ a driver and more than four people only to cut grass in the compound?

How he had trembled as the vision opened out, embracing new thoughts, new desires, new possibilities! To redeem the land: to fight so that the industries like the shoe-factory which had swallowed his sweat could belong to the people: so that his children could one day have enough to eat and to wear under adequate shelter from rain: so thay they would say in pride, my father died that I might live: this had transformed him from a slave before a boss into a man. That was the day of his true circumcision into a man. (136)

To see that this passage explains Abdulla's decision to join the movement in the early '50s is to grasp Ngũgĩ's reauthorization of Mau Mau as incipient class struggle that must continue in the spoilt aftermath of independence. Similarly, to read that "Mau Mau was only a link in the chain in the long struggle of African people through different times at different places" (137) while keeping in mind Ngũgĩ's definition of "the people"—peasant and worker—is to understand that, for this text, the values of Mau Mau still shape African popular resistance to racial oppression and to economic oppression. When the end of the novel reports the assassination of a slumlord carried out by "'Wakombozi—or the society of one world liberation,'" the young woman activist who gives Karega the details imagines that "'it's [Mau Mau leader] Stanley Mathenge returned from Ethiopia to complete the war he and Kimathi started ... There are rumours about a return to the forests and the mountains'" (344). All this then explains Abdulla's curious, reflexive formulation which I took as the title for this section: "we really were our people" (140).

Yet there is one further aspect of Ngũgĩ's Mau Mau vision worth pulling out, and that is the parallel between "the Movement" of the '50s and Ngũgĩ's cultural production in the '70s. By reinventing Mau Mau as the stirring of class consciousness, and even discovering it as the prototype of popular struggle, Ngũgĩ includes his own revisionist text in these two moments—the storied resistance tradition he celebrated in A Grain of Wheat and the new story he sees occurring around him. Committed to critiquing both colonialism and independence, Petals of Blood duplicates in its cultural work the heroic guerrilla work of forest fighters then and exploited masses now. It's a Mau Mau text, terrorizing both regimes with proof of corruption, hypocrisy and delegimization. Awakening, re-awakening; resistance, revision; above all, *re-authorization* : Ngũgĩ's novel continues the promise Dedan Kimathi made in his "Kenya Land and Freedom Army Charter": "Our people will chase away the foreign exploiters, wipe out the traitors and establish an independent government of the Kenyan people" (Kinyatti 17).

Ethnicity against Mau Mau

Abdulla's realization that "we really were our people," which he believes is the "knowledge" that kept Mau Mau going, handily introduces my second concern, to describe the reactionary discourse of ethnicity now being deployed by Kenyan elites to maintain the inequalities of their rule. Terence Ranger's contribution to *The Invention of Tradition*, "The Invention of Tradition in Colonial Africa," makes it clear that so-called "tribal" identifications and differences were codified by and heightened in the work of early European ethnographers and colonial administrators.[7] The British Protectorate of Kenya carefully nurtured the ethno-cultural distinctiveness and irreconcilable differences between the territory's peoples, in order to frustrate any pan-Kenyan—ie. national—sentiment. Now the inheritors of British rule, the bourgeois nationalists, can manipulate the same identifications.

The question of ethnicity should also be read in a context of delegitimized national leaders: delegitimized because they have failed to lead their nation beyond the rhetoric of Uhuru, and because their authority as figureheads of resistance has not necessarily translated into permanent competence to lead culturally diverse states caught between neocolonialism, neglect and reconstruction. Hence a crisis of authority. Of course, such elite authority was to be questioned by now anyway, as it was by Frantz Fanon in its early days: the role of the ex-colonial power in establishing the authority of the native elite tainted it from the start.[8] For a radical like Ngũgĩ, credibility as an anticolonial leader guarantees no automatic credibility as a national, postcolonial leader, especially given the Western orientation of Kenya in the Kenyatta years. Equally troubling, and more immediate for the populace, is the legitimacy-deficit of the intermediary representatives who ignore their constituencies, mix politics with the private enterprise, use their positions to enrich selves and families, and focus on preserving their privileges rather than extending and developing human and economic potential. Through Nderi wa Riera, Ilmorog's corrupt Member of

Parliament, *Petals of Blood* represents and then rejects these illegitimate leaders and in particular their attempt to rewrite Mau Mau for sectionalist purposes.

In the absence of legitimate leadership, the people search for new figures through whom to express their aspirations; in response, the figure himself (when official, the figure is usually a he) can condition the people's desire. Against this conditioning, I have suggested, Ngũgĩ's politics require that the historic discourse of resistance must motivate contemporary oppositional consciousness: the resistance of peasant (now joined by worker) will, the text implies, be far more efficacious than any newer discourse, whether that be bourgeois nationalism, Christianity or capitalism. Ngũgĩ's scrutiny of ethno-cultural chauvinism, or "tribalism," reveals it as an alienating and divisive weapon of the colonial rulers and their Kenyan successors. The text's victory over the tactic ensures that it will actually become an unwitting *participant* in the people's formation.

Ilmorog's M.P., Nderi wa Riera, has some popular prestige, accrued in his case during the drive for independence, which he quickly turns to private and sectarian profit. He is a typical character for Ngũgĩ to tear down: the standard corrupt politician-businessman, precursor to the thieves and robbers he attacks in *Devil on the Cross*, Nderi neglects his constituents, enriches himself by fronting foreign companies, competes manically with his colleagues for press attention and prestige, and shows himself thoroughly ignorant and negligent of popular needs. Of course, Nderi began right enough: "He was in those days also one of the most vocal and outspoken advocates of reform in and outside Parliament. He would champion such populist causes as putting a ceiling on land ownership; nationalisation of the major industries and commercial enterprises; abolition of illiteracy and unemployment and the East African Federation as a step to Pan-African Unity" (174). But by establishing himself as an antagonist to British interests he invites their attention, and "then he was flooded with offers of directorships in foreign-owned companies." By showing himself willing to participate he saves the system from any real adjustment, sacrificing his nationalist ideals and enriching himself. Beyond these standard postcolonial compromises, though, the text uses him to attack two symptoms of the contemporary malaise he helps spread through Kenya: tourism and ethnocentrism. Both stem from his collaboration with Western money, both are presented as tools for "development," yet both are seen to destroy the fabric of life.[9] For all this contradiction, apparent to people who have their property restricted and their freedom of association policed, Nderi can use the media to insist that his efforts prove him a "great advocate for African personality and

Black authenticity" (258): "'If you must wear wigs,'" he asks, "'why not natural African or black wigs?'" (174).[10] I concentrate here on ethno-centrism and the discourse of "tribalism" it uses.

A suitable word to describe what Nderi's "Kamwene Cultural Organization" seeks to do is "betrayal," on a number of levels. First, any factional grouping which promotes itself at the expense of the larger entity it inhabits—in this case the nation—relegates that entity to secondary status and effectively rejects its legitimacy. A factionalism along lines of ethno-cultural tradition, valorizing a "tribal identity" before citizenship or nationality (but without articulately rejecting the idea of a larger nation—or seceding from it), seeks to perform a double move. In its rationale it eclipses colonial intervention by returning to a prior, supposedly ageless and natural identity. And in its constitutive action it avoids the necessary negotiations and mutualism of nationhood. It rejects the hard task of nation-making in favor of an easier factionalism; like a parasite, it feeds off the nation but does not want the nation to die. Given a situation in which resources are distributed unequally across the national space, local defiance of other areas will only increase the centrifugal tendencies of a postcolonial state; Biafra proved this. There is, ironically, one way of seeing ethnocentrism within a postcolonial state as a movement to subvert Western hegemony, and such ethnic nationalisms usually claim this for their agenda. National boundaries in Africa were established by the various colonial powers, largely irrespective of pre-existing boundaries formed by language, ethnicity, ancient allegiance and so on. Thus to reject a modern, Western-fixed border for the sake of a new (ie. old) one is to reject Western organization of African space. The problem is that such an ahistorical rejection requires much larger, even continental, cooperation and adjudication at all levels of all societies than Nderi's KCO is interested in organizing.[11]

Second, KCO and the factionalism it promotes betray the ideology of Mau Mau as it has been represented in Ngũgĩ's text. When the text presents Mau Mau as a pan-tribal movement for unified territorial independence, it equates any subversion of that unity with subversion of the Mau Mau ethos—and thus of the historical moment at which Kenya's independence was guaranteed. In this way, the text sidesteps the challenge ethnic nationalism poses to its own "Kenyan nationalism": why is pan-ethnic nationalism better than the many nationalisms of separate ethnicities? Notably, and characteristically, Ngũgĩ delivers his response by means of textual advocacy, polemic and excoriation. To have Nderi expose the mean motivations behind ethnic separatism is enough to dismiss it and its sham anti-Westernism.

Worse still, KCO appropriates storied aspects of Mau Mau for antagonistic purposes. Oaths as social agreement existed long before any colonizers arrived, but their symbolic importance to Mau Mau (and to the British counter-insurgency) placed them in a special discursive realm reserved for nationally sacred artifacts. Since Uhuru, much official Kenyan historiography has minimized the role of Mau Mau in Kenyan's independence, while Kenyatta actively ignored guerrilla leaders and soldiers in his organization and policies. This disavowal opens up desacralized Mau Mau symbols for mis-appropriation by figures who want to use the aura of Mau Mau for new purposes. For Ngũgĩ, writing in prison several years later, "Kenyatta negated his past" (*Detained* 90).

The misuse of oathing offends in two ways. It oaths and militarizes the people (who, since this text is to be believed, were Mau Mau participants or supporters) as if they were continuing the struggle Mau Mau began, although in fact this new struggle opposes Mau Mau's goals. And it retrospectively devalues Mau Mau's goals by equating them with the new factionalism. The call for mobilization and sacramental sacrifice for this new identity erases Mau Mau's more valuable call for similar organization with larger purpose. Naturally enough, this coupling also opens up a very negative critique of Mau Mau that Ngũgĩ would surely reject but that textuality permits: to criticize as "ideological" such manipulation of Mau Mau is at the same time to grant the possibility that Mau Mau and "tribalism" actually had much in common. This is a problem of reading which the text can resolve only by producing so emotive a representation of Mau Mau that the reader responds with proper indignation to its misuse. In this regard, the text's work upon the reader replicates KCO's (and Mau Mau's) work upon its recruits: prostituting Mau Mau for the sake of ideological allegiance involves action *upon* reader/people rather than action *for and by* reader/people. The text can only plead that Mau Mau was a voluntarist, spontaneous continuation of local resistance, where KCO is an exploitative perversion. Such an attentuation of interpretation marks the crisis point of political fiction: however authoritatively the text insists that Mau Mau was this and not that, the textuality of its insistence always throws up the inverse claim. At this moment, when conviction rests upon the cumulative rhetorical persuasion of the text, the openness of the text itself threatens to betray the politics.

Third, Nderi's understanding of the new tribalism makes its reactionary purposes clear. It seeks to use supposedly indigenous and ancient identifications for authoritarian purposes: "He himself had recently been sent a secret invitation to join the Free Masons in Nairobi—a secret European business fraternity. Why not an African based counterpart to control Central Province where peasants and workers seemed very restive and this was dangerous [sic] because these people had had a history of anti-colonial violent resistance, a spirit of struggle, which could be misused by the enemies of progress and Economic Prosperity. Later the idea could be sold to other leaders of the other communities" (186). This rich passage, full of distance, desire, fear and collaboration, represents a political elite afraid of change, eager to mate Western models with local situations, unable to imagine that workers and peasants could act on their own initiative, concerned to reify into moral imperatives such bland duplicities as "Economic Progress" and determined to translate all discourses (of control, agency, resistance or manipulation) into money. So far as public consumption goes, Nderi feels as much urgency to "explain to the Western press that this was a different thing [from Mau Mau] all together—that it was not against progressive cooperation and active economic partnership with imperialism" as he feels to convince its victims that KCO is an expression of "cultural authenticity." The point to be made here is that KCO actually continues the colonial project of mapping out the other territory, of defining, assigning, separating, categorizing— and ruling. Modeled on Free Masonry, invoking difference in order to carve up the nation into discrete sectors of population whose membership can be monitored, whose separate (and of course unequal) development can be controlled from above and whose labor always goes for the greater good of their leaders, above all utterly *knowing* the contents of the state: KCO essentially replicates the greatest imperial project of all, apartheid.

Fourth, furthermore, even if KCO never accretes anywhere near that amount of control or organizes that scale of presence, its ideological premise sustains one of the central pillars of Western "knowledge" about Africa, the primacy of "tribal" identification, and thus offers the implicit, comforting inference that alternative senses of identity, say along class lines, cannot emerge. Like white colonizers before him, Nderi believes in the "primitiveness" of his economic inferiors: peasants, squatters and workers simply feel their customary ethno-linguistic origins so powerfully that other considerations fall to its power. To think that tribal or local or gender or racial allegiance infallibly conquers any other rational or irrational possibility for group consciousness is a very comfortable proposition for people who want to fashion the social fabric without appearing to do so. The invocation of the natural or the inevitable or the traditional always reinstates a particular and partial representation of the status quo. Nderi's call for cultural authenticity, even as he enjoys the perks of what on his own terms must be inauthenticity —the cars, the travel, the technology, the money—employs the language of a revived traditionalism to defend against one aspect of modernity elites always fear, the availability of new forms of *politicized* identities which as such recognize and reject naturalized and counter-progressive ways of being (together with the deracinated priests who market them). This is the burden of the connection I drew, at the beginning of this essay, about modernity, class and capitalism. In this sense anti-modern rather than pro-tradition, Nderi's ethnic organizations keep the masses outside both the circles of power operating around Western "investment" and the languages of empowerment offered by Marxism, feminism, human and civil rights, cultural production and critical consciousness. In their motives and their methods—the ethnic chauvinism stirred by powerful people using easy emotions to avoid deep problems and to keep potentially powerful communities divided and disenfranchised—Nderi's plans reveal the conservative applications of cultural moments such as Negritude, essentialism, African personality and other socio-political projects organized by elites after their relevant context of anti-colonial action has passed. The text's dismantling of his message in turn locates an authenticity based on the identification of interests, constituencies and critical understanding. Between Karega on one side and Nderi and Munira on the other, Ngũgĩ maps the difference between superficial and conscious authenticity : it's not just what you are *of*, it's what you are *for*. The abuse of coercively sentimental discourses such as ethnic essentialism can be deconstructed handily enough in this text and elsewhere; their persistence at the margins of supremacist or hegemonic institutions, local or foreign, overt or covert, legal or governmental or scientific, however, shows how successfully they can survive for later demagogues.

Containment and revision

Like all political fiction, *Petals of Blood* fights against the regime's containment of the people through direct or indirect coercion: stirring inter-ethnic tension, neglecting marginal areas, catering to offshore interests, masking general demagoguery as populism. At the same time, like all narrative, the novel inevitably re-contains regime, people and reader alike in its own coercive truths: the potential (and destined and proper) unity of "the people," the authenticity of suffering, the primacy of class struggle and so on. Mau Mau evidences one particularly complicated instance of such textual containment dialectically *recontaining* the social formations it represents. The struggle between a regime's power to contain, a text's power to contain and the power of each to *recontain* provides a compelling focus for cultural studies. For the regime's containment then sparks the anger of political literature: the need to expose coercion, division, illegitimacy. In turn, a text's exposure of power and of discourses it considers false exposes itself to the necessarily critical scrutiny of responsible and responsive reading. And, Ngũgĩ soon discovered, to state censorship.

Revision evolves, in a sense, backward. Revolution as desire looks forward, anticipates, promises the good telos, the new way. But in *Petals of Blood* the revolutionary desire undertakes a prior, foundational search: it *revises* the past, seeing it differently and writing it differently. Revolutionary prophecy is *a priori* a revisionary act, as revision is also a prophetic act. Ngũgĩ's revisionary history of Mau Mau contextualizes, authorizes, legitmizes and sanctifies working-class radicalism. By uncovering the working-class radicalism of Mau Mau, *Petals of Blood* contextualizes, authorizes, legitimizes and sanctifies it. The deployment of this mutually authenticating revision outlines the political desire of this text, since to *envision* is also always to *revision* . And in *Petals of Blood*'s desire we see Kenyan history, polity, territory and consciousness precisely at stake—the shapes of the political terrain this novel contests and the discursive habitat it seeks to control.

Notes

[1]Neil Lazarus, "Great Expectations and After: The Politics of Postcolonialism in African Fiction" *Social Text* 13-14 (1986): 49-63.

[2]A principal proponent of dependency theory is Samir Amin. See for example *Neocolonialism in West Africa* (New York: Monthly Review Press, 1973). Kwame Nkrumah's work in the early 1970s takes the same line. And see Ali Mazrui, *The African Condition: A Political Diagnosis* (New York: Cambridge UP, 1980). For a strong critique of dependency theory's theoretical weaknesses, see Bruce Berman, *Control and Crisis in Colonial Kenya: The Dialectic of Domination* (London: James Curry; Athens, OH: Ohio UP, 1990), ch. 1.

[3]Three recent studies revise the early historiography of Mau Mau, particularly the amateur and official British chronicles: Robert B. Edgerton, *Mau Mau: An African Crucible* (New York: Ballentine, 1989), Berman's *Control and Crisis in Colonial Kenya*, and Maina wa Kinyatti, ed., *Kenya's Freedom Struggle: The Dedan Kimathi Papers* (London: Zed, 1987), to which Ngũgĩ provides an introduction. Respectively popular, scholarly, and polemic, and written for different audiences, these three studies all present Mau Mau as much more than the atavistic 'tribal' revolt demonized by the British—and,

in Kinyatti's opinion, by Kenyan governments, too. Edgerton and Kimathi are particularly good on the post-independence rejection of Mau Mau politics.

[4]This novel's strong critique of religious motivation within political action furthers Ngũgĩ's extended examination of Christianity in Kenya. *Petals* offers the harshest criticism of messianic visions and, except for the Biblical import of the title for Parts 1-3 (drawn from Yeats), largely repudiates his earlier novels' appropriation of Biblical rhetoric for nationalist purposes. Here Christianity is initially imperialist, then reactionary.

[5]Another KANU slogan was "Uhuru na Kazi," freedom and work. An unfortunate and dreadful echo of Auschwitz's "Arbeit macht Frei."

[6]The British policeman who tracked and eventually captured Mau Mau leader Dedan Kimathi.

[7]The fondness of Western media for depicting every African social or political phenomenon through the lens of 'tribal' loyalties, evident in the very confused reporting of unrest in Kenya throughout 1991-2, makes it even more difficult to assess the role of political factions in fostering ethno-linguistic and regional identities rather than class or national allegiances.

[8]For example, "The Pitfalls of National Consciousness," in *The Wretched Earth* (New York: Grove, 1963).

[9]In *Homecoming: Essays on African and Caribbean Literature, Culture and Politics*, Ngũgĩ calls tourism "the virtual prostitution of the whole country" (59).

[10]This and a few other moments deliver Ngũgĩ's sharp critique of national media as propoganda vehicles for the dominant classes.

[11]In 1980, Moi's government conducted inquiries into the power and agendas of ethnic associations. GEMA (the Gĩkũyũ, Embu, Meru Association) was the largest among them; they included The Luo Union, The New Akamba Union, The Abaluhya Association, The Kalenjin Association, and The Miiji-Kenda Association. See Guy Arnold, *Modern Kenya* (London: Longman's, 1981) 91.

Works Cited

Edgerton, Robert B. *Mau Mau: An African Crucible.* New York: Ballentine Books, 1989.

Maina wa Kinyatti. Ed. *Kenya's Freedom Struggle: The Dedan Kimathi Papers.* London: Zed, 1987.

Ngũgĩ wa Thiong'o. *Homecoming: Essays on African and Caribbean Literature, Culture and Politics.* New York: Lawrence Hill, 1973.

—. *Petals of Blood.* London: Heinemann, 1977.

—. *Detained: A Writer's Prison Diary.* London: Heinemann, 1981.

Ranger, Terrance and Eric Hobsbawm, Eds. *The Invention of Tradition.* New York: Cambridge UP (1983), 1992.

Williams, Raymond. *Marxism and Literature.* New York: Oxford UP, 1977.

Gĩtahi Gĩtĩtĩ

Recuperating a 'Disappearing' Art Form: Resonances of 'Gĩcaandĩ' in Ngũgĩ wa Thiong'o's *Devil on the Cross*[1]

I

FOR ALL ITS limitations as political activity, writing has been an essential component of the process of decolonization in Africa, as well as in the rest of the formerly colonized world. If the imperial-colonial enterprise had relied on writing as a strategy of fixing reality, anti-colonial struggles at the cultural and political levels took recourse to writing as countering the suppression inherent in colonial discourse.

Ngũgĩ affirms that "it is impossible to understand what informs African writing, particularly novels written by Africans" (Ngũgĩ, 1986: 63), without reading Fanon's The Wretched of the Earth, among other books.

That the burden of emancipatory writing would be taken up by an easily recognizable élite from among the colonized or formerly colonized does not require much demonstration. In his *The Wretched of the Earth* (1961, 1965), especially in the chapters entitled "The Pitfalls of National Consciousness" and "On National Culture," Frantz Fanon wrote fairly prophetically about the tumultuous events that would characterize the period between insurrection and nominal independence in the formerly colonized world. Fanon's insight into the nature and character of the "national bourgeoisies" to emerge out of this maelstrom is particularly keen. While he vilified this "profiteering caste" as the bane of the post-independence moment, Fanon also recognized that this class would partly have enhanced the nationalist momentum. In their hands, writing, in one form or another, had played, and would continue to play, a central role in the process of colonial struggle and in the move toward self-determination.

It is not necessary here to demonstrate the influence of Fanon's thought on African (and other "Third World") ideological/political formations. Suffice it to say that there is ample evidence that Ngũgĩ wa Thiong'o would be familiar with

Fanon's politics of culture, language and autonomy. Indeed, Ngũgĩ affirms that "it is impossible to understand what informs African writing, particularly novels written by Africans" (Ngũgĩ,1986: 63), without reading Fanon's *The Wretched of the Earth*, among other books. Evidently, this observation is no less applicable to Ngũgĩ's own writings, creative as well as critical. Fanon's thesis on the (re)deployment of oral literature is a fitting point of departure for an examination of Ngũgĩ's language practice in the novel *Devil on the Cross* (1982), a practice further amplified in his aptly titled *Decolonizing the Mind* (1986).

Fanon postulated that, in the colonies, national(ist) literature is born at the juncture when the native intellectual moves away from addressing the colonizer and creates a completely new public—his own people:

> It is only from that moment on that we can speak of a national literature. Here there is, at the level of literary creation, the taking up and clarification of themes which are typically nationalist. This may be properly called a literature of combat, in the sense that it calls on the whole people to fight for their existence as a nation. It is a literature of combat, because it molds the national consciousness, giving it form and contours and flinging open before it new and boundless horizons; it is a literature of combat because it assumes responsibility, and because it is the will to liberty expressed in terms of time and space. (Fanon, 1968: 240)

According to Fanon, the nations arising out of the colonial project of territorial and cultural domination incorporate the oral tradition into the liberatory textual praxis that is part of the process of decolonization:

> On another level, the oral tradition—stories, epics and songs of the people—which formerly were filed away as set pieces are now beginning to change. The storytellers who used to relate inert episodes now bring them alive and introduce into them modifications which are increasingly fundamental. There is a tendency to bring conflicts up to date and to modernize the kinds of struggle which the stories evoke, together with the names of heroes and the types of weapons. The method of allusion is is more and more widely used. (Fanon, 1968: 240)

Ngũgĩ wa Thiong'o's writings, particularly those composed in the Gĩkũyũ language, fall within the ambit of Fanon's vision. There is a sense in which *Petals of Blood* (1977) can be seen to have aspired to be the post-independence *magnus opus* sufficient to the task outlined above. But *Petals of Blood* was written in English. Beginning in 1977, Ngũgĩ's involvement with the Kamĩrĩĩthũ "phenomenon" would be largely responsible for his determination to write in the Gĩkũyũ language, starting with *Ngaahika Ndeenda* (1977) and leading on to *Devil on the Cross* and its successor, *Matigari* (1989), among others. The themes which Ngũgĩ's Gĩkũyũ-language texts revisit and re-elaborate are very like the motifs in a *gĩcaandĩ* performance which are characterized less by their lack of resolution than by a dialectical indeterminancy.

II

Ngũgĩ has consistently written and spoken openly about "the history of Kenyan people creating a resistance culture, a revolutionary culture of courage and patriotic heroism ... A fight-back, creative culture, unleashing tremendous energies among the Kenyan people" (Ngũgĩ, 1981: 64). This history of resistance takes place at many levels—politically, economically, and in the realm of culture or socially creative labour. In literature, writes Ngũgĩ,

> the energy found creative expression in the many patriotic
> songs, poems, plays and dances over the years, giving rise to
> a great patriotic literary tradition of Kenyan poetry and
> theatre. There was for instance the Ituĩka, a revolutionary
> cultural festival among the Aagĩkũyũ which was enacted every
> twenty-five years both as a ceremony transferring power from
> one generation to the other; and as a communal renewal of
> their commitment to a struggle against tyrants, as their
> forefathers the Iregi generation had done. (1981: 65)

Devil on the Cross is obviously Ngũgĩ's test case for the adequacy of the Gĩkũyũ language to articulate political, economic, linguistic, religious, philosophical, and scientific concepts. Ngũgĩ also wanted to give central place to the oral tradition as an efficient conveyor of collective experience. Especially acute is Ngũgĩ's awareness of the sweeping colonial disparagement of non-European modalities of local expression. With reference to *gĩcaandĩ*,[2] W. Scoresby Routledge and Katherine Routledge had written in 1910 that

Occasionally a boy is seen going about by himself, dancing, singing, and accompanying the song by shaking a gourd which he holds in his hand, and which has been formed into a rattle. This proceeding he continues for a month or six weeks, and is termed ku-i'-nya ki-shan'-di (sic).

The words of the song are traditional; they are apparently gibberish, and convey nothing even to the performer. The gourd is scoured by him with signs which constitute a record of his travel. Instruction in the art of this singing and writing is given to the boy who wishes to learn it, by a "warrior" or young man. (Routledge and Routledge, 1910: 109)

There is a schizophrenic twist to the Routledge account at this point: are a people who indulge this "gibberish" capable of the following accomplishments?

The Akikūyu as a race (sic) are gifted with the musical ear. Their songs are almost always improvised solos with a chorus sung to a well-known air. Some hundreds of persons, strangers to one another, will join in a song with the dash and precision of a trained choir.

The rhythmical movements of their dances, too, show their marked sense of musical time .

By song and dance they give expression to their emotions with a spontaneity that is quite foreign to us. (Routledge and Routledge, 1910: 111)

It is also rather difficult to imagine that the Routledges did not witness an adult performance of gĩcaandĩ, or that they could have failed to see that the "boy" in question was undergoing the apprenticeship which would prepare him for his later years among his poetic peers.

Nor is it difficult to understand the reasons for the devaluation of African literary artefacts. Colonial description (which served also as a mode of containment and control) vacillated between the total dismissal and the *reductio ad absurdum* of the cultural production of the Other. In her *Oral Literature in Africa* (1970), Ruth Finnegan points out that the main characteristic of European study of African oral literature was the reduction of the latter to raw ethnographic material. Until the mid-1850s, European collections and translations

... contain narratives of various kinds (including stories about both animals and humans), historical texts, proverbs, riddles, vernacular texts describing local customs, and very occasionally songs or poems. (Finnegan, 1970: 28)

Early European academic, freelance, and missionary "interest" in African oral material is remarkable for its fragmentary and fragmenting nature, with a tendency to deny or obscure indigenous African literary traditions:

The main emphasis in these collections was, it is true, linguistic (or, in some cases, religio-educational, preoccupied with what it was thought fitting for children to know). There was little attempt to relate the texts to their social context, elucidate their literary significance, or describe the normal circumstances of their recitation. There are many questions, therefore, which these texts cannot answer. (Finnegan, 1970: 28)

Scant attention seems to have been paid to sung poetry: even when it was collected, its study was less rigorous:

Prose narrative was more often referred to than sung poetry, since it was easier to make a quick record of it and since it was more suitable, particularly in the form of 'myths', for use in functional analysis. Altogether the emphasis was on brief synopsis or paraphrase rather than a detailed recording of literary forms as actually recorded. (Finnegan, 1970: 38)

Finnegan further notes that obsession with primitivism and the "folkloristic" bias in European scholarship had the effect of relativizing and therefore devaluing the object of scholarship:

Because primitive tribes were supposed to be preoccupied with tradition rather than innovation, 'traditional' tales were sought and 'new' ones ignored or explained away. Because interest was focused on broad evolutionary stages, few questions were asked about the idiosyncratic history, culture, or literary conventions of a particular people. Finally because origins and early history assumed such importance in people's minds, there was little emphasis on the *contemporary* relevance of a piece of literature, so there seemed every excuse for collecting and publishing bits and pieces without attempting to relate them to their particular social and literary context. (Finnegan, 1970: 37)

It is precisely the contemporary relevance of the diverse indigenous African (or Kenyan) literary forms that Ngũgĩ is at pains to demonstrate and concretize. "The quest for relevance" is not only a chapter in *Decolonizing the Mind* but also Ngũgĩ's entire literary *modus vivendi*. However incomplete the task, the rendering of *Devil on the Cross* as a "gĩcaandĩ" novel represents an effort to contemporize *gĩcaandĩ*. There is ample evidence of Ngũgĩ's determination to attempt to repair, or at least arrest, the damage occasioned to the Kenyan (and by extension, African) political, cultural and spiritual body by decades of colonial and neo-colonial activity.

In a prefatory note to *Decolonizing the Mind* (1986), dedicated to "all those who write in African languages, and to all those who over the years have maintained the dignity of the literature, culture, philosophy, and other treasures carried by African languages," Ngũgĩ declared that he was bidding "farewell to English as a vehicle for any of my writings. From now on it is Gĩkũyũ and Kiswahili all the way." Time and necessity have already impinged on Ngũgĩ's pledge; nevertheless, Ngũgĩ has steadfastly blazed what is more than a symbolic trail in the campaign to foreground the question of the material and historical conditions of collective expression. Subsequent to the publication of *Petals of Blood* (1977), Ngũgĩ has written, published and lectured predominantly in Gĩkũyũ, relying on the medium of translation to bridge the linguistic gap.

Ngũgĩ's advocacy of writing in African languages is perhaps best summarized in his assertion that

> We African writers are bound by our calling to do for our languages what Spencer, Milton and Shakespeare did for English; what Pushkin and Tolstoy did for Russian; indeed what all writers in world history have done for their languages by meeting the challenge of creating a literature in them,

which process later opens the languages for philosophy, science, technology and all the other areas of human creative endeavours. (Ngũgĩ, 1986: 29)

Ngũgĩ is careful not to fetishize the mere gesture of writing in an African language, being conscious that

> [W]riting in our languages per se—although a necessary first step in the correct direction—will not in itself bring about the renaissance in African cultures if that literature does not carry the content of our people's anti-imperialist struggles to liberate their productive forces from foreign control .... (Ngũgĩ, 1986: 29)

Ngũgĩ has borrowed and made extensions to Amilcar Cabral's ideological concept of a "return to the source"[3] as a means of re-inventing a set of enabling, transformative modalities for social change. Proceeding from the truism that "the struggle of Kenyan national languages against domination by foreign languages is part of the wider historical struggle of the Kenyan national culture against imperialist domination" (1981: 61), Ngũgĩ urges Kenyan writers to remember that

> [N]o foreigners can ever develop our languages, our litera-tures, our theatre for us: that we in turn cannot develop our cultures and literatures through borrowed tongues and imitations.
>
> Only by a return to the roots of our being in the languages and cultures and heroic histories of the Kenyan people can we rise up to the challenge of helping in the creation of a Kenyan patriotic national literature and culture that will be the envy of many foreigners and the pride of Kenyans. (Ngũgĩ, 1981: 64-65)

In *Devil on the Cross*, Gatuĩria is Ngũgĩ's perfect example of the erstwhile "assimilated" intellectual groping his/her way back to a nativist or progressive consciousness, tripping over the syllables of his/her native language and despairing of ever regaining a coherent centredness:

Let us now look about us. Where are our national languages now? Where are the books written in the alphabets of our national languages? Where is our own literature now? Where is the wisdom and knowledge of our fathers now? Where is the philosophy of our fathers now? The centres of wisdom that used to guard the entrance to our national homestead have been demolished; the fire of wisdom has been allowed to die; the seats around the fireside have been thrown on to a rubbish heap; the guard posts have been destroyed; and the youth of the nation has hung up its shields and spears. It is a tragedy that there is nowhere we can go to learn the history of our country ... (1982: 58)

Gatuīria, the seeker-searcher-researcher who is also in part Ngūgī's *alter ego*, recounts that he and "some people at the university, students and teachers, are now attempting to unearth the roots of our culture. The roots of Kenyan national culture can be sought only in the traditions of all the nationalities of Kenya" (1982: 59). His dream is to compose "a piece of music for many human voices accompanied by an orchestra made up of all kinds of national instruments: skin, wind, string and brass ... " (1982: 59). Towards the end of the novel, Gatuīria has completed the score (it will never be played, it turns out) which is nothing short of the majestic harmony of a new and changed Kenya:

In his mind, of course, Gatuīria can reconstruct the whole process of mixing the various voices and the various sounds in harmony: how and where all the voices meet; how and where they part, each voice taking its own separate path, and finally how and where they come together again, the various voices floating in harmony like the Thīrīrīka River flowing through flat plains towards the sea, all the voices blending into each other like the colours of the rainbow. (1982: 226)

The *gīcaandī* instrument ranks high on the grand score that Gatuīria is composing. Significantly, its inclusion in the First Movement ("Voices from the past, before the coming of British imperialism") connotes a pre-colonial, pre-European knowledge-of-the-self. *Gīcaandī* as a questing (dialogic), multi-voiced text seems to have provided Gatuīria with a partial solution to the nagging question he has been wrestling with:

> Our stories, our riddles, our songs, our customs, our traditions, everything about our national heritage has been lost to us.
> Who can play the gīcaandī for us today and read and interpret the verses written on the gourd? (1982: 59)

And music as an inseparable component of the enactment (performance) of contemporary Kenyan history must reflect the vicissitudes of resistance and struggle as well as the desired triumph of the peasant-worker coalition against international monoply capital. When Warīīnga wonders why it has taken Gatuīria two whole years to compose a national oratorio, the latter replies:

> Music that tells the story of one's country? Music to be played by an orchestra of hundreds of instruments and sung by hundreds of human voices? And remember, you have to indicate where each instrument comes in. My friend, there is music and *the* music; there is song and *the* song! (1982: 226)

Like his own not-so-fictional creation, Gatuīria, Ngũgĩ is engaged in a search for suitable containers and conveyors of the various facets of individual African cultures—literature, philosophy, technology, politics, musicology, and so on. Ngũgĩ questions the role of research institutes at African universities (such as institutes of African Studies: what else should they be, Ngũgĩ has once asked). It is not Gatuīria's voice so much as Ngũgĩ's that we hear in the exploration of cultural ways and means:

> Gatuīria is trying to explain to Warīīnga the movement of the different voices and sounds. He is trying to explain to Warīīnga the kinds of instruments that might be made to represent the workers and peasants as they rescue the soul of the nation from imperialist slavery. He is trying to explain the difficulties of writing down African music, for the notation of African music has not yet been sufficiently developed and differentiated from that of European music. (1982: 230)

As we shall see later, the narrative structure of *Devil on the Cross* is undergirded by an interlacing network of genres—riddles, proverbs, songs, "tales," myths and legends, and so forth. Though no single genre is predominant, the proverb as a "condensing" narrative form (especially in the stacking so consciously conducted at the novel's opening) is worth some attention. The urgency to "reveal all that is hidden" is already forcefully articulated in the Gĩkũyũ proverb: *Kwa mwaria gũkĩhĩa, kwa mũkiri kwahĩire tene.* (The house of the person who does not call out for help is more likely to burn down than the house of the person who calls for help).

The narrative burden in *Devil on the Cross* is carried by the Prophet of Justice who is simultaneously/interchangeably the Gĩcaandĩ Player. The history of infamy of post-independence Kenya— the "story" of the reign of the devil of capital after he has been resuscitated by his local acolytes at the urging of and with the active support of international monopoly capital— is the burden weighing heavily upon the Prophet of Justice, inhibiting him from telling "this story [which] was too disgraceful, too shameful [and therefore] should be concealed in the depths of everlasting darkness" (1982: 1). But then

> Warĩĩnga's mother came to me when dawn was breaking, and in tears she beseeched me: Gĩcaandĩ Player, tell the story of the child I loved so dearly. Cast light upon all that happened, so that each may pass judgement only when he knows the whole truth. Gĩcaandĩ Player, reveal all that is hidden. (1982: 1)

It is demanded of the Prophet of Justice that he constitute himself into an oracle, in the best sense of the word. The task cannot ultimately remain an individual one: prophecy, the projection of what is (likely) to come to pass—which involves what has come to pass as well—is a collective concern.The Prophet of Justice is at first diffident, but after a ritual fast of seven days he is empowered to speak. A voice "like a great clap of thunder" admonishes him: "Who has told you that prophecy is yours alone, to keep to yourself?" It is the voice of the people, which is the voice of God, which mandates and authorizes the Gĩcaandĩ Player's complex narrative. The moment of the initiation of the many-layered *gĩcaandĩ* narrative is the beginning of an extended divination of the ills of the nation. The Prophet of Justice will henceforth discharge the office of diviner/priest, investigator, philosopher, counsellor, comforter, the voice of conscience, validating once again the multi-purpose function of *gīcaandī* as formulated in the coded utterance which comes at the beginning of virtually every *gīcaandī* performance:

Gīcaandī to ūgo kana ciira,
Kana ūthamaki wa riika;
Ti kūragūra matua kūragūra,
Na ti ciira. (Vittorio Merlo Pick, 1973: 167)

Gīcaandī is not only magical divination [or medicine];
nor is it just the government of the extant age-set;
it is more than diagnosing the cause of illness and
prescribing a remedial ceremony;
gīcaandī is not a law-suit. (My translation)

Although it is the form he most wants to rediscover and refashion as a powerful dramatic-narrative form in *Devil on the Cross* , Ngũgĩ had, by 1979, referred only obliquely to the *gīcaandī* tradition of the Aagīkũyũ. In *Writers in Politics*, Ngũgĩ describes how "the oppression of Kenyan languages during colonial and postcolonial times went hand in hand with the suppression of the cultures of the various nationalities" (1981: 63). He offers as examples the banning in Central Province of "the big Ituīka cultural festival of dances, songs, and poems, and instrumental music." In the period of British colonial rule, Ngũgĩ tells us, "the only poems and songs ever banned were those composed in Kenyan languages." Among these, Ngũgĩ enumerates the provocative *mũthīrĩgũ* dance and song in the 1930s and the Mau Mau patriotic songs in the 1950s. Curiously, Ngũgĩ makes no specific reference to *gīcaandī*. It is reasonable to speculate that the performance of *gīcaandī* was banned sometime between 1900 and the 1930s; there is, for all practical purposes, no official mention of this banning. The mystery is further deepened by the relative paucity of publishing, indigenous or otherwise, on the subject of what now persists as a severely endangered art form.

III

The *Kikuyu-English Dictionary* defines *gīcaandī* as follows:

n. (III), picture rattle shaken rhythmically as an accompaniment; a kind of dance, the song to which the rattle is an accompaniment; *ina* ~, sing the rattle-song which consists of riddles and conundrums in which two persons compete; cf. *irebeta*. (1964: 46)

The *Dictionary* further defines *irebeta* as follows:

> *irebeta*, ma-, n. (III), song with cryptic phrasing sung to the accompaniment of the picture rattle; see *gīcandī*. 2. wise witty saying, epigram; wise-cracking indulged in between young people in conversation as well as in song .... (1964: 374)

Clearly, then, *gīcaandī* and poetry are intricately linked, and their field of application is very broad.

The most extensive written *gīcaandī* text is Vittorio Merlo Pick's *Ndaī na Gīcandī: Kikuyu Enigmas/Enigmi Kikuyu*, first published in 1973. Part Two of the book contains 127 stanzas of a *gīcaandī* performance (out of an original 150). Merlo Pick, who after V. Ghilardi categorizes *gīcaandī* as "traditional poetry sung in the moonlight," is drawn to this particular genre for its ethnological value. He writes:

> The GICANDI is a poem which in the thirties [1930s] was still known to a few initiates, and is now almost forgotten. It is made up of elegantly elaborated enigmas which were sung by two people in competition. The song was accompanied by the shaking of a kind of rattle, itself called gīcandī , which was prepared specially and blessed by a medicine-man who had inherited the secret. This instrument is particularly interesting, because it bears, carved on its side, writings in the mnemonic-pictorial system, the only specimen of this kind, as far as I know, to be found among Bantu tribes. (Merlo Pick, 1973: 18)

It is necessary to state that *gīcaandī* , while it is a trade plied by the initiated (much like "poetry" which is still "read" to us by "poets" who are "better" than we are) is by no means a dead art form. At least in the 1970s and ˙ 80s, the Gīkūyū Service of The Voice of Kenya regularly aired *gīcaandī* performances and interviews with living *gīcaandī* poets. What is curious indeed is the silence in

Kenyan official circles surrounding the life and future of *gĩcaandĩ* as a representative of dialogue poetry in its myriad forms in Kenya. It is remarkable, too, that Jomo Kenyatta, in his *Facing Mount Kenya* (1938), his pioneering work on the life of the Aagĩkũyũ, wrote not a word about *gĩcaandĩ* .

Contrary to Merlo Pick's assertion, it is not at all probable that in the 1930s *gĩcaandĩ* was "known to a few initiates," given the numbers of performers whose texts have been recorded in the last few decades—for The Voice of Kenya radio and by researchers such as Wanjikũ Mũkabi Kabĩra (with Karega Mũtahi), Lee K. Kaguongo and Kĩmani Njogu, among others.

Merlo Pick's *Ndaĩ na Gĩcandĩ* presumes a total separation of genres such as riddles, proverbs, story and poetry. The reductive, ethnographic impulse is evident in this description of *ndaĩ* ("riddles") :

> The ndaĩ have as a subject, in most cases, matters and objects which belong to the environment in which the Kikuyu live and which they know in all details and circumstances: the hut and the homestead, the village, the members of the family, the domestic animals and their habits, the birds, the field, the crops, the forest, the different kinds of trees, the waste plains,—the whole nature with which a Kikuyu is unendingly in contact, observing its phenomena during the long hours spent over the grazing animals, in loneliness. (Merlo Pick, 1973: 26)

"Riddling," however, is creative activity, requiring the ability to metaphorize across time, space and event. In Merlo Pick's introduction, the literary value of *ndaĩ* is dismissed amid claims of the cultural exoticism of the Aagĩkũyũ whose intellectual faculties are *intrinsically* different from those of Europeans:

> [Riddles] often play on a double meaning, figures of speech, comparisons, metaphorical meanings, exaggerations of speech. The likeness between the object described and the one meant is very varied: the Kikuyu often space with their imagination in the realm of strangely grand representations, and we Europeans feel lost; very often we would find ourselves under obligation to «pay» in order to be told the solutions to the riddles; and even then we would be unable to see the

connection. (Merlo Pick, 1973: 26)

Even a cursory reading of a *gīcaandī* text reveals the complex interplay of genres—riddles, proverbs, biographical "information," history, commentary—and a performative dramatic quality which invests in voice, gesture and attention to the audience. Merlo Pick violently separates *ndaī* from *gīcaandī*, genres that are traditionally interdependent and integrated. He thus does violence to a discourse/tradition that recognises no such dichotomy.

The narrative tenor of *Devil on the Cross* is saturated with a "conversational," oral/aural dimension that demonstrates the dramatic sequence of challenge, response, conflict/tension, and reconciliation typical of *gīcaandī* performances. *Devil on the Cross* is Ngũgĩ's own translation of *Caitaani Mūtharaba-inī*. Ngũgĩ's profound interest in theatre is well demonstrated by *The Trial of Dedan Kimathi* (with Mĩcere Mũgo), *Ngaahika Ndeenda* (with Ngũgĩ wa Mĩriĩ) and *Maitū Njugĩra*, to name but a few. Yet Ngũgĩ translates the original *mūini wa gīcaandī* as "Gĩcaandī Player." In Gĩkũyũ the verb *kũina* means to sing, to dance, to perform a dance. In the Gĩkũyũ cultural milieu song and dance are, generally speaking, not separable, so even the phrase *kũina rwĩmbo* translates as both to sing (a song) *and* to perform a dance. There is an important dimension of performance which is omitted in the move from *mūini wa gīcaandī* (one who performs the *gīcaandī*) to "Gĩcaandī Player." The oral/aural dimension of *gīcaandī* is part of its inscription/creation. Performance is conveyed through the act of *kũina gīcaandī*—both "singing" and extemporaneous (but not haphazard) creation of verse. *Uini* (performance in its entirety) consists of "rhythming," "poetry-making," (dependent on a sense of movement, balance, structure) and prosody.

As Merlo Pick had noted, the object referred to in a *ndaī* is called *mũũndũ* (man), unlike the *gīcaandī* in which it is called *ngeithi* (greeting). While this is true enough, *ngeithi* can also mean subject, message, address, debate, point of view, discourse (or a variety of discourses). The pictographic inscriptions on the *gīcaandī* instrument itself are also called *ngeithi*. A typical *gīcaandī* "line" states:

Ngeithi nī hīrīrī nyiingī
Kũrī irũũngiī, kũrī ikĩĩgiī
Na kũrī ituramīire iria ingī

Ngeithi are of many stripes

There are those which stand upright; others
are horizontal
And others which face each other. (My translation)

The *gĩcaandĩ* instrument is made from a gourd which grows from a gourd
vine, *rũũngũ*, which is an annual plant. The gourd is easily broken, and in times
of drought there may be no vines to produce gourds to be made into *gĩcaandĩ*
instruments. The latter scenario is enacted in an excerpt of the *gĩcaandĩ* text
recorded by Merlo Pick, where one participant poses the crucial question:

> Q. Ngũũria kũrĩa mwarutire nyũngũ cia kũhaanda nĩguo
> mware gĩcandĩ: mwarutire kũ? Na Gĩkũyũ gĩothe kĩagĩte na
> Ikamba na Ukabi.
> (Merlo Pick, 1973: 199)

> I wonder where you obtained the seeds for planting, that you
> might start *gĩcaandĩ*,
> when none could be found in the land of the Gĩkũyũ and
> Ikaamba and Ukabi.

> A. Uigue: kaheti cũcũ gakĩruta tũgoto twĩrĩ: tũgoto twohete
> mbegũ ya nyũngũ, rĩrĩa gũkoira ahande.

> Listen: My old grandmother took them out of a purse made
> of banana-bark, and planted them when the rains started. (My
> translation)

Besides, a performer can always lose his instrument to a competitor. What
would happen to *gĩcaandĩ* as an art form or tradition if its very source were
destroyed or lost? Seeds of the gourd vine must always be saved, so that a future
planting can be insured. *Gĩcaandĩ* is, ultimately, about self-generation and
continuity: the storing of the seed for future planting involves a selection of the
best. The continuity of *gĩcaandĩ* as a productive text requires discursive strategies
that accommodate diverse interpretations and points of view. Hence the call to
be adaptable: *Garũrĩra mbeũ, ti ya kĩnya kĩmwe.* (Change, for the seeds in the
gourd are not all of one kind.)
Kĩnya is the generic name for a gourd or calabash in the Gĩkũyũ language.

The proverb refers to the practice of storing seeds in gourds. There is an important parallel to be drawn between the gourd used as a seed store and the *gīcaandī* gourd as an emblem of a people's cultural "wisdom." This self-signifying gesture demonstrates not only the consciousness of the danger posed by the vagaries of the natural world on community survival, but also the literary encoding of the requisite strategies for the continuance of *gīcaandī* as a cultural artistic form. In this regard, *gīcaandī* is the equivalent of *kīgīīna* (treasury). Besides, as the Aagīkūyū are fond of saying, *[Mūūndū] Utamerithīītie ndaigaga kīgīīna thī.* (S/he whose seeds have not germinated does not put away the seed-hoard.)

As an event that takes place in the public square, *gīcaandī* is not only a performance but a site of performance, providing a model for interpersonal and public discourse. Practically every *gīcaandī* performance concludes with the formula: *Hau twacemania ūmūūthī, no ho tūgaacemania rūūciū.* (We will meet again tomorrow in the same place where we met today). Far from signifying changelessness, this formulaic line promises future encounters between performers in which new themes will be introduced and old ones re-examined. The public, let it not be forgotten, will be in attendance.

Incidentally, the instrument of divination, the *mwano*, is also made from a gourd/calabash and contains rattling seeds. The *gīcaandī* and the *mwano* are both means of discerning the nature of that which is not always clearly understood. The "answers" in a *gīcaandī* contest and the prognosis given by a "medicine-man" are almost never the same, even for the same "seeker" or quest(ion). Herein lies the value of the implied connection between *kūina gīcaandī* and *gūthiī ūgo-inī* (to go to a diviner).

The relationship between individual *perform*-ance and collective participation is cogently dramatized in the exchange where one *mūini wa gīcaandī* enjoins the other to

Nyambīkīra ngeithi, amu ndingīhota ūtambīkīte.

Start the weaving of the *ngeithi* for me, for I cannot begin without your collaboration. (My translation)

The fellow *mūini* responds with a most complex formulation of the communal ethos within which *gīcaandī* is performed:

Mūtumi wa kīondo. Mwambīrīria wa ūhandi. Mūgo agīkunūrwo

ambīrīrie ūgo akīambīrīria na ndawoine. (Merlo Pick, 1973: 297)

The weaver of a string basket. The young girl who ritually initiates the season's planting of the seed. The diviner/ medicine man, when he is first "initiated," has no prior experience. (My translation)

Throughout most of his writing, Ngūgī pays homage to the enormous contribution of peasants and workers to the Kenyan economy and culture. The Kenya Land and Freedom Army (or "Mau Mau") figures prominently in Ngūgī's musings on Kenyan history. The metaphor of the weaving of the *kīondo* finds its ultimate articulation in a stanza of a "Mau Mau" song of the 1950s and ' 60s in which what was apparently started by an individual or a small group matures and is borne to its conclusion by collaborative enterprise:

> Kīondo kīambirwo nī Kenyatta wa Mūigai
> Mūingī ūkīogothera ndigi
> Mau Mau īgītiriha
> Kamūingī kooyaga ndīrī
> Kīondo kīambirwo

> The *kīondo* was "started" by Kenyatta son of Mūigai
> The patriotic collective spun the uprights and the cross strings
> "Mau Mau" put the finishing touches
> The *kīondo* was thus woven. (My translation)

In *Matigari*, Ngūgī pays particular attention to the lessons to be gleaned from the Mau Mau struggle and how those lessons might be applied to the continuing engagement between the producers and the parasites in contemporary Kenya. Change and innovation are key words in both *Matigari* and *Devil on the Cross*; both ideas proceed from the construction of "the other heart," a humanity motivated by the collective good:

> That humanity is in turn born of many hands working together, for, as Gīkūyū once said, a single finger cannot kill

a louse; a single log cannot make a fire last through the night; a single man, however strong, cannot build a bridge across a river; and many hands can lift a weight, however heavy. The unity of our sweat is what makes us able to change the laws of nature, able to harness them to the needs of our lives, instead of our lives remaining slaves of the laws of nature. That's why Gĩkũyũ also said: Change, for the seeds in the gourd are not all of one kind. (Ngũgĩ, 1982: 52)

In Ngũgĩ's reckoning, Mau Mau and their ideological offspring, *matigari ma njirũũngi* (those who survived the bullets), become the logical descendants of the Iregi generation, that

> ... generation of revolutionary rebels, who had overthrown the corrupt dictatorial regime of King Gĩkũyũ, established ruling councils and established (sic) the procedure for handing over power, an event commemorated in the Ituĩka festival of music, dance, poetry and theatre. The last such festival was held towards the end of the nineteenth century. The next, due in about 1930, was banned by the colonial overlords as a threat to public peace and order. (Ngũgĩ, 1981: 65)

Gĩcaandĩ celebrates this long history of resistance, throwing its weight behind the party of Iregi (the ones who said 'NO!') and their descendants:

> Kuuma Wanyahoro gũũka
> Gũtirĩ kĩama giũkĩĩte
> No kĩrĩa kĩa Iregi na Mũũriũ (Mũkabi Kabĩra and Karega Mũtahi, 1988: 167)

> Since the arrival of Wanyahoro
> No [new] party has arisen
> Except that of Iregi and his descendants.[4] (My translation)

The "open endings" of both *Devil on the Cross* ("Warĩĩnga walked on, without once looking back. But she knew with all her heart that the hardest struggles of her life's journey lay ahead ... " [1982: 254]) and *Matigari* ("And suddenly he seemed to hear the workers' voices, the voices of the peasants, the voices of the students and of other patriots of all the different nationalities of the land, singing in harmony: Victory shall be ours ... " [1987: 175]) no doubt reweave a *gĩcaandĩ* theme:

> Hau twacemania ũmũũthĩ,
> No ho tũgaacemania rũũciũ ...

Notes

[1]This is an abbreviated version of a work-in-progress on the subject of *gĩcaandĩ* as dialogue/dialogic poetry.

[2]My orthography, including the spelling of *gĩcaandĩ*, is in accordance with the recommendations of the Gĩkũyũ Language Committee of 1980/81 (not to be mistaken for the colonial United Kikuyu Language Committee [1949]). Merlo Pick's orthography follows the latter.

[3]See especially "National Liberation and Culture," in *Return to the Source: Selected Speeches of Amilcar Cabral.* (New York: Monthly Review Press, 1973).

[4]Wanyahoro is the "corrupted" name of Francis Hall, an early colonial administrator in the Mũrang'a district of Central Kenya. The implication of the statement: We hold steadfastly to the tradition of resistance of the Iregi generation. Our embrace of other political "parties" is merely strategic.

Works Cited

Benson, T. G. *Kikuyu-English Dictionary.* Oxford: The Clarendon Press, 1964.

Fanon, Frantz. *The Wretched of the Earth.* New York: Grove Press, 1968.

Finnegan, Ruth. *Oral Literature in Africa.* Oxford: The Clarendon Press, 1970.

Merlo Pick, Vittorio. *Ndaĩ na Gĩcandĩ.* Bologna: Editrice Missionaria Italiana, 1973.

Mũkabi Kabĩra, Wanjikũ, and Mũtahi, Karega. *Gĩkũyũ Oral Literature.* Nairobi: Heinemann, 1988.

Ngũgĩ wa Thiong'o. *Decolonizing the Mind.* London: James Currey, 1986.

—. *Detained: A Writer's Prison Diary.* Nairobi: Heinemann, 1981.

—. *Devil on the Cross.* Nairobi: Heinemann, 1982.

—. *Matigari.* Trans. by Wangũi wa Goro. Nairobi/London: Heinemann, 1989.

—. *Writers in Politics.* Nairobi/London: Heinemann, 1981.

Routledge, W. Scoresby, and Routledge, Katherine. *With a Prehistoric People: The Akikuyu of British East Africa.* London: Frank Cass & Co. Ltd. , 1910 (1968).

Decolonizing the Child

> For the majority of Third World peoples brutalized by the nightmare reality of a colonial past and a neocolonial present, art is literally a matter of life and death. It reflects in varied forms the ongoing class struggle .... Art cannot deny its social origin nor its historical destiny.
>
> —Juan E.S Jnr, 1988

CHILDREN IN LITERATURE and in the real world are generally seen as representing promise, hope, and optimism. They epitomize renewal and regeneration. Quite often, their lives are used as a basis for reflection on the world in which we live. In literature oriented towards social change, the child is used as a take-off for the conflicted representation of existing educational theory and practice.

Throughout the chil-dren's books, Ngũgĩ uses problematization as both a strategy and as a methodology of getting children to know their world. He poses a problem and, together with the child, works through the problem in order to resolve it.

In God's Bits of
not comprehend N'deye
awareness of the sig-
strike. Touti's Eurocen-
cated her from her so-
that she neither under-
physical geography and
around her nor the basis
La Guma's In the Fog of
racist South African
teaching that "repres-
and any attempts at

Wood Mama Sofi can-
Touti's apparent un-
nificance of the worker's
tric education has extri-
cial fabric to the extent
stands her immediate
the socio-political set up
of labour law. In Alex
the Season's End, the
regime is depicted as
sion is God-ordained
changing things is sin-

ful" (87). Education is used in the legitimation of oppressive racist policies. But through the efforts of teacher's like Flotman, students are exposed to an alternative education that may lead to individual and national liberation. Some of them start getting involved in real liberative pursuits; they distribute antigovernment leaflets and read books on guerrilla warfare in preparation for military action against apartheid. And in Viera's The Real Life of Domingoes Xavier young Timothy reads critical books and liberation pamphlets from Luanda in order to understand his people's struggle against Portuguese colonialism. Furthermore, the school going Abidjibidji in *God's Bits of Wood* and Joseph and Akinyi in *Petals of Blood* are directly linked with those involved in the struggle against international monopoly capitalism.

There is no doubt that children have been centralized in African literature as embodiments of the principle of hope of a better future amidst the gravity of today. Any attempt, therefore, at writing *specifically* for them can only be a step forward. It is an endeavour to get them to see for themselves how they are represented by adult writers instead of such representation being viewed mainly by adult readers. Ngũgĩ's attempt at linking directly with children is evident in his *Njamba Nene* series. The relevant texts are: *Njamba Nene na Mbaathi ĩ Mathagu* (*Njamba Nene and the Flying Bus*), *Bathitoora ya Njamba Nene* (*Njamba Nene's Pistol*), and *Njamba Nene na Chibũ Kĩng'ang'i* (*Njamba Nene and Chief King'angi*). As we shall see presently, the issues presented in the children's texts are as complex as those in the other texts. However, these issues are here presented simply and idealistically for the benefit of the child. The storyline in the series is supported by powerful illustrations which reinforce the message in the narrative.

Throughout the children's books, Ngũgĩ uses *problematization* as both a strategy and as a methodology of getting children to know their world. He poses a problem and, together with the child, works through the problem in order to resolve it. Problematization, for Ngũgĩ, is both a method of reflection and knowing. It is a deconditioning strategy. The essential premise of such an approach is that children are capable of knowing that which conditions them. In other words, they are capable of reflecting on their actions and behaviour and, in the process, changing the world.

In *Njamba Nene na Mbaathi ĩ Mathagu*, Ngũgĩ calls into question educational theory and practice in a colonial setting. He shows it as a negation of liberation. Education, during the last days of colonialism in Kenya, was viewed by colonialists as a tool for the preparation of a social class that would owe unswerving allegiance to the colonial master. The main objective of the primary school TAPS[1] (Tie and Tie Primary School) where Njamba Nene is enrolled is to tap children while they are still young in order to prepare them for "service" at the advent of independence. The school is modelled on the British Grammar School of the post Second World War period. TAPS is the fictional locus where the worst in colonial education is assembled. The school is committed to the perpetuation of an education that is totally Eurocentric in content and perception. Indeed, TAPS is the culmination of a long process of conditioning African children so that they are culturally disoriented.

Ngũgĩ's project is to reverse that relation by endeavouring to decondition the child. In *Njamba Nene na Mbaathi ĩ Mathagu*, Ngũgĩ is clearly in harmony with Paulo Freire's perception of the role of education. Freire asserts:

> There is no neutral education. Education is either for domes-
> tication or for freedom. Although it is customarily conceived
> as a conditioning process, education can equally be an
> instrument for deconditioning. An initial choice is required of
> the educator. (Freire 1972: 9)

The colonial educator had certainly chosen the path of domestication. In contrast, Ngũgĩ as teacher, has chosen decolonizing the child as a necessary route to the decolonization of the nation-state. In the decolonized child, Ngũgĩ sees promise and hope. The decolonized child represents for him the *matigari* (the remains) of Kenya's history of resistance.

At the onset of colonialism in Africa, African societies were destabilized politically, economically, socially and culturally. This destabilization was a necessary prerequisite for the sustenance of economic exploitation which was the backbone of classical colonialism. African societies responded against this onslaught by resisting in varied forms and affirming their inalienable right to life in freedom and liberty. In Kenya the resistance was principally cultural and military. This resistance is at the centre of the children's books as much as it is the concern of the other texts.

The children's books address the issue of *relevance* both of content and methodology in Kenyan educational institutions during the colonial era. But, by focusing on the colonial period, Ngũgĩ is simultaneously seeking to question educational theory and practice in neocolonial Kenya. For example, Njamba Nene revisits the issue of indigenous languages. For him "*rũthiomi nĩ rũthiomi na gũtirĩ rũthiomi rũthiomaga gũkĩra rũrĩa rũũngĩ*"[2] (A language is a language and no language is superior to the other). Yet, Njamba Nene perpetually wears the plate "I AM AN ASS" for speaking in his language at school. Wearing the plate was not only meant to humiliate the child in the face of his peers and thus erode his self confidence, but it was also meant to translate into strokes of the cane at the end of the day.

It will be appreciated that *Njamba Nene na Mbaathi ĩ Mathagu* was written at a time when Ngũgĩ was reexamining his use of the English language to address his primary audience, the Kenyan people[3]. Njamba Nene's argument may therefore be seen as a "voicing" of Ngũgĩ's own internal struggles to come to terms with the contradictions, at least at the level of language, in his earlier works. He not only aspires to talk *about* the Kenyan people but (especially) *with* them. In this quest for relevance, Ngũgĩ has consistently re-emphasized the use of African languages in communicating with the workers and peasants of Africa. In a similar vein, Ngara says:

> To fulfil its social function adequately, literature must be able to speak to the widest spectrum of society possible .... It must reach the masses of the people in the writer's society and at the same time speak to universal man. (Ngara 1985: 46)

In a sense, the use of African languages in different arenas of social intercourse ceases being seen as an emotive and romantic retreat into "what is our own" but a disconnection and a simultaneous reconnection dialectically linked up with the search for a reversal of the prevailing lopsided economic and cultural relations. The continued valorization of colonial languages for the intellectual development of the Third World presupposes a continuation of the perpetuation of a world view so well represented in John Bull[4] and his teacher Kĩgorogoru in *Njamba Nene na Mbaathi ĩ Mathagu*.

Teacher Kĩgorogoru represents the emerging petty bourgeoisie during the final days of classical colonialism in Kenya. In its quest for a Western value system, this social class has acted as an umbilical cord for cultural imperialism; and in its eagerness to embrace the alien, it has sacrificed relevance. This class is characterized by an uncritical imitative tendency. In it, we witness an excessive urge to shed its African identity and to identify with the foreign; in dress, language and ceremony.

Inevitably, animosity develops between Kĩgorogoru and his pupil Njamba Nene because of the former's obsession with things foreign. He asks Njamba Nene:

> I thiomi cia kĩĩrĩu, thiomi cia ũthitarabu na]thii na mbere ta Kĩng'enũ, Gĩĩtariani, Kĩĩbaranja, na Kĩĩnjeremaani? ... One ningĩ   njiongirabĩ! Wee ndwendaga kũmenya   njũũi cia

rūraaya; irīma cia rūraaya; ndia cia rūraaya; mītī ya rūraaya!
Wendaga atī wambe ūmenye ūhoro wa njūūī na irīma
na ndia na mītī   na   mīūmbīre yoothe ya gūkū kwanyu.
Ugakīūhīga rī?   Njīīra. (Ngūgī 1982 a: 3)

[... when will you learn to speak civilized languages like
English, French, or German?... Now come to geography, you
are not interested in knowing the rivers, mountains, lakes, and
trees of Europe .... You say that you want to first know those
rivers, mountains and animals in your own country. When
will you ever learn?]

The pedagogic dictum of moving from "the known to the unknown" is
completely alien to Kīgorogoru. So are the concepts of relevance and student
motivation. Predictably, he is all praises for children who can sing incomprehen-
sible Western songs while castigating and ridiculing Njamba Nene for singing
freedom songs.

Kīgorogoru's perception is consistent with the depiction of the members of
his social class in *Devil on the Cross*. During the abortive Gatuīria-Warīīnga party
at Ngorika Heavenly Orchards, for example, Gatuīria's parents and guests emerge
as caricatures of a Western culture they hardly comprehend:

The men had on dark suits, white frilled shirts and bow ties.
The women wore very expensive clothes of different colours.
But they all wore hats and white gloves. On the outer edges
stood foreign guests and tourists, dressed very lightly for a
sunny day and bemusedly watching the drama unfolding
before them as if they were studying the ridiculous products of
their own civilizing missions. (Ngūgī 1982b: 247)

In contrast, Warīīnga dresses like a true Gīkūyū woman proud of her history and
culture.

The uncritical imitative tendency of this emerging social class is a manifestation of its disconnection with an indigenous value system to which it can resort.
The school, as evidenced in TAPS, plays a very crucial role in capturing children
and catapulting them from their cultural base. It is this capture that Njamba
Nene courageously and consistently resists. Njamba Nene's courage and clear

headedness prepare him for revolutionary duty at the peak of the Mau Mau liberation war which Ngũgĩ takes up in *Bathitoora ya Njamba Nene* (Njamba Nene's Pistol) and *Njamba Nene na Chibũ Kĩng'ang'i*. On the other hand, teacher Kĩgorogoru becomes a guardian of Western interests as a colonial chief and is finally eliminated by the freedom fighters.

Kĩgorogoru's elimination is a symbolic erasure of negative values being inculcated in the minds of the community. It is a delinking of the conditioning project perpetuated by colonial Britain. Kĩgorogoru as a school teacher and as a colonial chief does not have a mind of his own; his life-blood emanates from Brainwash. He is a custodian of colonial thought and practice. El Hadji in Ousmane's *Xala* is an agent of economic imperialism and Kĩgorogoru is an agent of cultural imperialism. Regarding this midwifery socio-economic class, El Hadji has this to say:

> We are a bunch of clodhoppers. Who owns the banks? The insurance companies? The factories? The businesses? The wholesale trade? The cinemas? The bookshops? The hotels? All these and more are out of our control .... The colonialist is stronger, more powerful than ever before, hidden inside us .... He promises us the left overs of the feast if we behave ourselves .... What are we? Clodhoppers! Agents! Petty traders! In our fatuity we call ourselves 'businessmen'! Businessmen without funds. (Ousmane 1983: 84)

Kĩgorogoru aligns himself against nationalists in the struggle for independence so that he may be "rewarded" by the colonial government. So does Chibũ Kĩng'ang'i. Ngũgĩ's statement to the child is this: that in the Mau Mau war of liberation certain colonial chiefs worked rigorously for the continuation of colonial rule. Some of them tortured and killed Kenyan nationalists just as Chibũ Kĩng'ang'i tortures and kills Njamba Nene's mother, Wacũ. Because of the violence they meted on the Kenyan people, such colonial chiefs had to go violently. Unfortunately for Kenya, the Kĩgorogoru and Kĩng'ang'i of colonial Kenya live on and as a result nationalist history is seldom taught in Kenyan schools. In writing the *Njamba Nene* series, Ngũgĩ is attempting to teach a nationalist history to the Kenyan child.

Children play a very important role in Ngũgĩ's books. They clearly represent for him a vision of the possibilities of subverting the lopsided socio-economic relations and political subjugation in a colonial and neo-colonial situation. In *Matigari ma Njiruungi* Muriuki retrieves Matigari's AK-47 in readiness for liberative work and, in the same vein, in *Bathitoora ya Njamba Nene*, Njamba Nene rescues General Ruheni and joins the freedom fighters. Clearly, Ngugi's children are historical subjects with a historical vocation. By writing for children, Ngugi is simultaneously educating them into appreciating their liberative potential and, in a sense, calling upon them to rise up to the challenge.

Njamba Nene's mother, Wacu, (clearly an allusion to the legendary Wacu in Gikuyu orature) represents a crucial reference point for Njamba Nene's actions. In moments of doubt and indecision, he seeks guidance by recalling her words of wisdom. Although we never come face to face with Wacu, her presence pervades the *Njamba Nene* series. This presence is, however, distant because it is felt through Njamba Nene. She is for Njamba Nene an epitome of the Gikuyu people's wisdom. This wisdom comes in the form of stories, songs, proverbs and anecdotes. That is, it is grounded in Gikuyu orature. This grounding is clearly Ngugi's way of historicizing the Kenyan people's collective consciousness. It is his way of reemphasizing the need to retain an African authenticity and to recreate, from that basis, a new set of values attendant to the historical demands of the Kenyan situation.

Njamba Nene's turning point occurs during a school trip to the museum but the social class conflicts that shape him are acted out prior to and during the trip. Because of his poor economic background, Njamba Nene is the odd pupil out at TAPS. He is isolated and discriminated against by his teacher and fellow pupils. They see in him a negation of all TAPS stands for in the form of social background, attire, physical appearance, food, and perception. Njamba Nene has clearly rebelled against what the settler Pious Brainwash meant for the school; the centre of colonial interests.

Yet during the trip to the museum the hitherto neglected child assumes instantaneous leadership by displaying an amazing familiarity and adaptability to his environment. The journey to the museum needs to be conceived in allegorical terms as an attempt by TAPS to reconnect with the past. But because the basis of that reconnection is Eurocentric, the bus overturns and the pupils find themselves in the forest completely unable to function in an alien environment.

In the forest, the pupils under the guidance of Njamba Nene undergo a process of reflection. They come to grips with Wacu's teachings. Colonialism, individualism and the worship of material things are problematized. The irrelevance of a Eurocentric world view becomes even more evident. Indeed, that world view has so intellectually deformed John Bull that he wishes "they were in a British forest." He could easily figure out where they were for "he knows the geography of Britain so well!" John Bull is, however, completely ignorant of his immediate environment. Under the tutelage of his teacher, John Bull has persistently scorned everything unWestern and anticolonial.

In contrast, Njamba Nene is on familiar ground. He has been learning relevant education from Wacū. He has also learnt that collective thought and generosity based on concern for fellow human beings are possible ways of overcoming difficulty. He selflessly shares his food with others, organizes them into groups and utilizes his knowledge in order to help rescue his colleagues both physically and intellectually. The forest experience is later to lead to Njamba Nene's expulsion from TAPS and his logical link with the freedom fighters: the subject of *Bathitoora ya Njamba Nene*

Ngũgĩ's reflection on the children in school and the place of Eurocentrism in education may be mistakenly viewed as a rejection of Western contributions to knowledge. What emerges from *Njamba Nene na Mbaathi ĩ Mathagu*, however, is a call for the shifting of the basis of perception from Europe to other "multiple centers in the world" (Ngũgĩ 1993). Such a perception would contribute in not only decolonizing the child in Third World countries but it would also decolonize the Western child. This would have the effect of creating a universe of decolonized children appreciative of the contribution of other cultures to world knowledge.

Moreover, there is also a sense in which Ngũgĩ is appealing for a shift from the tendency to locate knowledge in Western institutions, such as schools, in which teachers like Fartwell Kigorugoru act as umbilical cords for the actualization of Western thought to centres like homes in which the teachers are the Wacūs of the world. Ngũgĩ's argument is that these shifts are crucial if education is going to fulfill the historical role of liberating human kind from natural and social forces.

Njamba Nene is significantly shaped and made conscientious by his daily struggles at school and beyond. The contradictions borne out of the formal Eurocentric educational system and the experiential informal school in the streets reinforce each other in preparing him for the liberative project. In *Bathitoora ya Njamba Nene* and *Njamba Nene na Chibū Kĩng'ang'i* Njamba Nene is engaged in the practicalities of the Kenyan freedom struggle. Ngũgĩ's treatment of the Mau Mau war of liberation has a double advantage for the child in view of the turn of events in postcolonial Kenya. Those that have held the reigns of power since independence have been uncomfortable with the possibility of centralizing the struggle in schools and national festivities. Some of them supported British colonialism directly while others did so indirectly. At independence the ruling class engaged in what has come to be known as "grabbing." They grabbed virtually anything that would lead to economic and political power. The broad masses of the people were betrayed and sidelined; the cause for which so may people lost their lives was forgotten.

As a result, Kenyan nationalist history is glossed over at different levels of the educational spectrum. There is no initiative on the part of the postcolonial Kenya governments to provide a space for the Kenyan child to know who really contributed in the creation of an independent Kenya. Ngūgī's texts lead the child towards reflection on this question. Secondly, children *did*, in fact, participate in the liberation war. Their contribution has never been acknowledged. In a sense, Ngūgī's texts lead the child to reflect on the possibilities of children participating in liberative pursuits and specifically in the Mau Mau war of liberation. Such a reflection would invariably lead to an empowerment of the child.

In *Bathitoora ya Njamba Nene* Ngūgī poses this problem: how is a child living in a situation of liberative pursuits supposed to respond? After expulsion from TAPS, Njamba Nene is employed by Gacerū Mwendanda (the spy who loves his stomach). This is at the peak of the Mau Mau war of liberation. This was a period of total economic and social destabilization. Families were torn apart, people were placed in concentration camps, the Kenyan people's rhythm of life was totally disrupted. It was a period of physical and spiritual hunger. It was also a period of personal aggrandizement for those who supported the colonial power. The narrative voice affirms:

> Andū aingī nī manyariiriītwo mūno nī thirikari ya
> gīīkoroni, indo ciao ikaharaganio, mītūūrīre yaao
> īkaagagio na mīoyo yaao īkanyamaario. No maūndū ma
> Gacerū Mwendanda mathiaga nywee, indo ciake
> igatheerema wega, makai maake magatendera wega, na
> muoyo waake ūkaiganīra wega.Gacerū Mwendanda aarī
> gītoonga kīnene mūno mwena-inī ūcio wa Rīmuuru.
> (Ngūgī 1984: 1)

[Many were greatly troubled by the colonial government. Their property was destroyed, their livelihood was severely destabilised, and their hearts greatly troubled. But not so for Gacerū Mwendanda. Everything went pretty well for him. His property increased abundantly, his cheeks smoothed and his heart was at peace with the world. Gacerū Mwendanda was a very rich man in Limuru.]

In his quest for more property, Mwendanda is extremely mean, insensitive and devoid of basic human feelings. Njamba Nene works for Mwendanda. Yet for two days he has not eaten anything. Like other people in Limuru, Njamba Nene goes scavenging for stale bread discarded by the Asian bakery merchant Manu. But for a week Manu has not thrown away any bread at the dumping ground. Moreover, Mwendanda would not give Njamba Nene his wages in spite of the latter's pleas for food money. Njamba Nene is on the verge of collapse for want of life-giving-food. How is a working child supposed to respond to this situation?

At the Green Hotel, Njamba Nene hears the news that the freedom fighters have warned people against eating bread and, as a rejoinder, the government tells them not to heed that warning. Njamba Nene learns also that Kīgorogoru (the TAPS teacher-turned- chief) has been killed and that children are being hanged for assisting the freedom fighters. What then is the connection between Njamba Nene's hunger, Kīgorogoru's death and bread? That is the problem that the child has to resolve in order understand his or her role in a liberative situation.

It is at the Limuru Hotel that we get a glimpse of the bread as the carrier of the instrument of freedom. Bread and gun are merged. A possible way out for the hungry Njamba Nene is presented. That it is at the Limuru Hotel that this unity of bread and gun emerges is significant. The Limuru Hotel is pervaded by mutually reinforcing voices of liberation. Outside it are to be found such nationalist newspapers as Mūmenyereri, Inooro, Waigua Atīa?, Mwaranīria, Wīhūūge, and inside it are to be found key fighters such as the hat-wearing General Rūheni. One also finds the gun bearing bread.

The individual's physical hunger is juxtaposed with the people's hunger for freedom. Naturally, for Ngũgĩ, the quest for collective freedom takes precedence over the physical hunger of an individual. Or, to put it in other words, the individual's physical satiation is subsumed in the realization of collective freedom. Njamba Nene breaks the bread and uses the gun to save General Rūheni and others. The child, Njamba Nene, is initiated into fighting for his country and a bond is created between him and General Rūheni. Conversely, the white settler's child is initiated into safeguarding colonial interests by humiliating suspected freedom fighters. They occupy different ideological positions.

Njamba Nene's search for freedom jeopardizes the safety of his family and specifically that of his mother. In *Njamba Nene na Chibū Kīng'ang'i* Wacū is tortured by Chief Kīng'ang'i so that she may reveal Njamba Nene's whereabouts but she does not. She eventually dies. How is the young Njamba Nene supposed to respond to the death of a loved one in the hands of a colonial chief? Njamba Nene once more has to make a decision. He decides to settle scores with Chibū Kīng'ang'i. This is achieved through an ingenious utilization of his knowledge of the enemy. Through a play of sycophancy, creative camouflage, linguistic manipulation and sheer bravery, Njamba Nene avenges Wacū's death. Thus, *Njamba Nene na Chibū Kīng'ang'i* is a continuation of the practical liberative project approximated in *Bathitoora ya Njamba Nene* and theorized in *Njamba Nene na Mbaathi ī Mathagu*. These works, though meant for the child, clearly deal with similar issues treated in greater detail in Ngūgī's other texts.

Through the utilization of a partially distanced perspective and historical sources, the narrator in the *Njamba Nene* texts attains a certain level of structural and verbal delineation which is necessary for the articulation of colonial and postcolonial contradictions. The unyielding shifts in the narrator-character voices, the intersection of theoretical knowledge and practical experiences and the occasional intrusion of the authorial voice are clearly Ngūgī's strategy in decolonizing the child.

Notes

[1]This reminds us of the New Primary Approach (NPA) pilot program in Kenyan primary schools a few years prior to "independence". The NPA project aimed at introducing English as the only medium of instruction in all primary schools right from grade one irrespective of the child's linguistic background. The pilot was later rejected as untenable.

[2]All translations in this paper are mine.

[3]However, the contradiction does seem to persist. Ideally, of course, he would have opted for Kiswahili which is the national language of Kenya. The choice of Gīkūyū has to do with the specific community which gives him the raw materials for his creative enterprise, at the level of culture at least, namely the Gīkūyū people. In any case, a reading

of his works does betray a familiarity with Kiswahili literature to which he makes constant reference. Ngũgĩ's consistent claim is that it is possible to develop different literary centres which would enrich each other. In a sense, then, he is able to resolve the apparent contradiction. A few of his books have been translated into Kiswahili.

⁴The boy's name was John Ndegwa. The translation of "Ndegwa" to "Bull" is significant in so far as it represents a disconnection with the indigenous culture in view of names acting as signs of identification.

Works Cited

Freire, Paulo. *Cultural Action for Freedom*. New York: Penguin, 1972.

Juan, E. S, Jnr. *Ruptures, Schisms, Interventions: Cultural Revolution in the Third World*. Manila: De La Salle University Press, 1988.

Ngara, Emmanuel. *Art and Ideology in the African Novel: A Study of the Influence of Marxism on African Writing*. London: Heinemann, 1985.

Ngũgĩ wa Thiong'o. *Njamba Nene na Mbaathi ĩ Mathagu*. Nairobi: Heinemann Educational Books, 1982.

—. *Devil on the Cross*. Nairobi: Heinemann Educational Books, 1982.

—. *Bathitoora ya Njamba Nene*. Nairobi: Heinemann Educational Books, 1984.

—. *Njamba Nene na Chibũ Kĩng'ang'i*. Nairobi: Heinemann Educational Books, 1986.

—. *Moving the Centre: The Struggle for Cultural Freedoms*. London: James Currey, 1993.

Ousmane, Sembene. *Xala*. Connecticut: Lawrence Hill & Co., 1983.

Matigari ma Njirũũngi: What Grows from Leftover Seeds of "Chat" Trees?[1]

"Karega ... " she said aloud. "What a funny name!" "Ritwa ni mbukio," Karega quoted the proverb (Ngũgĩ, Petals of Blood 61)

Aka matirĩ cia ndiiro no cia nyiniko (Barra 2)[2]

There is no democracy. You can't say; if you say, you are in for it. (Macharia)

When all was said and done and revolutions had been fought and won perhaps only dreamers longed for a voice like that of the man who was as beautiful as the coming of the Christ-Child. (Head 140)

AT THE LAUNCHING of Petals of Blood Ngũgĩ wa Thiong'o hypothesized that, "if the peasants and workers were to write in ink the history that they have

and sweat, their stand- that of the worker look- Brecht's poem that be- seven gates of Thebes?"[3] ma Njirũũngi resistance peasants and workers are critiqued by the voice among other voices. The est detail and most of- own earlier writings. Ndeenda, and Caitaani tiqued and revised from and parodied by Rewriting, rereading, re-

Matigari ma Njirũũngi as it re-names the resistance history of the struggle of the Kenya Land Freedom Army, the resistance history of Kenya, and resistance narration more generally, also specifies as potentially revolutionary the role of speakers and writers in these resistance histories.

already written in blood point would be [like] ing at history" in gins, "Who built the In the novel Matigari texts told and sung by rigorously critique and of Brecht's worker works critiqued in great- ten parodied are Ngũgĩ's Petals of Blood, Ngaahika Mũtharaba-Inĩ are cri- progressive standpoints postmodernist practices. vision and parody,

Matigari ma Njirũũngi provides plural, and sometimes, in Kwame Anthony

Appiah's sense of the postmodern, "more playful—though not necessarily less serious" (142) standpoints from which to raise questions about workers, writing and history.

Like Brecht's worker, the character Matigari asks the same rhetorical questions asked in the poem quoted in *Decolonizing the Mind*, but in this revised version Matigari asks the questions after first specifying them in a narrative of his resistance experience. In this the first resistance narrative in the novel, Matigari also questions a Kiswahili proverb used by Muyaka bin Haji, a 19th-century Mombasa poet, in a poem cautioning the leaders of the Lamu city state against accepting assistance from Oman. In Muyaka's poem each verse is concluded with the line: "Mjenga nyumba halele, yulele ukumbizani"/"The builder of a house does not sleep there, he sleeps outside on the verandah"(Abdulaziz 124).[4] Matigari provides a first person literal translation of the line from Muyaka's poem and makes this line relevant to his own specific experience. He tells Ngarūro, "You see. I built the house with my own hands. But Settler Williams slept in it. I would sleep outside on the veranda" (21). Subsequently, in this first version that he tells of his resistance experience Matigari places the proverb used by Muyaka in the context of related proverbs: "the tailor wears rags", "the tiller eats wild berries" (21). Matigari addresses the second version to John Boy Junior. In this revised version of his resistance narrative Matigari speaks as Brecht's worker, as Muyaka, and as he did in his first narrative, but now he not only asks rhetorical questions, he asks specific local questions, answers them with demands, and insists upon attentiveness: "Who built this house? Who cleared and tilled this land? Listen to me carefully. The builder demands back his house and the tiller his land"(46).

"Who?" is an interrogative used both by Matigari and by other characters with respect to Matigari, and has also been a central question of much of the criticism of *Matigari ma Njirūūngi*. Critics, like characters in the novels, have posed the rhetorical question "Who is Matigari?" And they have answered that "Matigari" is, or is to some readers, Jesus,[5] General Stanley Mathenge,[6] Elijah Masinde,[7] Superman,[8] the Terminator,[9] and Ngũgĩ writing as prophet.[10] Karl Marx, Frantz Fanon, and Dedan Kĩmaathi might also be suggested. Bertolt Brecht, Shaaban Robert, Muyaka bin Haji, Martin Luther King, Jr., Abdilatif Abdalla, Gakaara wa Wanjaū, and Ngũgĩ writing as socialist and gĩcaandū player[11] are some additional possibilities. Robert Sobukwe as depicted by Bessie Head in "The Coming of the Christ Child" might also be considered. In the note to the English edition, Ngũgĩ himself suggests "Old Man Ndiiro."

It is easy to read the novel as an allegory and also to note the obvious, and sometimes not so obvious, intertexuality at work. Like Abdulrazak Gurnah, Simon Gikandi, and David Maughan Brown, I also initially read *Matigari ma Njirũũngi* as an allegory. But the allegory that Gurnah and Maughan Brown read in Christian and Kenyan terms, and that Gikandi defined in terms of biblical parables ("The Epistemology of Translation" 165) and those of "Gĩkũyũ oral traditions" ("Ngũgĩ's Conversion" 139) is one that I read in socialist terms. Gurnah read Matigari as a Christ figure, Gũthera as Mary Magdalena, and Mũriuki as "the lost boy" (170). Gikandi read an allegory based upon a Gĩkũyũ tale about Thĩĩrũ, "a man who can transform himself" ("The Epistemology of Translation" 165). I read an allegory in which surviving memory of struggle that has become individualized confronts contemporary social reproduction and workers' struggles, is liberated by praxis that has repudiated idealism, and becomes the source that informs a revolutionary quest for truth and justice based in praxis and social reproduction.

I was convinced that my reading of the novel as a socialist allegory was plausible, but as I re-read Ngũgĩ's preface to the English edition and re-read Maughan Brown's article, an article that discusses the allegory as Christian in more detail than does Gurnah's or Gikandi's, it seemed obvious that I could not argue persuasively for my reading of the allegory as socialist without considering more carefully the plausibility of readings based on biblical and Gĩkũyũ language stories as is suggested by Gikandi.

In discussing the sources of the novel Gikandi ("The Epistemology of Translation" 165) cites a Gĩkũyũ oral narrative involving transformation that is included in Rose Gecau Mwangi's collection (114-119). Additional related versions of the story are also available (Mbiti 133, Gakahũ 34-39). In a prefatory note to the English language edition Ngũgĩ states that:

> [T]his novel is based partly on an oral story about a man looking for a cure for an illness. He is told of old man Ndiiro, who can cure his illness, but he does not know how to get to him. So he undertakes a journey of search. He meets different people on the way and to each he sings the same description of old man Ndiiro:
>
>> Tell me where lives old man Ndiiro
>> Who, when he shakes his foot, jingles.

And the bells ring out his name: Ndiiro
And again: Ndiiro.
Helped on by the different people, he eventually reaches
his destination, where he finds the necessary cure.

Ngũgĩ says of this story:

> The story is simple and direct, and it dispenses with fixed time
> and place. For effect, it depends on the rhythmic restatement
> of the motif of search; and for suspense, on the urgency of the
> man's need for a cure. As the story progresses, old man Ndiiro,
> whom we never actually meet, looms large and dominant, a
> force, a god, a destiny.

In the novel a song is composed about Matigari by the residents of Trampville.
Their version in Gĩ[gĩkũyũ corresponds to the song in Ngũgĩ's preface except that
the name "Ndiiro" and "njiingiri"/"ankle rattles" have both been changed to
"Njirũũngi," and "tell me" has been changed to "show me."

Nyonia kwa mũthuuri ũreetwo Njirũũngi
Mũthuuri ũrĩ na kĩĩgaamba kũgũrũ
Ariingithagia kĩĩgaamba
Njirũũngi ikagaamba
Na rĩĩngi ikagaamba (69)

Show me the way to a man
Whose name is Njirũũngi
Who stamps his feet to the rhythm of bells.
And the bullets jingle
And the bullets jingle (71)

The published versions of stories about Thĩĩrũ involve transformation and
exploitation. In Gecau Mwangi's and Gakahũ's versions a bird clears, plants and
hoes Thiirũ's field, but is captured and imprisoned by Thiirũ when it claims its
portion of the harvest. The bird is inadvertently enabled to escape by Thiirũ's
daughter, but remains trapped by Thiirũ's medicine and sings variations on the
following song as it attempts to find Thiirũ:

Tūhīī tūtū	Young boys
Ndinamūruma	I do not abuse you
Ndinamūcinūra	I do not insult you
Mūnyonererie gwa Thiirū-ī	But show me the home of
Thīīrū Mūndū mūgo	Thiirū the medicine man
(Gakahū 37)	(Mwangi/Gecau 117)

Thiirū eventually hears the song and recaptures the bird who then informs Thiirū that the daughter's action enabled it to escape. Ngūgī's preface version speaks of a "cure," rather than of transformation. In addition, the character's name is changed. His name in the English preface version is "Ndiiro," and in the workers' song, "Njirūūngi."

Maughan Brown argues that Ngūgī, "presents Matigari as a Christ-like figure," and this argument seems plausible to the extent that Matigari is both presented by the novel and viewed within the novel as "Christ-like." Maughan Brown cites the following passage:

> "No," he answered them. "The God who is prophesied is in you, in me and in the other humans. He has always been there inside us since the beginning of time. Imperialism has tried to kill that God within us. But one day that God will return from the dead. Yes, one day that God within us will come alive and liberate us who believe in Him. I am not dreaming.
>
> "He will return on the day when His followers will be able to stand up without worrying about tribe, race or colour, and say in one voice: Our labour produced all the wealth in this land. So from today onwards we refuse to sleep out in the cold, to walk about in rags, to go to bed in empty bellies. Let the earth return to those to whom it belongs. Let the soil return to the tiller, the factory to the worker ... But that God lives more in you children of this land; and therefore if you let this country go to the imperialist enemy and its local watchdogs, it is the same thing as killing the God who is inside you. It is the same thing as stopping Him from resurrecting. That God will come back only when you want Him to." (156)

Maughan Brown argues that in this passage Ngūgī "is insisting on the Christ-like nature of the Kenyan dispossessed in the interests of fostering resistance to that dispossession"(177). But it is Matigari who is speaking here, who is citing a Kiswahili proverb as cited by Muyaka and a Gīkūyū proverb, "Mūrīmi ti we mūrīi," that is cited by Gakaara wa Wanjaū in the conclusion of his detention diary and translated by Ngigi wa Njoroge, "It is not the farmer who eats the food he has grown" (212). Matigari revises the Martin Carter poem often cited by Ngūgī,[13] to declare "I am not dreaming" and predicts not just "resistance" in "Kenya," as Maughan Brown reads into the passage, but the possibility for socialist revolution everywhere where there is resistance to exploitation, mystification and division of the oppressed by "tribe, race, or colour." It seems at least ambiguous as to whether Matigari is, as Maughan Brown suggests, "theologizing the impulse towards a socialist revolution." As I read this passage Matigari is, on the contrary, liberating the impulse towards theology. In either case, Ngūgī has created a character who is successful in convincing children who recognize him and who give him shelter to reject prophesy unless it is of socialist revolution and to reject "Christ-like" figures unless those spoken of as "god-like" are they themselves speaking in their own voices of resistance. More obviously, the parody of Christian communion ritual in the prison scenes (57) and the depiction of the priest(s) who betray(s) Gūthera (36) and also betray(s) Matigari (116) make reading the novel strictly as a Christian allegory, even a liberation Christian allegory, seem naive at best. The resistance potential of liberation theology is not denied in the novel, but it is given a minor role: that of Gūthera's father, as is noted by Maughan Brown (174).

The novel resists strictly allegorical readings, whether they be based upon Christian, Gīkūyū or even socialist narratives. In the prefatory poem to the novel Ngūgī invites readers to situate, "the story in the country of your choice," "the place of your choice," "the time of your choice," and "to allocate the duration of your choice" (i,ix). The prefatory poem ends and the narrative begins, "Tene tene mūno būrūri ūtarī rīītwa"/"Long long ago in a country with no name"(i,ix). We are invited to make choices, to read according to our inclinations, but clearly there are senses in which "Kenya" and "ūūgīkūyū," two names that do not occur in the novel, are two names that we should read into the novel in some ways, and not read into the novel in other ways, however else we choose to read it.

On this basis it seemed essential to me to reconsider "naming" in the novel and my reading of the novel as a socialist allegory starting with a question of language and a personal narrative. When I first read the novel *Matigari* I realized that my intertextual reading was limited because I am only familiar with some of the voices and languages upon which Ngũgĩ draws. To comprehend a wider range of the voices and languages that are used in the novel I discussed the work with colleagues and friends, began carefully reading *Matigari ma Njirũũngi*, the Gĩkũyũ edition, and re-read the available criticism of the novel.

I initially had read "matigari," the Gĩkũyũ term, literally as "leftovers of food or dregs in drinks"[14] and symbolically in the context of the Gĩkũyũ title of the novel as "the remains of the bullets." I read the term as dually symbolic both of the people who were destroyed by colonial and neo-colonial conquest and oppression and of those who survived and continue to resist. I also read the term as symbolic of memories and narratives of this destruction that are not part of official histories, but that "remain" as demands for liberation. My sense of "Matigari" as name of character, of movements, and as term was also informed by a discussion with Gĩtahi Gĩtĩtĩ, who drew my attention to the use in the novel of "Matigari" as an inherently plural name/term and "Matigari" as a singular name; always a surprising name for a person to characters in the novel (see, for example, 18 and 20), because it means both "the people" and "memory of the people's struggles," but is just a name in the English title.

My understanding of "Matigari" was also informed by a discussion with Carol Sicherman following a presentation of an earlier version of this paper. She told me that when Wangũi wa Goro began translating the novel she attempted to avoid English pronouns marking gender. Pronouns are not marked for gender in Gĩĩgĩkũyũ and thus the gender of Matigari is ambiguous, in the sense of multi-gendered for much of the novel, and in the sense gender free throughout the novel.

I also re-read Simon Gikandi's discussion of the novel, a discussion that begins with an explanation of the meaning of the title/the title character's name. Gikandi relates that he, "first heard the word "Matigari" used in its current politicized version" as "a signifier of Mau Mau" and "as a trope mediating the colonial past and the post colonial moment," "sometime in the early 1960s" ("The Epistemology of Translation" 164). He states that:

> At this time, "Matigari" represented an attempt to celebrate the once unmentioned "Mau Mau" and to introduce it into the political vocabulary of Kenya, now that Kenyatta was Prime Minister. ("The Epistemology of Translation" 162)

But when some of those who fought in the forest refused to discontinue their struggle, they were hunted down and became known as "Matigari." Gikandi indicates that:

> By the late 1960s, when there was a lot of discontent with the politics of neocolonialism, popular notions of independence were also being transformed: from being the apotheosis of national consciousness, or—as the legends would have it—the fulfillment of Waiyaki's prophesy, independence was now represented as an incomplete project, a project awaiting a future time when the "Matigaris" [sic] would return from the forest to reverse the betrayal of independence. ("The Epistemology of Translation" 162)

I had not realized that "Matigari" as a name has had such resonance. In my limited understanding of Kenyan history and Gĩgĩkũyũ I had metaphorically interpreted a narrow literal reading of the title/the title character's name. My initial literal and symbolic readings now seemed based upon an incomplete and limited understanding of the history of the multiple meanings of "Matigari"/"matigari." With the history of the collective name provided by Gikandi as well as Gĩtahi's and Sicherman's explanations of the inherent ambiguity of the name in the novel, I had a more complete understanding of how the sources drawn upon for the novel and of how the name and term Matigari ma Njirũũngi work in the novel.

Matigari ma Njirũũngi as ambiguous name reconnects with the "whispers and ciphered euphemisms" ("The Epistemology of Translation" 161) used to name the struggle between the Kenya Land Freedom Army and the British colonial forces. 'Matigari ma Njirũũngi' also replaces the English/British, generally derogatory name, "Mau Mau." Matigari ma Njirũũngi as name also revives the name used to refer to those in the Kenya Land Freedom Army who refused to join the Kenyatta government. The name personifies heroic resistance by specifically, abundantly, and historically personifying a particular struggle. As noted by Gikandi, the name Matigari ma Njirũũngi also refers to, and the novel draws upon, the legends prophesying the return of the Matigari ("The Epistemology of Translation" 162). Gikandi specifically mentions the legend of General Stanley Mathenge, but the legends of Kĩmaathi, Kenyatta, and Waiyaki might also be mentioned, as should be the Gĩkũyũ resistance songs that demanded and that have continued to demand the return of those unjustly detained and imprisoned.

A resistance history told in Gĩĩgĩkũyũ named Matigari, the character; just as Matigari the collective character names a resistance history. Matigari ma Njirũũngi as history supplies the name for "the country without a name." It replaces the obvious names we might read into the novel, such as ũũgĩkũyũ and Kenya, with a name that specifies all in ũũgĩkũyũ and Kenya, and includes everyone elsewhere, who has resisted colonialism and neo-colonialism.

I next re-examined other names in the novel. Gũthera is also ambiguous in that it is a verb that means to be pure, clear, have commonsense. It is distinct from "gũthambia"/"to cleanse" a term much appropriated in Christian and anti-Mau Mau discourse. Gũthera, in current Kenyan terms, means "to be transparent;" i.e., to be uncorrupted, honest, unambiguous. Gũthera, the character, in the beginning of the novel does not appear to be this. She is a prostitute who has been victimized by the police. She tries to pick up Matigari and mocks Matigari. When Gũthera meets Matigari she has rejected Christianity, but she has retained one bit of idealism, her absolute refusal to have sex with a policeman, a refusal that makes her a victim of her persecutors. It is only when she repudiates this last shred of idealism that Gũthera is able to free the imprisoned Matigari, liberate herself from prostitution and false consciousness and reconcile the apparent ambiguity of her name. Gũthera, whose name literally means clarity and commonsense, thus personifies ideology as theory that has rejected idealism and become praxis in struggle.

Similarly, workers' resistance is personified by Ngarũro wa Kĩrĩro, whose name literally means "wiping away tears" or "from mourning to change." Ngarũro first rescues Matigari and becomes a leader of the strike as his calls for the strike come to be informed by metaphors and symbolism learned from Matigari. Matigari, the character, provides a resistance history to Ngarũro that the latter uses as a discourse of strategic concealment in organizing the workers (24, 60, 74). Through this experience Ngarũro becomes capable of articulating the position of the workers to the Minister for Truth and Justice (109-110). When imprisoned with Matigari:

> [They] talked nearly the whole night about the workers ... peasants ... freedom fighters ... revolutionaries ... about all the forces committed to building a new tomorrow for all our children ....
>
> They became like student and teacher. Each was both a student and teacher to the other. (126)

Social reproduction that is informed by history (Matigari), praxis (Gũthera), and social change (Ngarũro) is personified by Mũriuki, whose name literally means "resurrection and rebirth;" or, in this case, "revolutionary change." Mũriũki is the first person to whom Matigari speaks in the novel and he is Matigari's guide, shelterer, and interpreter, throughout the novel. It is Mũriũki who leads Ngarũro to Matigari when the latter is stoned by the childen and it is Mũriũki who takes Matigari to the bar where he meets Gũthera. Mũriũki literally becomes Matigari in the concluding section of the novel as he returns to the Mũgumo tree and dons the weapons that Matigari has buried there. Social reproduction that has linked history to praxis and contemporary social change has become a revolutionary force that concludes the opening of the suppressed and coded history of Matigari ma Njirũũngi and begins a revolutionary narrative.

Matigari ma Njirũũngi as it re-names the resistance history of the struggle of the Kenya Land Freedom Army, the resistance history of Kenya, and resistance narration more generally, also specifies as potentially revolutionary the role of speakers and writers in these resistance histories. The novel indicates the potentially revolutionary role of intellectual workers as it cites resistance speakers and writers, depicts resistance speech actions, and names characters and sections of the novel after processes of resistance articulation (i.e., "Ngarũro wa Kĩrĩro"/"From Mourning to Change," "Macaria ma na Kĩhooto"/"Searches for Truth and Justice," "Gũthera na Mũriũki"/"Praxis and Social Reproduction"). *Matigari ma Njirũrũngi* also revises histories of resistance articulation, specifically histories composed in Gĩĩgĩkũyũ, Kiswahili, Afro-European, and socialist languages, but certainly the revisions are made in ways that include narrations of resistance in additional languages. The example of naming is illustrative. Gĩkũyũ and Kiswahili names such as "Karega," "Mzigo," "Kĩmeria," and "Chui" match character names to behavior patterns and traits in *Petals of Blood*. Not naming the country in which a novel or play is set has enabled countless progressive books to be published and read and sometimes become required reading for students. Changing the names in songs allowed Christian hymns to be used to celebrate the struggle of the Kenya Land Freedom Army and, more recently, for KANU songs to be used to celebrate the newly formed FORD (Forum for the Restoration of Democracy).[15] Using euphemisms like "progressive" or "socialist," or even the lower case initial letter "marxist," has allowed Marxist writing to be published. Simply, translating or not translating words and/or defining or not defining words in obvious ways may change a text or language constructively. For example, if we have read *Matigari ma Njirūūngi*, whether in Gīgīkūyū or English or both languages, we have probably changed our lexicons by adding some sense of "matigari"/"Matigari" that we did not have previously. These are, of course, only a few examples.

Just as the name Matigari ma Njirūūngi changes in the novel from the name of a character and a suppressed history to the name of the vanguard of a revolutionary movement (126) and the names of its members (names that define this vanguard as children) (145), the potentially revolutionary calls of progressive speakers and writers become revolutionary in the novel as they are revised critically and used by workers in organizing a strike. The example of Muyaka's poem sent to Zahidi Mngumi of Lamu early in the nineteenth century is illustrative. This poem was composed in the Kiamu dialect of Kiswahili and in proverbs to prevent decoding by Omani speakers of Arabic. It is a poem that along with others was preserved by progressive scholars to become published in a series of editions that provided codes used by twentieth century progressive articulators in organizing the Tanganyika African National Union and in resisting the Kenyatta and Moi regimes. This poem and this entire corpus is revised in *Matigari ma Njirūūngi*. The proverb cited in Muyaka's well known poem is revised more than ten times in the novel. In two of the final versions Matigari addresses his poem and his prose translation of it as demands to the Minister of Truth and Justice. His poem melds the voices of Muyaka and Brecht and connects both of their voices to a history of resistance poetry that includes Shaaban Robert and Abdilatif Abdalla as well as to a history of resistance texts constructed in the novel. Matigari's prose version translates his poem and at the same time as the poem is rewritten so too is a new conclusion written for Gakaara wa Wanjaū's *Agīkūyū, Mau Mau na Wīyathi and Mwandīki wa Mau Mau Ithaamīrio-inī*, among other works:

> The house is mine because I built it. The land is mine too because I tilled it with these hands. The industries are mine because my labour built and worked them. I shall never stop struggling for all the products of my sweat. I shed blood and I did not shed it in vain. One day the land shall return to the tiller, and the wealth of our land to those who produce it. Poverty and sorrow shall be banished from our land!
> [... .]

And you, imperialist, and your servant Boy—with all your other lackeys, ministers and leaders of the police force, the army and the courts, the prisons and the administration—your days are numbered! I shall come back tomorrow. We are the patriots who survived: Matigari ma Njirūūngi! And many more of us are being born each day. John Boy, you shall not sleep in my house again. It's either you or me and the future belongs to me! [124]

In a subsequent version Matigari tells Gūthera:

"This world is upside down .... The robber call the robbed "robber." The murderer calls the murdered "murderer," and the wicked calls the righteous "evil." The one uprooting evil is accused of planting evil. The seeker of truth and justice ends up in prison and detention camps. Yes, those who sow good seeds are accused of sowing weeds. As for the sell-outs, they are too busy locking up our patriots in gaols, or sending them into exile to let outsiders come in and bask in the comfort wrought by others. Those we have left in the wilderness are not the only ones doing evil. Yes, this world is upside-down. Those to whom it belongs must set it to rights again!" (150)

Decolonizing the Mind concludes with a call for "regenerative reconnection with the millions of revolutionary tongues in Africa and the world demanding liberation" (108). My reading of Matigari ma Njirūūngi is of the novel as a response to this call. I read it as a novel that reinvigorates links between past and present insistence upon truth and justice by revitalizing, restoring, and critiquing revolutionary and resistance voices and languages that have been and are being silenced when they demand liberation. Matigari ma Njirūūngi is a novel that provides challenges and guidance for progressive writing and study, through the ways it demands of us revolutionary change in our reading and writing practices.

As Gikandi notes Ngūgī in Matigari ma Njirūūngi "skillfully reestablishes links with African oral literature," but it is arguable whether he does "much the same thing" as "Chinua Achebe and Wole Soyinka had done ... in their English language works"("Conversion" 138). Rather than valorizing "oral literature" as authenticizing mythic tradition in the sense that Soyinka and Achebe did, Ngũgĩ explicitly identifies a Gĩkũyũ folktale that seems to valorize exploitation, mystification, and informing on innocents. The story of Thiirũ in Gecau Mwangi's and Gakahũ's versions seems basically reactionary, but it does include a passage in which the bird when first captured asks/tells Thiirũ, "Didn't I clear the bush, dig it, and plant my own maize seeds?" (Gecau Mwangi 116)/ "No, I'm not taking your sweet potatoes, but only my sweet potatoes that I've dug up" (Gakahũ 36). In *Matigari ma Njirũũngi* the bird's straightforward words, his "ndiiro," have replaced the story of Thiirũ, become a version of Matigari's most often used proverb and provided the name for the character in Ngũgĩ's English edition preface.

As a reader I am challenged and intrigued by the revisions in *Matigari ma Njirũũngi* of Brecht, Muyaka, Martin Carter, Shaaban Robert, Gakaara wa Wanjaũ, and Gĩkũyũ folktales, among other texts. The novel raises questions about revision, parody, critique and appropriation concerning texts that I personally have taken very seriously. It raises these questions, and in fact I think forces confrontation of them, particularly for those of us who have read Ngũgĩ's writing, because the works most extensively critiqued and revised in *Matigari ma Njirũũngi* are Ngũgĩ's previous works, including *Ngaahika Ndeenda*, *Detained*, *Decolonizing the Mind*, and *Caitaani Mũtharaba-Inĩ*. In *Decolonizing the Mind* Ngũgĩ said of *Ngaahika Ndeenda*:

> I did and I have been telling the Kamĩrĩĩthũ story wherever and whenever I have a chance. For on a personal level it has changed my life. It has led me to prison, yes; it got me banned from teaching at the University of Nairobi, yes; and it has now led me into exile. But as a writer it has also made me confront the whole question of the language of African theatre—which then led me to confront the language of African fiction. (62)

In the same work he also said in the description of his experience of writing *Caitaani Mũtharaba-Inĩ* in prison:

> [T]he biggest problem then, and what I still think is the biggest problem facing the growth and the development of the African novel, is finding the appropriate 'fiction language,' that is with fiction itself taken as a form of language, with which to

effectively communicate with one's targeted audience: that is, in my case, the people I left behind. (75)

These two statements, as well as *Detained*, Ngũgĩ's prison diary, seem to be mocked in the second prison scene in *Matigari ma Njirũũngi* where Matigari and Ngarũro talk. The passage that I cited above in my discussion of the novel as allegory and the name Ngarũro wa Kĩrĩro and decided to end as follows, "building a new tomorrow for all our children ....," actually ends with "Amen":

> [They] talked nearly the whole night about the workers ... peasants ... freedom fighters ... revolutionaries ... about all the forces committed to building a new tomorrow for all our children ... Amen. (126)

In the earlier section of the paper I have criticized other writers for their Christian readings of *Matigari ma Njirũũngi*, but in incompletely quoting I changed a passage in the novel where Ngũgĩ uses "Amen" to parody his own writing and, thus, eliminated his parody.

In the first prefatory poem in *Caitaani Mũtharaba-inĩ*, the "Gĩcaandĩ player," "Prophet of Justice" narrator, invokes the titles of *Weep Not, Child* and *The River Between* as he agrees that he should, "Wipe away the tears of the heart ... ," and asks, "But why am I lingering on the bank of the river?" (8). Matigari remembers a similar song in the first chapter of *Matigari ma Njirũũngi* (4) and also sings this revised version in the mental hospital with Ngarũro (126). In the revised *Matigari ma Njirũũngi* version "bathing" is not "stripping off clothes" (*Caitaani Mũtharaba-inĩ* 8) and "swimming" is not "plunging into the river" (*Caitaani Mũtharaba-inĩ* 8). "Bathing" and "swimming" have changed to become the action of "sharing the water with swimming creatures" (4,4).[16] In the final line of the *Matigari ma Njirũũngi* version of the song, "nĩgũkĩire na gwathererũka," the sun-setting sequence that provided the names for the parts of *Weep Not, Child* is reversed to become a dawning sequence and the name of the first part of *Matigari ma Njirũũngi*, "Wiping Your Tears Away"(2), is explained. The Gĩcaandũ player of *Caitaani Mũtharaba-inĩ*, agreed to "silence the cries of the heart." In *Matigari ma Njirũũngi* the cries are not "silenced," but "changed" and become the name of the first part of the novel and of the character Ngarũro wa Kĩrĩro. Similarly, the narrator is not identified as a "prophet of justice" nor as a gĩcaandũ player, but as a story teller who tells a story that asks questions about "prophecy," even prophecy of justice; and about expertise with language even that of gīcaandū players.

In *Decolonizing the Mind* Ngũgĩ asked, "Why should not the African peasantry and working class appropriate the novel?"(68). In *Matigari ma Njirũũngi* this question becomes a completed action as a line in a song that changed in *Ngaahika Ndeenda* from "makeenyūrana"(34)/"they would share"(27) to "tūkeenyūrana"(117)/"we will share" (115) is remembered in its revised version in *Matigari ma Njirũũngi*. Progressive peasants and workers and resistance writers including Ngũgĩ along with non-progressive voices among the African peasantry and working class, Voices of Truth, Ministers for Truth and Justice, and the rest of us "appropriate"; not just the novel, but poetry, histories, philosophies, and orature. It is critique, systematic, as well as parodic, particularly of our own work, as is evidenced by Matigari's and Ngũgĩ's revisions in *Matigari ma Njirũũngi*, that distinguishes progressive use of prior and parallel resistance texts from the appropriation of resistance texts by the Minister for Truth and Justice and those of his ilk. Such critique also enables parody of reactionary appropriation and the refinement of resistance strategies.

Matigari insists that workers and peasants have articulated their histories, novels, and philosophies through the pens of progressive writers as well as through their songs and stories and everyday languages of struggle. Just as progressive writers have "regenerated" and "reconnected" by basing their writing in the languages, discourses, texts and daily language of workers and peasants. The novel challenges us to respond as progressive readers who choose to join a project of critical study, reconnecting, revising, translating and re-writing; a project we may choose to call "kuuga nĩ gwĩka" (141), resistance articulation, or the praxis of social reproduction; but one in which the choice of names is an action.

Gikandi has argued that Ngũgĩ's decision to write in Gĩĩgĩkũyũ, "enabled him to reject realism without renouncing it, and to experiment with modernist and postmodernist forms without acknowledging their legitimacy" ("Conversion" 139). He has also suggested that, "Ngũgĩ's recourse to Gĩkũyũ oral traditions (especially in *Matigari*) allowed him to accept a hitherto unrecognized affinity between modernist and postmodernist forms and African oral traditions ("Conversion" 139). Similarly, Kwame Anthony Appiah has suggested that, "Ngũgĩ's conception of the writer's potential in politics is essentially that of the avant garde, of Left Modernism" (149). I would argue that, on the contrary, Ngũgĩ has enabled us as his readers to recognize connections between modernist and postmodernist forms and contemporary orature and literature in African and other languages. As Matigari "smiled to himself"(4), wrapped his AK47 (*Barrel of the Pen*?) in "a plastic sheet" and buried it next to "the central root" of a mūgumo tree, so too Ngũgĩ has hidden a history of his writing, even a history of his writing as a socialist realist and a gĩcaandũ player. He has invited us as postmodernist readers to become, if we chose to do so, revolutionary readers, in a circular sense if no other, who smile, as we read that "Mũriũki dug up all the things that Matigari had hidden"(175), and consider, for example, that "Mũgumo"/"Fig Tree" was the title of Ngũgĩ's first short story (*Decolonising* 70), but now is a term that does not require English translation, or that *Matigari ma Njirũũngi* may be as much a postmodernist as a Gĩkũyũ translation and revision of both *Petals of Blood* and *Ngaahika Ndeenda.*

Notes

[1]I am indebted to, along with those cited elsewhere, Kĩmani Njogu, Tracie Hall and Debra Amory, who listened carefully to my arguments and tactfully suggested substantive revisions, and Tom Brokaw who on the NBC "Nightly News" of 7 December 1992 inadvertently mispronounced a word and provided me with the sub-title of this essay. "Njirũũngi," a "word used, maybe coined, by "Mau Mau" guerillas as a euphemism for bullets" (Gikandi, "The Epistemology of Translation" 165), also means "fruit of C. [Catha] Edulis, inedible" (Benson 190). The qat tree, "muirũũngi" in Gĩĩgĩkũyũ, produces leaves that, according to Benson, are "used by Masai as well as Somalis as an aphrodisiac and to prevent sleep while escorting sheep"(190). These leaves, have also been discussed recently in American media sources as the "addictive" and "lethal" "drug" ingested by "gun-toting" Somali teenagers (See, for example, Perlez). In response to such discussions, my daughter asked me, "Isn't that what I chewed with bubble gum as a teenager in Malindi?"

It is, of course. The "muirũũngi" (qat tree) produces leaves that peasants in Igembe are said to chew at weddings, that tourists in Malindi chew with bubble gum on beach holidays, and that East African truck drivers chew as their American counterparts ingest No-Doz. Contrary to the expert opinions of Benson and Perlez, qat tree leaves are neither an "aphrodisiac" nor "lethal," although the contexts of their use may make them seem such.

The novel *Matigari ma Njirũrũngi* seems to me to be less about qat tree leaves than about the seeds of this tree, and less about the seeds that produce more trees, than about the leftover ungerminated seeds; seeds that might be used as bells or other musical instruments; seeds, the name of which was used as a code-name for bullets.

[2]Barra translates the proverb, "Women have no upright words, but only crooked

ones." A more accurate translation of the proverb might be, "Women have no straight-forward words, but only inverted ones."

³*Decolonizing the Mind*, 97.

⁴This translation is based upon those of Mohamed Abdulaziz (who uses "shelter in the yard" as a translation of "ukumbizani" in his English version of the poem [126], but supplies the term "verandah" in a footnote to the Kiswahili version) as well as upon a translation that I did with Ibrahim Noor Shariff in *Mashairi ya Vita vya Kuduhu* that was based upon a range of additional earlier translations. Unless otherwise noted, I am responsible (in the sense that I have devised a translation or revised earlier translations) for translations from Gĩĩgĩkũyũ and Kiswahili in this essay, except those from *Matigari ma Njirũũngi*. Translations of *Matigari ma Njirũũngi* are from Wangũi wa Goro's translation, except where otherwise noted.

⁵See Abdulrazak Gurnah and David Maughan Brown.

⁶See Simon Gikandi, "The Epistemology of Translation: Ngũgĩ, *Matigari* and the Politics of Language," 162.

⁷See Maughan Brown 178.

⁸See Crehan 123.

⁹See Crehan 123.

¹⁰See Maughan Brown 180.

¹¹This possibility was suggested to me in conversations with Gĩtahi Gĩtĩtĩ and Kĩmani Njogu.

¹²I'm grateful to Gĩtahi Gĩtĩtĩ for drawing my attention to the use in the song of "njiingiri."

¹³See, for example, *Decolonizing the Mind*, 3, 108.

¹⁴Gikandi's literal translation, "The Epistemology of Translation," 161.

¹⁵On December 31, 1991 I heard a song with the following refrain sung in Nairobi, "Wakimeza, wakitema, chama chetu ni FORD." I thought it was a spontaneous humorous song, and upon my return to the U.S. repeated the refrain to Thiong'o wa Ngũgĩ who explained to me that it had been a KANU song. Kĩmani Njogu added that the KANU song was based upon a popular song by the taarab singer Malika.

¹⁶My translation of "Ngagayane maaĩ na thaambĩri."

Works Cited

Abdulaziz, Mohamed H. *Muyaka: 19th Century Swahili Popular Poetry*. Nairobi: Kenya Literature Bureau, 1979.

Appiah, Kwame Anthony. *In My Father's House: Africa in the Philosophy of Culture*. New York: Oxford University Press, 1992.

Barra, G. *1000 Kikuyu Proverbs*. Nairobi: Kenya Literature Bureau, 1939.

Biersteker, Ann and Ibrahim Noor Shariff. *Mashairi ya Vita vya Kuduhu: War Poetry in*

Kiswahili Exchanged at the Time of the Battle of Kuduhu. East Lansing, Michigan: Michigan State University Press, forthcoming.

Benson, T.G. *Kikuyu-English Dictionary.* Oxford: Oxford University Press, 1964.

Crehan, Stewart. Review of Herta Meyer's *"Justice for the Oppressed ... ": The Political Dimension in the Language Use of Ngũgĩ wa Thiong'o, Research in African Literatures,* 24,i (1993): 121-123.

Gakaara wa Wanjaũ. *Agĩkũyũ, Mau Mau na Wĩyathi* (trans. title: *The Gĩkũyũ, Mau Mau and Freedom*). Karatina: Gakaara Press, n.d.

Gakahũ, Benson. "Mũthuri Wetagwo Thiirũ waarĩ Mũndũ Mũgo." *Ng'ano Ikũmi na Ithano cia ũgĩkũyũ.* Nairobi: East African Literature Bureau, 1957, 34-39.

Gecau Mwangi, Rose N. *Kikuyu Folktales.* Nairobi: East African Literature Bureau, 1970.

Gikandi, Simon. "The Epistemology of Translation: Ngũgĩ, Matigari and the Politics of Language," *Research in African Literatures,* 22, iv (1991): 161-167.

—. "Ngũgĩ's Conversion: Writing and the Politics of Language," *Research in African Literatures,* 23, i (1992): 130-144.

Gurnah, Abdulrazak. "*Matigari*: A Tract of Resistance," *Research in African Literatures,* 22, iv (1991): 169-172.

Head, Bessie. "The Coming of the Christ-Child" in *Tales of Tenderness and Power.* Johannesburg: Ad. Donker, 1989: 131-140. [Originally published in *Marang* (1980-88), no. 3].

Macharia, CNN transcript of interviews in Kenya, NEXIS, 11 November 1992.

Maina wa Kĩnyattĩ. Ed. *Thunder from the Mountains: Mau Mau Patriotic Songs.* London: Zed, 1980.

Maughan Brown, David. "*Matigari* and the Rehabilitation of Religion" *Research in African Literatures,* 22, iv (1991): 173-180.

Ngũgĩ wa Thiong'o. *Barrel of a Pen.* Trenton, New Jersey: African World Press, 1983.

—. *Caitaani Mũtharaba-Inĩ.* Nairobi: Heinemann, 1980.

—. *Decolonizing the Mind.* London: James Currey, 1986.

—. *Detained: A Writer's Prison Diary.* London: Heinemann, 1981.

—. *A Grain of Wheat.* Nairobi: Heinemann, 1967.

— and Ngũgĩ wa Mĩriĩ. *Ngaahika Ndeenda/I Will Marry When I Want.* Nairobi: Heinemann, 1980, 1982.

—. *Matigari ma Njirũũngi/Matigari.* Trans. by Wangũi wa Goro. Nairobi/London: Heinemann, 1986, 1989.

—. *Petals of Blood.* New York: Dutton, 1977.

—. *The River Between.* Nairobi: Heinemann, 1965.

—. *Weep Not, Child.* Nairobi: Heinemann, 1964.

—. *Mwandĩki wa Mau Mau Ithaamĩrio-inĩ/ Mau Mau Writer in Detention.* Trans. by Ngigi wa Njoroge. Nairobi: Heinemann, 1983, 1986.

Perlez, Jane. *New York Times,* 7 December 1992: 1.

Alamin Mazrui and *Lupenga Mphande*

Orality and the Literature of Combat: The Legacy of Fanon

1.

PRIOR TO THE inception of European colonial rule in Africa many of the societies on the continent had modes of communication that tended to preclude the medium of writing. Such societies have sometimes been described as belonging to the "oral tradition" in the wider sense of the term that includes not only expression in speech form, but also in its "complimentaries" like the drum, the dance, the performance and other paralinguistic practices. But even in societies, like that of the Amhara in Ethiopia, which had indigenous scripts centuries before their encounter with European invaders, the production of texts continued to be primarily a function of the oral domain. Writing can, and does often, take a life of its own. But in these precolonial, scripted African societies, writing was not only relatively restricted in its functions, but it also remained, to a large extent, a mere expression of the oral word.

> *In colonial scholarship, in particular, this supposedly Western orientation towards writing and the supposedly African orientation towards orality often assumed the form of the grand racialist divide between "civilization" and "primitivity".*

This particular configuration of orality, writing and literacy is, of course, a product of certain material and social conditions obtaining in specific societies, and indeed globally, at a certain historical juncture. But there has often been a tendency to regard writing as an exclusive preserve of the Western mind, and orality as a peculiarly African predisposition. In colonial scholarship, in particular, this supposedly Western orientation towards writing and the supposedly African orientation towards orality often assumed the form of the grand racialist divide between "civilization" and "primitivity". Oral literature, for instance, was seen as nothing more than a manifestation of an earlier stage in the historical evolution of society towards a more advanced state of a writing "culture." It is this colonial legacy that led Ama Ata Aidoo to state:

One doesn't have to really assume that all literature has to be written. I mean one doesn't have to be so patronizing about oral literature. There is present validity to oral literary communication. I totally disagree with people who feel that literature is one stage in the development of man's artistic genius. (1972: 23-24)

But even when orality has been freed from negative associations, the tendency to regard it as something peculiarly African has remained strong. It is not uncommon to find claims that the distinction between the oral and the written underlie the entire relationship between sub-Saharan Africa and the West (1990: 69).

Partly as a result of this ahistorical dichotomy between the writing West and "oralizing" Africa, many Africans came to see the advance of writing in the Roman script in Africa as an aspect of the continent's capitulation to European imperialist designs. The colonial conception of "African" orality as an undeveloped form of expression that does not do justice to the human creative potential was now met with an anti-colonial view of "Western" writing as a pervasive form of cultural tyranny.

This juxtaposition of the Western-African divide on a dichotomous view of the orality-literacy continuum expectedly led to the emergence of a neonationalist school which sought to "reclaim" orality as one of the many glories of the indigenous heritage of Africa. Oral literature came to be regarded as a hallmark, *sui generis*, of the African creative mind which needed to be "conserved" and protected against the imperialist onslaught of the written word. Orality now came to be romanticized. It came to carry the entire weight of African civilization and its historical longevity. In some instances it came to help define the very soul of a preconceived Africanity. In Negritudist circles, for example, the supposed oralness of African societies came to be a mark of their humanism (Leopold Senghor, 1965: 84-85), in contrast to the supposedly detached and impersonal character of writing.

But the neonationalist cultural struggle was by no means restricted to the revalorization of orality as an independent mode of discourse and literary creativity. Evidence of orality in written texts, and especially in the novel, became part of the quest for an authentically African literature. According to Mbye Baboucar Cham, the process of conflating the oral with the written is seen by some as "an act of literary authenticity clearly meant to put an imprint of legitimate Africanness on the work" (1982: 24).

Some have acknowledged that the novel in Africa is indeed part of the Western legacy. Nonetheless, they have proceeded to argue that the indigenous force of orality managed to Africanize it to a point where we can now talk of a novel that is peculiarly African in style. Phanuel Egejuru has described how elements from the oral tradition are sometimes inserted in contemporary African novels to "add a specific African flavor to the work" (1990: 1-2).

Others have sought a complete break with the West, seeking instead to place the origins of the novel in Africa in a progressive path of development from Africa's own heritage, rather than in a more recent history of Western imposition. Chinweizu, Jemie and Madubuike, for example, have contended:

> Since there are these pre-European narratives, both oral and written, some of which are comparable to European novels, and others which have contributed to the development of the African novel, there is no reason why they should not be considered African antecedents to the African novel, antecedents out of which the African novel might entirely have evolved, without hybridization by the European novel. (1985: 22)

Similarly, Harold Scheub criticizes the common assumption that the novel evolved first in the West only to be later transported to the rest of the world. Describing this view as blind as it is arrogant Scheub concludes that "the early literary traditions were beneficiaries of the oral genres, and there is no doubt that the epic and its hero are the predecessors of the African novel and its central characters" (1985: 1).

But the ahistorical opposition between orality as African and writing as Western, and the undialectical relegation of orality to Africa's precolonial heritage have combined to make the oral literature of African intellectuals and academia frozen in time and virtually closed to organic growth. Contrary to its dynamic, growing, and creative character, oral literature is often regarded as a static heritage that can only be passed on "intact" from one generation to another. Many African writers come to see their role as one of digging into this "past" to uncover material for display in their writing as an affirmation of their Africanness. It is precisely this kind of orientation that led Christopher Miller to suggest that,

> Orality in its broadest sense thus has a clear political connotation in Africa, representing the authenticity of the precolonial world: "tradition" and orality are synonymous. The traditional African verbal arts, however, while extant, are fast disappearing or becoming something else. It is said that every time an old African dies another museum disappears. (1990: 70-71)

The very terminology used in placing oral literature within a historical time-frame betrays the extent to which the tradition has become fossilized in our imagination.

All these tendencies described above are products of a particular phase of a more general phenomenon that Frantz Fanon described as alienation or estrangement from one's existential and cultural being. This phenomenon begins with a stage of attempted assimilation into the culture of the oppressor, in which the writer is virtually completely inspired by the aesthetics of European creative writing. His or her works can easily be linked up "with definite trends in the literature of the mother country" (Fanon, 1967:179).

The "native" writer is soon shaken into a rude awakening that the desperately sought doors of Europeanness are, in fact, completely closed. At this point the writer is forced to remember and to express his or her Africanity. But with lost cultural roots, the writer is no longer

> a part of his people, since he has only exterior relations with his people, he is content to recall their life only. Past happenings of the bygone days of his childhood will be brought up out of the depth of his memory; old legends will be reinterpreted in the light of a borrowed aestheticism and of a conception of the world which was discovered under other skies. (Fanon, 1967:179)

Precisely because the African writer or intellectual now seeks to be attached to the people without actually being an integral part of them, he or she only manages "to catch hold of their garments." Yet these garments are merely the reflection of a hidden life, teeming and perpetually in motion. As Fanon observes, "The man of culture, instead of setting out to find this substance, will let himself be hypnotized by these mummified fragments which, because they are static, are in fact symbols of negation and outworn contrivances" (1967:180).

Operating within the boundaries of this particular psychology of culture, the early Ngũgĩ as well as many other African writers, incorporate into their works fragments from the oral tradition in a manner that is mummified, exotic and usually unrelated to the dynamics and realities of the lives of their people. However, the fossilization of oral literature reminiscent, to some extent, in Ngũgĩ's early works, is a tendency which he manages to overcome in his later writings. After *Petals of Blood* in particular Ngũgĩ begins to use oral literature in a way that maintains its life and vibrancy. Whether drawn from a pre-existing pool or newly created, and whether its presence is substantive or stylistic, orality in Ngũgĩ's writing comes to have an existence that is in an organic and rhythmic communion with the dynamics and counter-dynamics of life at present.

This development in Ngũgĩ's writing is partly a product of a maturation of national consciousness on his part. A manifestation of this national conscious-ness is described by Frantz Fanon as that habit of the "native" writer, acquired progressively over time, to turn away from addressing the audience defined by the oppressor, and seeking to address, instead, his or her own people. Ngũgĩ's increasing use of his native language, Gĩkũyũ, and his campaign for the promotion of African indigenous languages in African writing, is partly a product of this attempt to redefine the audience of African literature. Precisely at this point, in Fanon's view, when the focus on a new audience has taken root, can national literature be said to have come into being (1967: 193).

This redefinition of the audience, this creation of a completely new public, necessarily disrupts the entire vocation of literary creation. In the process new forms, new styles and new themes may emerge to characterize the emergent national literature. In Fanon's conception a national literature may properly be called a literature of combat, in the sense that

> it calls on the whole people to fight for their existence as a nation. It is a literature of combat, because it moulds the national consciousness, giving it form and contours and flinging open before it new and boundless horizons; it is a literature of combat because it assumes responsibility, and because it is the will to liberty expressed in terms of time and space. (1967: 193)

The revolutionary nature of this literature, its fighting spirit, comes to provide oral literature with a new value and a new orientation altogether. Again, in the words of Fanon:

> the oral tradition—stories, epics and songs of the people—
> which formerly were filed away as set pieces are now beginning
> to change. The storytellers who used to relate inert episodes
> now bring them alive and introduce into them modifications
> which are increasingly fundamental. There is a tendency to
> bring conflicts up to date and to modernize the kinds of
> struggle which the stories evoke, together with the names of
> heroes and the types of weapons. (1967: 193)

It is these attributes of national literature, which Fanon saw as developing independently in oral literature, that came to manifest themselves in substance and style in Ngūgī's creative writing. In the area of literature, Ngūgī can rightly be described as a follower of the legacy of the literature of combat that was described by Frantz Fanon over thirty years ago. The multifarious utilitarian potential of orality particularly vitalizes Ngūgī's own literature of combat.

2.

The history of the Mau Mau movement against British colonialism in Kenya has been a central feature of virtually all of Ngūgī's creative works. Furthermore as Ngūgī has moved more and more to the political left, and as he has increasingly come to espouse the quasi-Marxist view of history as a potential weapon of revolution, the more his own conception of Mau Mau has changed. Ultimately Mau Mau has assumed a more radical character with greater emphasis being placed on issues like class alliances, the trans-ethnic quality of the movement, the active role of women in the war front, the primacy of local over foreign factors as immediate causes of the revolutionary upsurge, and the collective nature of its leadership. All this has had a certain impact on Ngūgī's literary style. Employing history as a kind of weapon to transcend the boundaries of mere description of reality and negate the notion of individual consciousness, he has broken away from the traditional conception of the novel. As he has revolutionized his perspective of African history, his mode of creative discourse about that history has molded a new kind of novel.

Ngūgī's political radicalization seems to have affected his views not only in relation to the substance and nature of the Mau Mau movement, but also in terms of what should be considered the more "authentic" and more "reliable" source of the history of the movement. And it is here that the question of orality versus writing comes into prominence once again.

By the time Kenya attained its independence in 1963, virtually all records on the Mau Mau movement that existed in writing could be described as colonial in perspective. The Mau Mau combatants were described as blood-thirsty terrorists and some of their leaders, like Kīmaathi, as lunatics. Partly because most written sources were colonial, and partly because of the mental colonization precipitated by both colonial and neocolonial education, the history written by Kenyans in the postcolonial period continued to assume a colonial character. Because of these twin factors, Ngũgĩ came to regard most written sources on Mau Mau as highly unreliable, and the resort to oral sources became a compelling quest.

The opposition between written and oral sources of history has centered around the fundamental question of whose history we seek to represent. Is it the history of the colonial and neocolonial bourgeoisie and their ideologues, or is it the history of the mass of the exploited people from whose ranks the Mau Mau emerged? It is against this background that Ngũgĩ and Mīcere Gīthae Mūgo found it necessary to make the following remarks as they were preparing to compose their play on Kīmaathi:

> There was no single historical work by a Kenyan telling of the grandeur of the heroic resistance of Kenyan people fighting foreign forces of exploitation and domination, a resistance movement whose history goes back to the 15th and 16th centuries when Kenyans and other East African people first took up arms against European colonial power.... Our historians, our political scientists, and even some of our literary figures were too busy spewing out, elaborating and trying to document the same colonial myths .... For whose benefit were these intellectuals writing? (1976: ii)

Maina wa Kīnyattī went even further by describing leading Kenyan historians like B.A. Ogot, William Ochieng, E.S. Atieno Odhiambo and B.E. Kipkorir as essentially anti-Mau Mau in their intellectual orientation (1980:9, fn.70). The oral versus the written, posed not only the question of whose history were we drawing from, but also whose history were we documenting for posterity.

Consequently, Ngũgĩ and Mīcere Mūgo decided, for the first time, to turn to the oral tradition, and to elicit a first hand oral account of Kĩmaathi directly "from the people who had known him as a child, a villager and a guerilla hero" (1976:iii). In the process they discovered a history of Kĩmaathi, and a history of Mau Mau, that was in direct contra-distinction to the one they had read in most written texts. Historians trained in the Eurocentric tradition that put primacy on written records, and on the fetish of "objectivity", were quick to condemn Ngũgĩ and Mũgo's play, The Trial of Dedan Kĩmaathi, as lacking in historical veracity. The two writers were condemned for "creating" a Kĩmaathi who was not in conformity with the "historical" Kĩmaathi (See, for example, E.S. Atieno Odhiambo, 1977). Apart from the fact that The Trial of Dedan Kĩmaathi was essentially a work of fiction, Ngũgĩ and Mũgo were not interested in producing anybody's "objective history" of the Mau Mau. Their aim was to present an aspect of Kenyan history as seen by the people, from their point of view and in conformity with their class interests. That people's history, emanating from the womb of the oral tradition, necessarily entailed an element of myth-making as a way of empowering it and hightening its liberative essence. Yet such history, both in its factual and mythological dimensions, was a genuine product of the people's oral tradition on which Ngũgĩ and Mũgo had come to rely. The Trial of Dedan Kĩmaathi recreated it, albeit in a fictionalized manner.

While oral tradition as a source of information influences all of Ngũgĩ's subsequent creative writing, Matigari attains a new level of involvement. The novel can be seen as a reincarnation of the collective Mau Mau, yet the main character can also be regarded as a return of Kĩmaathi who survived the colonial bullets. This is in conformity with the oral account in which Ngũgĩ and Mũgo were told by a woman: "Kĩmaathi will never die .... But of course if you people have killed him, go and show us his grave!" (1976:iii).

Matigari can be considered a rekindling of the spirit of the people's oral history of Mau Mau not only in its substance but also in its orientation. The thematic development of the novel is, at the same time, a process of creating a myth of the Mau Mau character that is Matigari. This process of myth creation is both a product of the oral tradition and a revalidation of a people's oral history in the politics of power.

The critical achievement of Matigari notwithstanding, important to remember is that at the early stages of Ngũgĩ's quest for information directly from "the people", Ngũgĩ was drawn to the oral tradition more by default than by design. He was forced to turn to the oral tradition only because the history he sought to represent existed primarily in the oral mold. At first, Ngũgĩ had difficulty transcending the "museum" conception of the oral tradition. His use of orality in *Petals of Blood*, which was published at more or less the same time as *The Trial of Dedan Kīmaathi*, did not show much progress from its use in his early novels. Nevertheless, these efforts to seek a non-colonial interpretation of Kenyan history from the people who were a part of it, also brought him directly into contact with them. He forced himself to submit, almost as a student, to the wisdom of peasants and workers of Kenya, a phenomenon that was later extended to his work at the Kamīrīīthū Center. In this process, Ngũgĩ came to discover the wider dimensions of orality and its utilitarian potential as an instrument of combat, which ultimately led him to accord orality a different kind of treatment altogether in his writings after *Petals of Blood*.

3.

One of the earliest uses of orality to be found in Ngũgĩ's works is as a component of his writing. In his first two novels, Ngũgĩ delves into the themes of colonialism, alienation from Gĩkũyũ land, and peoples' resistance to the politics of occupation. In this connection, Ngũgĩ uses orality in the form of the myth of Mũũmbi and Gĩkũyũ as the progenitors of the displaced Gĩkũyũ people. At the beginning of things, it is reported in *The River Between*, "there was only one man (Gĩkũyũ) and one woman (Mũũmbi)." God, the myth continues, brought these two progenitors to Kĩrĩnyaga hill and "showed them the whole vastness of the land. He gave the country to them and their children and the children of their children, tene na tene, world without end" (1965:18). Inserted into the text, the myth legitimizes the Gĩkũyũ peoples' claim to the land in their conflict with European settler forces and establishes how and why life in Gĩkũyũ land comes to be the way it is.

Prophecy is another oral strand that Ngũgĩ uses in the early works to legitimize the Gĩkũyũ's claims to the land, justify their political protest, and give credence to its leadership. In *Weep Not, Child*, for example, after making huge sacrifices to fight the white man's war, the Gĩkũyũ come home to find that "The land was gone:"

> My father and many others had been moved from our ancestral lands. He died lonely, a poor man waiting for the white man to go. Mugo had said this would come to be. The white man did not go and he died a Muhoi on this very land. It then belonged to Chahira before he sold it to Jacobo. I grew up here,

but working .... (1969:48)

The old seer, Mugo wa Kibiro, had prophesied, "There shall come a people with clothes like butterflies," and the people did not believe him: "They would not listen to his voice, which warned them: 'Beware!'" The people of the ridges "gave him no clothes and no food. He became bitter and hid himself, refusing to tell them more." The nationalists triumphantly claim association with Gīkūyū seers and prophets of long ago from whom they purposefully derive their authority: "We are his offspring. His blood flows in your veins" (1965:18-19). Being a descendant of the great Gīkūyū seer, Mugo wa Kibiro, for example, gives Chege a greater claim to Gīkūyū religious leadership, and Waiyaki to the Kenyan political leadership. Similarly, the name "Mugo" gives the character with that name in A Grain of Wheat a greater claim to heroism in the Mau Mau movement in the eyes of the people than his actual role, and helps to depict the movement as the natural heir to the prophecy.

Exemplifying Ngūgī's use of the oral tradition, these Mau Mau myths were used by the movement itself to validate its military campaign and its claim to the land. They can also be found in Mau Mau songs (Maina wa Kīnyattī, 1980). In other words, these myths and prophecies come as part of the Mau Mau "baggage," and Ngūgī uses them within the boundaries of a realistic rendering of the Mau Mau oral history. The Mau Mau used them not only to fire up nationalistic sentiment and resolve against colonial oppression and land alienation in Kenya, but also to project their nationalist leaders in the form of biblical seers, prophets who had come to remind the people that this lush land now in European settlers' hands was once given to them by God. Furthermore, the approach of these modern seers resembled that of the prophets of old who had warned their fellow countrymen against the impending doom with the arrival of the white man.

In Ngūgī's early works, the tragic seer/nationalist heroes like Mugo wa Kibiro and Chege in the River Between only preach at their people: "Now, listen my son. Listen carefully, for this is the ancient prophecy. ... I could do no more. When the white man came and fixed himself in Siriana, I warned all the people. But they laughed at me ..." (1965:20). In his later works, however, Ngūgī transforms this type of tragic hero to a more combative hero like Dedan Kīmaathi in The Trial of Dedan Kīmaathi, and Matigari, who works with the people instead of preaching at them. Through this transformation Matigari becomes the reincarnation of the old prophets, going from community to community seeking for truth and justice. However, instead of his words ringing in the wilderness they are now repeated again and again at workers' rallies, in prison, and everywhere where people dwell. Ngũgĩ makes it explicit that Matigari is in fact to be understood as the re-incarnation of the old prophets when the farmers, unaware that they were talking to Matigari, say: "Go back ... and look for a man called Matigari ma Njirũũngi. He is the one who now beats the rhythm to the tune, 'truth and again truth'" (1987:79).

Yet the impression we get at the end is that Matigari is much more than just the incarnation of the old prophets. To the people he is the messiah, the redeemer, the one who survives the bullets to fulfill the prophecy the way Jesus survives the nails on the cross. Ngũgĩ also uses the oral tradition of prophecy to universalize his themes by unifying the traditional Gĩkũyũ prophecy of old with the biblical prophecy into one. Thus to the question "Who is Matigari?" at the court scene, another person answers "Don't you know that the Bible says he shall come back again?" "Do you mean to say," the other persists, "he's the One prophesied about? The Son of Man?" (1987:81).

Ngũgĩ's later works remold the old inherited myths and prophecies into new forms to serve his own ideological purposes rather than merely to describe the ideological foundations of Mau Mau. He begins to explore orality as a creative process rather than as a received tradition. Even biblical myths are re-assessed and re-created. The very title of *Devil on the Cross*, for example, is an ironic twist of the original story of the crucifixion: The Devil, the ruthless genius of capitalism, is crucified by workers and peasants. The myth of the resurrection is also re-moulded so that now it is Satan who is rescued from the cross and nurtured back to life by the rich and powerful who adhere to His creed. Thus, instead of accepting the biblical myth as received from the Bible, Ngũgĩ re-creates it and inverts its meaning to sharpen the contrasts in the abstract concept of good and evil within a capitalist setting.

The myth of the hereafter too, with its provision of heaven and hell, is re-created in a new way and made relevant to the present living conditions of the people. As Mũturi puts it, "Heaven and Hell? ... Both exist... Listen. Our lives are a battlefield on which is fought a continuous war between the forces that are pledged to confirm our humanity and those determined to dismantle it" (1982:53).

In *Matigari*, too, there is a creative rather than merely traditional use of the biblical myth. In the prison scene, for example, in a re-enactment of the Last Supper and the Chrisitan Communion service, Matigari shares with other prisoners his food and beer—items that miraculously evade the stringent prison security checks. Matigari, we are told, "took the food, broke it and gave it to them ... Then he took the bottle of beer, opened it with his teeth, poured a little of it on the floor in libation and gave them to drink and pass round" (1987:57). The collective capitalist oppressor, who acts as the Devil in the *Devil on the Cross*, is pitted against the collective revolutionary patriot who acts like Jesus in *Matigari*. The title of the Minister of Truth and Justice in *Matigari* is a similar inversion for the same purpose.

Orality is similarly transformed in the realm of song and ritual. In his early novels, Ngũgĩ often introduces songs and ritual with sometimes elaborate explanations: Waiyaki's initiation and Muthoni's decision to undergo circumcision in *The River Between*, for example, are introduced by lengthy preambles about their intentions and reasons for wanting to undergo the rituals. Circumcision, in fact, generates a heated argument between Muthoni and her sister, Nyambura. To the charge of being demonically possessed and that "Every man of God knew that this was a pagan rite against which, time and time again, the white missionaries had warned," Muthoni answers: "Look, please, I - I want to be a woman. I want to be a real girl, a real woman, knowing all the ways of the hills and ridges" (1965:25-26). This example highlights Ngũgĩ's reaction to the overzealous anthropologists who condemned Africa's cultures and practices, including its ritual and songs. In the early novels, partly because of his focus on a Western defined audience, Ngũgĩ is inclined to use his writing to answer the charge that African customs were barbaric and a sign of backwardness.

Similarly, songs and chants are sometimes accompanied with elaborative explanation, and if they are in Gĩkũyũ they are usually accompanied by an English translation. This becomes necessary partly because the songs themselves as a tradition of the oral are detached from the central narrative. At this stage Ngũgĩ's inclination to throw in chunks from the oral tradition into his writing within the specifications of the Western concept of the novel leaves such oral forms undigested.

After *Petals of Blood* and in the process of redefining his audience, Ngũgĩ integrates song, dance and formal patterns of celebration into his writing without feeling the need to explain or justify. In the *Devil on the Cross*, for example, Mũturi constantly describes himself as talking into song:

> They have been taught new songs, new hymns that celebrate
> the acquisition of money. That's why today Nairobi teaches:

Crooked to the upright,
Meanness to the loving
Civil to the good .... (1982:15-16)

Warīīnga also employs song simultaneously in a semi-autobiographical narrative:

For today Kareendi has decided that she does not know the
difference between
To straighten and to bend,
To swallow and to spit out,
To ascend and to descend
To go and to return.

Yes, for from today she'll never be able to distinguish between
The crooked and the straight,
The foolish and the wise ... (1982:25)

In *Matigari*, Matigari confronts the cowardly priest by asking him: "You, wise man, did you say that this world is not upside-down? A world in which

The builder sleeps in the open,
The worker is left empty-handed,
The tailor goes naked,
And the tiller goes to sleep on an empty stomach?

Tell me! Where are the truth and justice in all this? Where in
the world can one find justice? (1987:98)

As Ngūgī modifies his use of song and ritual so that they relate more directly to the kinds of struggle which they evoke, he starts to use song and ritual as media of communication in their own right, and in the process transforms the singer and ritual performer into a Brechtian type of collective agents. In this transformation Ngūgī's central intention is to present ideas, and not just to entertain. In his early novels, Ngūgī draws his audience into his descriptions emotionally; but now he wants his audience to comprehend the action intellectually as well. The singer-as-chorus technique keeps the audience captivated yet alert. In his early novels, Ngūgī uses orality to argue (for example, about the validity of the peoples' claim to their land). The use of singer as chorus in the later novels enables him more subtly to suggest. In this way, the creative employment of song and ritual with their own rhythms, call and response technique, and borrowings from the Bible, all directed at a new audience, give his narrative style a combative thrust that goes beyond the traditional use of orality for mere authentication.

There is, therefore, a transformation in Ngũgĩ's use of orality in his writing. In the early works, he uses orality in a "chunking" fashion partly to reproduce the Mau Mau narrative and partly to authenticate his work. Orality is treated as a pristine, static and unchangeable phenomenon, employed within the Western concept of the novel, and necessitating, in Fanon's words, a "borrowed aesthetics" for its interpretation. In his later works, however, Ngũgĩ uses orality as a dynamic vibrant reality, and as part of the call and response pattern that brings out its collective power. As his own creative development leads him to re-define his audience, Ngũgĩ modifies his use of the most identifiable oral forms by enlivening them to maximize their revolutionary potential. Nevertheless, to accomplish this Ngũgĩ had first to totally identify himself with the people, and see history from their point of view.

4.

The adoption of orality in its Brechtian didactic form is most apparent in Ngũgĩ's later works. He uses different oral features to establish an oral form and style that help him to deliver his moral lessons and to clarify the issues on which those moral decisions are based. In his early novels, Ngũgĩ tends to restrict his use of oral style to epithets or stock phrases, starting with names, such as Joshua (Christian), or Livingston (Colonial), or mythological names, such as Mũũmbi, Mugo, Chege, and others. Such names and phrases become easy to remember, both for the narrator and for the audience, and handy to exaggerate certain characteristics that the writer wants to emphasize. This epic narrative style gives the reader a vivid and concrete impression of what the issues are and how the characters contrast with each other. Even when he reverts to mythology, Ngũgĩ is quick to create a contrast of mythological figures:

> Kameno threw up more heroes and leaders than any other ridge. Mugo wa Kibiro, that great Gĩkũyũ seer of old .... Or there was that great witch, Kamiri, whose witchery bewildered even the white men at Muranga. Another was Wachiori, a

great warrior, who had led the whole tribe against Ukabi, Masai. As a young man he had killed a lion, by himself ....
(1965:2)

Effective as this narrative style is in his early novels, its scope remains constrained by Ngũgĩ's use of orality as a received tradition rather than as a creative process.

Ngũgĩ's later work continues to employ epithets in a kind of epic style, yet it powerfully exploits additional epic and oral techniques like fantasy, exaggeration, and prophesying to impart specific moral lessons to his audience. For instance, *Matigari* contains many stock phrases to describe characters and situations that the author wants to render familiar to the audience: "His eyes shone brightly" describes Matigari; "those-who-reap-where-they-never-sowed" describes the capitalists. To articulate and characterize the central theme of "truth and justice" that runs throughout the novel, certain phrases are repeated again and again: "a seeker of justice never tires;" "A farmer whose seeds have not germinated does not give up planting;" "girded with a belt of peace;" and "too much fear breeds misery." Like epithets or stock phrases, songs, too, are repeated throughout the novel; as are episodes such as the one about the hunter-and-hunted confrontation between Matigari and Settler Williams. Also typical of oral tradition, these episodes, whic are told over and over again, are never repeated in exactly the same way. Each version differs from the others, depending on the particular audience, much like the repeated news broadcasts.

Simultaneously redefining his style and his audience, Ngũgĩ also bases his transformation of oral narrative on prophesying, gospel preaching, and public address. To take an early example, when Mugo was Kibiro, the great Gĩkũyũ seer, says, "'There shall come a people with clothes like butterflies,'" the reader can practically hear the voice. A similar oral power enlivens the preaching and debating encounters between adversaries like Waiyaki and Joshua in the church, or Waiyaki and Kabonyi at the Kiama in *The River Between*, or Mugo's public address at the independence anniversary rally in *A Grain of Wheat*. However, the settings in these early novels are formalistic, their rhetorical style stilted, the characters warped in their individualistic psychological impotence, and their speeches like the muffled voices of hermits preaching disjointedly to an empty space. Prophets are neither met nor heard. There are only reports about them. Similarly, there is a mere description of what Waiyaki and Kabonyi say at the Kiama rally. Even Chege appears as somebody beyond this world: a recluse isolated from his people and forced into hiding and talking in riddles. In Fanon's terms, the use of preaching, prophesying, and public address in Ngūgī's early narratives cannot be considered an example of national literature because it is not of the people and from the people!

When Matigari goes to an old woman hermit in the wilderness in the fashion of the old prophets to seek for truth and justice, he is told: "My dear wanderer, you cannot find answers here where nobody lives. Truth and justice are to be found in peoples' actions" (1987:87). This statement corresponds to Ngūgī's own re-assessment of his early use of the prophesying narrative style. Ngūgī radically modifies the narrative style of his later works to become more informal and more combative. In both the gathering of thieves in *Devil on the Cross* and the political assembly by the Minister of Truth and Justice in *Matigari*, Ngūgī uses the oral narrative style of prophesying and public address to portray his characters as persuasive verbal combatants. Furthermore, he punctuates the text with songs of praises from the hymn-book entitled *Songs of a Parrot!*

Transforming a biblical type of prophesying instead of preaching from the wilderness, Matigari stamps through the country to confront his enemies on country-roads, farms, political rallies, churches, courtyards and prisons. He cries, "You breed of parasites! Give back the keys to these houses and these lands which you took away from the people .... This country has its owners" (1987:78-79). The tone is messianic. Yet when asked whether he is the Second Coming of Jesus prophesied long ago, Matigari replies: "The God who is prophesied is in you, in me and in other human beings. He has always been there inside us since the beginning of time" (1987:156).

The beginning of *Matigari* sounds thoroughly oral: "So say yes, and I'll tell you a story! Once upon a time, in a country with no name ..." (1987: ix). The story of Matigari also ends as it begins: "This day, rumour has it that the torrential rain that fell was what put out the fires that had earlier consumed the houses. Across the land children came out to sing" (1987:174). In *Matigari* Ngūgī warns us from the outset that "This novel is based partly on an oral story. ... The story is simple and direct, and it dispenses with fixed time and place" (1987: vii). In Matigari, the character, we are confronted with a phantom: someone belonging to no particular time and space, someone we never actually see. Later he warns the policeman who attempts to arrest him: "Don't you dare touch me! I am as old as this country" (1987:112).

Ngūgī uses oral narrative style to characterize Matigari as a folk character, a form of Everyman. He is alleged to be "there at the time of the Portuguese, and the time of the Arabs, and the time of the British." Nobody knows if Matigari is a man or woman, adult or child, solitary as the old prophets or part of a group—in fact he is sometimes addressed in the plural: "Can't you guess who Matigari ma Njirũũngi are?" (1987:72). Nobody knows either his nationality or his size. The woman returning from the river describes him as "a tiny, ordinary-looking man," and yet other people describe him as "a giant who could almost touch the sky above" with smoke gushing out of his nose, mouth and ears (1987:75-77). Matigari suddenly appears wherever he wants to go; and he instantly meets the person he is looking for. He does not eat, yet he is described as supernaturally strong. Even the weather around him, in a typical fairy tales style, is constantly described as "neither hot nor cold," at least in the earlier part of the novel, to characterize a form of lifelessness in the country arising from the oppressive atmosphere in which "nothing was clear." Yet when Matigari eventually leads an insurrection against that oppression, the weather suddenly changes, and we are told that "The sun was blazing hotter than the hottest coals" (1987:137).

Transforming the conventional, individualistic and hermitic prophet trapped in the impotency of his own stream of consciousness, Ngũgĩ's oral narrative style reveals an enigmatic voice that is truly collective in character. While in early works like A Grain of Wheat combatants are usually portrayed as brave individuals displaying their bravery against overwhelming odds, Matigari faces the Minister of Truth and Justice, who is flanked by an awesome paramilitary force, by standing right in the middle of the crowd. Yet he is the crowd, too. In a typically collective style, the individual stands for the whole. Wherever he is, Matigari is surrounded by other people, reinforcing his own adage: "Those who eat alone die alone."

In a typical Western novel, character portrayal is individualized. Emphasis is placed on the psychological predisposition of the individual character and the various dimensions of his or her life. In Ngũgĩ's later works, however, there is a tendency, typical of the oral tradition, to use archetypal characters, who are often flat, as a way of reinforcing the social and collective voice rather than the individual voice. In the Devil on the Cross and Matigari, Ngũgĩ even "exaggerates" the very use of the oral style of exaggeration. In the former, when he uses the biblical parable of the citizens given talents to suggest its capitalist implication of the exploitation of the masses, he presents the whole issue of international capitalism in a graphically exaggerated way:

> And now before I sit down, I shall call upon the leader of the
> foreign delegation from the International Organization of

Thieves and Robbers (IOTR), whose headquarters are in New York, USA, to talk to you. I think you all know that we have already applied to become full members of IOTR. There are many tricks we can learn from them. We should never be afraid to acknowledge the fact that we don't know as much as foreigners do, and we should not feel ashamed to drink from foreign fountains of knowledge. (1982:87)

The cave scene in general reminds one of names like "Chief Rat" in primary school folklore, "Mr. All of You" in Achebe's folk tales, or even Dickensian satirical names like Mr. Pumblechook and Mr. Magwitch. They provide a kind of visual symbolism, right down to physical appearance and mode of dress. The characters are over-portrayed. Their characteristic mannerisms and activities are over-emphasized. The final item on the agenda of the Devil's Feast is a scheme to market human organs for transplants so that the elite will be able to purchase physical immortality and leave death to the workers!

To represent the collective voice rather than the individualistic in *Matigari*, Ngũgĩ avoids naming characters. Matigari's "real" name is not known. The name "Matigari" simply stands for those who survived the guerrilla war against the European settlers. The Minister's name is not known; nor are those of his VIPs. We see the diplomats from America, Japan and Europe through their parroty mannerisms: "All the guests on the platform took their handkerchiefs out of their pockets at about the same time" (1987:115). None of the characters are named. The only way to identify them is through such exaggerated description of their actions or appearance. The MP is identified as the one "who wore a silk suit, a KKK tie and thick-rimmed sunglasses" (1987:119).

This narrative style of exaggeration reveals dexterity with language and culture on the part of the narrator. Ngũgĩ's role in the composition of his tales can be taken as really that of the griot or *imbongi* of the oral tradition. He is "a master of words," versatile, and willing to engage all shades of his audience. A griot takes a tale, a trait or character and embellishes it by exaggerating, extolling, praising, or parodying. Both in his writing and in his profession as a teacher Ngũgĩ wa Thiong'o could be compared to a griot or an *imbongi* on several different levels. A griot has different functions in society, but as a teller of tales and a chronicler of the peoples' history, he may, as did the griot in the epic of Sundiata, describe himself as follows:

I am a griot. It is I, Djeli Mamoudou Kouyate, son of Bintou
Kouyate and Djeli Kedian Kouyate, master in the art of
eloquence. Since time immemorial the Kouyates have been in
the service of the Keita princes of Mali; we are vehicles of
speech, we are the repositories which harbour secrets many
centuries old .... I derive my knowledge from my father Djeli
Kedian, who also got it from his father .... I teach kings the
history of their ancestors so that the lives of the ancients might
serve them as an example. (Okpehwo, 1992:26)

Ngũgĩ's use of the griot tradition is present in his early writings, too. In *The
River Between*, for example, Ngũgĩ describes Chege as knowing "more than any
other person, the ways of the land and the hidden things of the tribe. He knew
the meaning of every ritual and every sign. So, he was all the head of every
important ceremony" (1965:7). In adopting the oral style of a griot, Ngũgĩ, like
Chege, wants to "guard this knowledge and divulge it to none but the right
one(s)." Yet Ngũgĩ's "right ones" become the children, students, farmers, and
workers that he eventually discovers in his later works. As a "master of eloquence"
in his early novels, Ngũgĩ chronicles Gĩkũyũ genealogy and Kenyan history as
portrayed by the deeds of the Mau Mau movement. This use of orality serves
the purpose primarily of a master of the spoken word who also has the power
to charm, to heal, to divine. Narrating the troubled history of his people, Ngũgĩ
offers a healing remedy for those wounded and betrayed by the Mau Mau war.
Nevertheless, in these early works Ngũgĩ "divulges" this knowledge primarily
within the confines of the realistic form of the novel.

The griot oral narrative style of Ngũgĩ's later works transcends realism to
chronicle his own interpretation of that knowledge and history. Matigari says
that for people to seize their own history, "one had to have the right words; but
these words had to be strengthened by the force of arms. In pursuit of truth and
justice," he continues, "one had to be armed with armed words" (1987:131). In
typical Fanonian fashion, the only way a griot can fashion a new language and
a new aesthetics that can enable him to interpret the peoples' heritage in
accordance with the peoples' interests is to become an active participant in their
struggle.

As a griot, Ngũgĩ is very methodical with his use of orality as a style of delivery.
Even the prison reminiscences in *Detained* demonstrate that Ngũgĩ does not
choose his literary strategies lightly, but carefully selects those oral devices that not

only enable him to tell a story, or give information, but also to give moral counsel (1981:8). In a typical griot tradition, Ngũgĩ employs oral tradition in the form of fable, fantasy, exaggeration, and song to bring issues for public debate, with himself acting as a moderator: in other words, not only praising but also criticizing. By the time he writes *Devil on the Cross*, Ngũgĩ abandons his earlier attempts to act as an omnipotent author indicting his characters and describing their deeds, and now uses orality to create a satiric world in which villains themselves assert their own villainy. Ngũgĩ transforms the narrative style of exaggeration deliberattely to blur the boundary between reality and fantasy: a device he employs effectively in the cave scene shifting from the real to the unreal. Ngũgĩ's newly developed skills in oral narrative succeed in creating stereotypical characters which enable him to present more clear-cut contrasts between social classes which these characters represent: more adequately expressing the horrors created by class antagonism in a capitalistic world. Ngũgĩ's adoption of a bolder oral tradition style leads not to a cruder technique but to a brilliantly new and more appropriate kind of literary tool.

Ngũgĩ's development of an oral narrative style is crucial to his own auctorial identity as a committed writer activist. Yet orality itself is the product of the griot tradition that comes from the peoples' voice and assures that the linkage between the griot and the people is immediate. Thus works like *Devil on the Cross* and *Matigari* go beyond the Western boundaries set by Ngũgĩ's early novels, and instead become unique events in language based on the imperatives of an immediate and direct communion with peasants and workers. Ironically, it is a double tragedy for Ngũgĩ that just at a time when his work is becoming orally "accessible" to the people of Kenya, since he turns to writing in Gĩkũyũ language and adopts a more dynamic oral form and style, that his primary audience will not "read" his books until the political and literary conditions in Kenya make reading possible. Yet Ngũgĩ's active participation in Kenyan politics re-directs his work from its early tendencies of being a mere product of the colonial discourse of domination and neo-colonialism towards becoming a very important event in Gĩkũyũ language and the struggle of the Kenyan people against oppression. His works become a clear organizational project intended to create a popular narrative style that is of the people, yet simultaneously the Kenyan people are changing themselves and the world around them. In the project, Ngũgĩ re-invents the Gĩkũyũ language in a new context as an oral granary of symbolic traditions, and in the process he also re-invents the novel. As a new griot in a new political situation, Ngũgĩ reclaims oral tradition and liberates it from its traditional, relatively passive use as a vehicle for authentication and passing messages from generation to generation.

5.

The question of orality in Ngũgĩ's writing relates to the audience for whom he writes. As indicated earlier, Fanon describes a national literature as a literature of combat partly because it appeals to the potential revolutionary consciousness of a non-elitist local audience, rather than to the sentiments of a more elitist trans-local audience that is defined by its proficiency in a shared European language. But in many instances the decision to "go local" in Africa entails, in linguistic terms, composing in languages that are predominantly ethnic bound: which is precisely the linguistic path that Ngũgĩ takes in his quest for a truly national literature of the Kenyan people.

Is Ngũgĩ's decision to write in Gĩkũyũ merely a manifestation of his ethnic chauvinism?[1] According to a section of Kenyan writers and scholars, a "modern, secular" education partly functions to transform people into "intellectuals" who would have, as some of their characteristics, a trans-ethnic world outlook and a commitment to a trans-ethnic community.[2] Responsibility and allegiance to such a community demands, of necessity, the use of an international medium of intellectual exchange like English and French. Nevertheless, this group does not find objectionable the idea of an Oromo, for example, who has not had any schooling, composing in his or her native Orominya. They would contend that such an individual has not acquired an international medium of exchange; and lacking in "education"—the "intellectualizing" agent—he or she cannot be expected to conceive of an individual's responsibility and commitment in relation to a community wider than the ethnic one. However, to them, for an educated intellectual like Ngũgĩ to write in a language that is ethnic bound is seen as an act of betrayal of the international community and the universal value of ideas, and a capitulation to a merely parochial melody of ethnicity.

To counter this argument, Ngũgĩ asks if the children of Kenya have been educated by their peasant and proletarian parents, often under very strenuous and almost unbearable financial hardships, only to come and express the knowledge they have acquired over the years in foreign language? Furthermore, do such oppressed peasants and proletarians finance the education of their children for the benefit of foreigners?[3] According to Ngũgĩ, to write in European languages demonstrates precisely such a socio-political orientation towards an audience that has been defined by "foreigners." In an attempt to break away from this sociolinguistic prison-house of imperialism, he writes in his mother tongue, Gīkūyū.

This language of Ngũgĩ's new writing, however, like many other African languages, exists primarily as an oral medium. There is, as yet, very little that has been written in Gīkūyū. Furthermore, written Gīkūyū has not yet assumed a life of its own apart from the "linguistic culture" of orality. The Gīkūyū language is yet to develop discernible features that can be considered to belong primarily to its written mode of discourse. In a sense, the very act of writing in Gīkūyū necessarily demands from Ngũgĩ's works a certain degree of orality. Both *Devil on the Cross* and *Matigari*, Ngũgĩ's two novels composed originally in Gīkūyū, are replete with linguistic conventions of orality rather than those of writing. That the oral aspect of the Gīkūyū language would have a certain impact on his novels is, of course, a matter that Ngũgĩ himself was fully conscious of from the very beginning (1986:77-78).

To turn to Ngũgĩ's audience in Gīkūyū, the majority of Gīkūyū peasants and workers have not had the opportunity to attend the formal institutions within which precincts the skills of reading and writing are often imparted. Those who have acquired literacy in local languages through the efforts of church and other literacy societies usually belong to a class of people who cannot afford to buy published materials in those languages. Also, the pedagogic approach used in many literacy classes produce learners that are less than functionally literate. Reading in local languages in Kenya seems to have remained a relatively undeveloped activity.[4] Therefore, Ngũgĩ writes in Gīkūyū for an audience that is predominantly oral in that language.

A result of this incongruence between written works and an oral audience is the transformation of Ngũgĩ's works in Gīkūyū into orally transmitted extended stories. Just as children once used to sit around their parents and grandparents to listen to stories from the oral tradition, adults may now be seen sitting with members of their own generation or younger, listening to narrations from Ngũgĩ's novels. Commenting on the transmission of his *Caitaani Mūtharaba-inĩ*, Ngũgĩ writes: "A family would get together every evening and one of their literate members would read it for them. Workers would also sit in groups, particularly during the lunch break, and would get one of them to read the book. It was read in buses; it was read in taxis; it was read in public bars" (1986:83). Ngũgĩ formally identifies this process as "the appropriation of the novel into the oral tradition." Through oral transmission *The Devil on the Cross* and *Matigari* are embellished and enriched, both substantively and aesthetically, by the immediate, collective and participatory response of the listening audience, both in their linguistic and para-linguistic reactions.

6.

Orality serves a variety of functions and assumes a variety of forms in Ngũgĩ's creative writing, especially after *Petals of Blood*. Orality features at the levels of inspiration, composition, narration, and transmission,[5] each feeding into the other to produce a cohesive product that is at once conventional and revolutionary, old and new. Furthermore, orality in Ngũgĩ's post-*Petals*' novels takes an even more creative, dynamic and natural character that distinguishes it, to a large extent, from the more static and "museum-type" of orality found in his early novels and in the novels of many other African writers.

Developing a literary style informed by the powers of orality, Ngũgĩ creates a literature that represents the interests of the "masses" and, in the process, a literature of combat that is both national and anti-imperialist in character. Radical as *Petals of Blood* may be in its theme and message, the book is bound by the imperialist terms of reference of an audience that served the ends of neocolonialism at the expense of the national interest. *Devil on the Cross* and *Matigari* are a radical attempt to depart from this tradition and chart out a new course towards a national literature, specifically, and a national culture in general. But the growth, maturation and consolidation of a national culture ultimately depend on the presence of politico-economic conditions necessary to support and sustain that new culture. Attempts at creating a national culture must go hand-in-hand with efforts to create a new political environment altogether. As Fanon states: "To fight for a national culture means in the first place to fight for the liberation of the nation, that material keystone which makes the building of a culture possible. There is no other fight for culture which can develop apart from the popular struggle" (1967:187). No person can purport to be contributing to the creation of a national culture and yet distance himself or herself from the popular struggle for liberation. In the words of Fanon: "No one can truly wish for the spread of African culture if he does not give practical support to the creation of the conditions necessary to the existence of that culture; in other words to the liberation of the whole continent" (1967:189).

Precisely this Fanonian legacy requires the national artist to be, at the same time, a political activist, and this distinguishes Ngũgĩ from many other creative writers in Africa. In addition to being a producer of elements of a national culture, Ngũgĩ is a staunch political activist who has earned the wrath of the successive neocolonial regimes of his home-country, Kenya. Through his political involvement, orality emerges as an organic dimension of Ngũgĩ's later works.

Notes

[1]Much of this discussion took place informally within the corridors of Kenya's universities.

[2]Of course the reality in Africa has been quite different. While there has indeed been a trend towards declining ethnic behavior, there seems to have been a rise in ethnic consciousness which has been most pronounced precisely among the "educated" elite.

[3]This argument is contained in the introduction of the Gĩkũyũ original, *Caitaani Mũtharaba-inĩ* (1980).

[4]According to Onyango Ogutu, Marketing Manager of East African Publishing House (formerly, Heinemann (kenya) Ltd.), there has been very little demand for their publications in local languages other than Kiswahili. Among these Ngũgĩ's two novels in Gĩkũyũ have shown the highest sales.

[5]In his two plays originally written in Gĩkũyũ, *I Will Marry When I Want* and *Mother Sing for Me*, Ngũgĩ also experimented with orality as a method of composition. Actors and actresses among the Gĩkũyũ peasants and workers affiliated with the Kamĩrĩĩthũ Center were provided only with outlines of the plays, and collectively developed them into complete scripts. Through this process, Kamĩrĩĩthũ Center became a venue for producing a Kenyan "participatory literature."

Works Cited

Aidoo, Ama Ata. Interview. *African Writers Talking*. Ed. C. Pieterse and D. Duerden. New York: Africana, 1973.

Atieno-Odhiambo, E.S. "Rebutting "Theory" with Correct Theory: A Comment on *The Trial of Dedan Kĩmaathi* by Ngũgĩ wa Thiong'o and Micere Githae Mugo." *Kenya Historical Review* 5. 2. 1977: 385-88.

Cham, Mbye Baboucar. "Ousmane Sembene and the Aesthetics of African Oral Traditions." *Africana Journal* 13. 1-4. 1982: 24-40.

Chinweizu, Onwuchekwa Jemie and Ikechukwu Madubuike. *Toward the Decolonization of African Literature*. London: KPI Ltd., 1985.

Egejuru, Phanuel. "Traditional Oral Aesthetics in Modern African Literature: Oka Okwu in Theme and Character Exploration in *The Lands Lord*." *The Literary Griot* 2.2. Fall 1990: 1-22.

Fanon, Frantz. *The Wretched of the Earth*. Harmondsworth: Penguin. 1967.

Maina wa Kīnyattī. Ed. *Thunder from the Mountains*. London: Zed Press, 1980.

Miller, Christopher L. *Theories of Africans: Francophone Literature and Anthropology in Africa*. Chicago: University of Chicago Press, 1990.

Ngūgī wa Thiong'o. *The River Between*. London: Heinemann, 1965.

—. *A Grain of Wheat*. London: Heinemann, 1967.

—. *Weep Not, Child*. New York: Collier Books. 1969.

—. (With Micere Githae Mugo). *The Trial of Dedan Kīmaathi*. London: Heinemann, 1976.

—. *Petals of Blood*. London: Heinemann, 1977.

—. Introduction. *Caitaani Mūtharaba-inī*. Nairobi: Heinemann, 1980.

—. *Detained: A Writer's Prison Diary*. London: Heinemann, 1981.

—. *Devil on the Cross*. London: Heinemann, 1982.

—. (With Ngūgī wa Mirii). *I Will Marry When I Want*. London: Heinemann, 1982.

—. *Decolonizing the Mind: The Politics of Language in African Literature*. London: James Currey, 1986.

—. *Matigari*. Oxford: Heinemann, 1987.

Okpewho, I. *African Oral Literature*. Bloomington: Indiana University Press, 1992.

Senghor, Leopold Sedar. *Senghor: Prose and Poetry*. (selected and translated by John Reed and Clive Wake). London: Oxford University Press, 1965.

Scheub, Harold. "A Review of African Oral Traditions and Literature." *African Studies Review*. 28.2/3. June/September 1985: 1-72.

F. Odun Balogun

Ngũgĩ's *Matigari* and the Refiguration of the Novel as Genre

A FASCINATING DIAMETRIC OPPOSITION characterizes the reception of Ngũgĩ's latest novel *Matigari*. Ngũgĩ was encouraged to write *Matigari*, his second Gĩkũyũ-language novel, by the enormous success of its predecessor *Devil on the Cross*, which had enjoyed enthusiastic reception in Kenya (*Decolonizing the Mind* 83-84). *Matigari* was equally successful in Kenya, the primary audience. It was so artistically successful that the Kenyan government had mistaken its protagonist for a real life revolutionary seeking government overthrow and had issued a warrant for his arrest. By contrast, critics' reception of the English translation of *Matigari* has been anything but enthusiastic.

> *Ngũgĩ's historic decision to abandon English for his native Gĩkũyũ and Kiswahili as his primary languages for writing (Decolonizing the Mind xiv) can be seen as the most significant achievement of Obi Wali's school of language discourse in African literature.*

At least three major reasons can be advanced to explain the current lukewarm critical reception of the novel. The first relates to the language ideology that brought *Matigari* into being, the second concerns the political ideology privileged by the novel's thematic discourse, and the third arises from Ngũgĩ's experimental use of *Matigari* as a medium for genre refiguration.

Ngũgĩ's historic decision to abandon English for his native Gĩkũyũ and Kiswahili as his primary languages for writing (*Decolonizing the Mind* xiv) can be seen as the most significant achievement of Obi Wali's school of language discourse in African literature. In *Decolonizing the Mind*, Ngũgĩ provides an ideological articulation of his reasons for adopting the language philosophy of the Obi Wali school which argues that only those works of African literature that are written in indigenous African languages can be considered authentic and relevant. Just as Obi Wali's enunciation of this philosophy at the now famous 1962 African writers' Makarere conference instantly created a counter-discourse as to what constituted the appropriate language of African literature, so has

Ngũgĩ's actualization of Obi Wali's dream aroused immediate contestation. For example, Joseph Mbele suggests that Ngũgĩ's novel evidences entrapment by a kind of Oedipal complex. According to Mbele, Ngũgĩ "is bent on killing the father, the former colonial master, who, through a process of displacement, is represented by the colonizer's language" (150).

The most easily recognizable reason for this kind of hasty dismissal of *Matigari* as an unsuccessful novel is the extreme overtness, pointedness, and harshness of its anti-imperialist rhetoric. For critics brought up to believe that genuine art and propaganda do not mix, *Matigari* cannot be anything other than seriously flawed. However, in a *A Grain of Wheat* and *Petals of Blood* Ngũgĩ proves that he can be as subtle a propagandist as anyone else when he chooses. His extreme overtness in *Matigari* is a conscious artistic strategy. Furthermore, the practice of stretching a literary device beyond its limits is one of the deliberate means by which postmodernist writers attempt to engage the minds of their readers.

We have traditionally conceived of nineteenth-century novels as realistic, twentieth-century novels as modernist, and contemporary novels as postmodernist. Similarly, we have labelled individual novels as romance, picaresque, or science fiction; as historical, political, or satiric; or as autobiographical, symbolic, or mythic. Broadening this purist view of the genre, we would say a novel is realistic, but with elements of naturalism or modernism. A symbolic novel might also be a political satire. Quite often, Third World novels have been perceived primarily as novels that have incorporated native elements of the oral narrative tradition. In other words, we have operated under the assumption that a novel could function safely as a novel only if it has carried so much generic load, but no more.

However, the premodernist assurance concerning the novel and its definite, almost inviolate, generic boundaries has at last given place to the postmodernist diffusion about the relationship between genres. We no longer think, as Ian Watt, for instance, that the novel is necessarily realistic; Latin Americans have shown us that it can be marvelous. In fact, we no longer care to circumvent the freedom of literary creativity by insisting on iron-clad generic boundaries. On the contrary, the current tendency is to privilege faction over fiction largely because the former traverses at will the worlds of fantasy and realism. Due in part to this development, but even more as a result of certain internal dynamics of his art and ideology, Ngũgĩ wa Thiong'o has succeeded in creating a fascinating and revolutionary concept of genre in his recent novels

Devil on the Cross and *Matigari*.

Ngũgĩ's earlier novels have consistently exhibited certain stylistic tendencies which have conflated in the recent experimental novels. First, his early realistic novels were autobiographical and emphasis in them was on presenting a certain span of the life (biography) of the protagonist. Second, there has always been a pronounced religious strain and love of religious myths and motifs in all of Ngũgĩ's novels. Third and lastly, the communalist and nationalist ideology which permeated all of Ngũgĩ's novels has recently led to the radical and historic switch from the English-language novel with an aesthetic that was primarily rooted in Western literary history to the Gĩkũyũ-language novel with aesthetic principles that privilege oral narrative techniques at the same time as they permit synthesis with useable elements of other traditions. The purpose of the language switch was not to repudiate all aspects of the Western tradition of the novel; rather, it was to exchange the dominance of the Western tradition within his own writing with the predominance of the native literary tradition.

Indeed, it would be naive of anyone to assume that Ngũgĩ intended the total isolation of cultures at this time in human history. Far from it, Ngũgĩ switched to a native language-based literature because he wished to liberate his art from the constraints of the Western tradition and broaden its scope by situating it within the primary control of the less exclusivist and more accommodating aesthetic philosophy of the oral narrative tradition. The exchange of primary influence between aesthetics was well conceived, for it has opened greater possibilities not only to Ngũgĩ's individual art but also to the genre of the novel as a whole.

Matigari initiates the commencement of a qualitatively different novelistic genre—one that incorporates several genres on equal footing. Some of the genres that harmoniously coexist in *Matigari* are those that were traditionally thought to be antithetical. In the past, for instance, we have meticulously distinguished written literature from oral narrative performance, but in *Matigari* this traditional distinction is invalidated: *Matigari* is both a novel at the same time as it is an oral narrative performance. *Matigari* is likewise equally a hagiography as it is a myth. Hence *Matigari*, to borrow the language of Walter Ong in *Orality and Literacy*, is not exactly a post-literate narrative aspiring to orality, but one that unites literacy and orality with equal respect for both. *Matigari* might even remind the Western reader of Homer's *Odyssey* and of some books of *The Bible*, although Ngũgĩ's work is the sophisticated product of centuries of the history of narrative literature from the age of orality to the period of post-structuralist literacy. *Matigari* is also not only a politically satiric and realistic novel, but also a multivocal postmodernist deconstructivist experiment. In other words, we have a new kind of novel that is equivalently multiform and multigenre, requiring a set of critical questions that goes beyond traditional analytic methodologies.

One of the primary distinctions between the literatures of Africa and the Western world is the centrality of the role of the oral tradition in the former and its progressive extinction from the latter. Thus, critical concern with the character of the relationship between the written and oral traditions within the works of African writers has been a permanent feature of literary analysis. Emmanuel Obiechina, for instance, in *Culture, Tradition and Society in the West African Novel* suggests that African writers' borrowing from the oral tradition does not constitute "a literary fad or an attempt to exoticize West African literature" (26). In fact, Bernth Lindfors believes that the best works emerging from Africa are those that artfully blend elements of the oral and written traditions. Lindfors particularly finds this tendency in the works of Amos Tutuola (*Folklore in Nigerian Literature* 32, 59). The same awareness made Chinweizu, Jemie, and Madubuike prescribe a return to oral traditions as the primary source of inspiration for African writers (*Toward the Decolization of African Literature* 146, 290, 291). Ngũgĩ, himself, in *Homecoming* designated this blend resulting from the mix of oral and written traditions as *orature* (76).

More recent studies such as Eldred Durosimi Jones' *Oral and Written Poetry in African Literature Today*, and *Tradition and Innovation: New Wine in Old Bottles?* by Sienaert, Bell, and Lewis show that *orature* is the most dominant trend in African literature today. *Matigari* is an illustration of how this trend has been taken to its most logical development. Whereas earlier classical instances of *orature* such as Achebe's *Things Fall Apart*, Soyinka's *Death and the King's Horseman*, and Okot p'Bitek's *Song of Lawino* negotiate the contour of their genres on terms dictated to one degree or another by the Western literary tradition, *Matigari*, defines its own artistic nature in terms dictated by the oral tradition. Thus, in *Matigari* oral tradition does not, as in the past, serve, but rather, it is served by, the Western novelistic tradition.

Since traditional novel criticism has not provided tools to analyze a work like *Matigari*, we must turn to the scholarship in oral tradition and critics who have recognized the so-called "gray areas" (Foley 164) in which orality and literacy interface to produce texts that exhibit what Walter Ong calls "'literate orality' of the secondary oral culture" (160). Ong distinguishes "orality" that emerges from a primary oral culture from "literate orality" that emerges in a literate culture as a choice creating secondary orality. Orally derived texts have distinctive characteristics that set them apart from genres that are determined by the norms of the written tradition such as the novel; the history of which is almost synonymous with the history of writing and literacy in the West. The characteristics exhibited by *Matigari*, on the other hand, show the greatest affinity to the most developed genre of oral narrative—the oral epic.

Initial doubts concerning the existence of the epic genre in Africa have been dispelled by Isidore Okpewho, John William Johnson, and a host of others who continue to elaborate on both the peculiarly African as well as the universal traits of the African epic.[1] Catherine Williams notes a shift in the narrative forms of Ngūgī's recent novels and has also remarked, on Ngūgī's use of "mixed genres" (Williams 59-61). A central characteristic of the epic is its multiformism, that is, the quality of incorporating diverse genres. This trait is clearly evident in *Matigari*, structurally made up of narratives such as history, legends, proverbs, parables; performance that is comprised of music, songs, dialogues, and mimicry; and other diverse elements such as description, etiology, radio broadcasts, and borrowings from Hollywood films and from the traditions of the realistic novel.

Although *Matigari*'s narrative is episodically structured—another primary quality of the epic—its story line—is clear and strong. This, too, is no accident, for the core of the epic narrator's art is the story that is to be told. As Albert Lord observes, in epic "the tale's the thing" (*Singer of Tales* 68). However, because the tale must be made to be engaging, the singer dramatizes it in performance. Isidore Okpewho, emphasized the vital importance of the performance element in the African epic. He suggests that drama and music are "the thing" (52-66). *Matigari* as an epic justifies this view, for it is dramatically composed; the narration moves rapidly, enhanced by vivid descriptions, frequent dialogues, perpetually tense atmosphere, and dramatic, often explosive, actions.

In the tradition of the typical epic, *Matigari*'s multiform and episodic structure also operates under a cataloguing and framing principle of composition that formulaically links themes. When closely examined, *Matigari* manifests what Ong calls "prefabricated" formulary parts (23). The themes, the framed stories, and the language of *Matigari* are made up of formulary units. The novel opens with a variant of the theme of weapon description—a beloved device by European epic bards. This theme is also quickly linked with another popular epic theme—the return of a long absent hero—because the reader soon learns that the ex-fighter who is hiding his weapon under a *mūgumo* tree is a Mau Mau patriot. Popular legend, built on a historical Kenyan reality, holds that the patriots, who have been hiding in the forests and mountains since the end of the war for independence, would return to restore true independence to the Kenyan people, already disfranchised by post-independence rulers. Another popular epic theme, the quest, is then introduced: Matigari, the returning hero, starts on a search for his "family and children." Several other quests will succeed each other later in the novel as Matigari goes all over the country, seeking truth and justice. Additional formulaic themes include pursuit and rescue, which are associated with government officials' attempts to liquidate Matigari and Gūthera.

At least nine framed stories are narrated in *Matigari* in the ornamental digressive manner of the traditional epic. The stories are ornamental because they do not belong to the main story line. Most frequently, the framed story is presented through the device of the ring composition by which epic narrators neatly bracket off their ornamental narrative insertions. A typical example of the framed story in *Matigari* is the history of Gūthera. In a typical epic formulary manner, this story is repeated almost word for word on two separate occasions (33-37 and 94-97).

Ngūgī's use of formulary epic principles is most evident in *Matigari*'s diction and syntax, especially in the earlier sections of the narrative. Here the sentences are strung together in an additive, paratactic, rather than aggregative manner, thus creating parallelism. A typical example is section 2 of part one of the novel (5-6). Instead of using a mixture of simple, complex, and compound sentences in the passage, there is a succession of simple sentences repetitively beginning every time, in the English translation, with a third person masculine singular personal pronoun "He." The most easily recognizable formula in *Matigari* is the epithets which proliferate throughout: "flaming sword" (78), "Minister of Truth and Justice" (102), "His Excellency Ole Excellence" (*passim*), "Hooded Truth" (117, 120), "You who Eat what another has sown" (*passim*).

Finally, Matigari is a typical epic hero. His legendary background as a Mau Mau fighter returning on a mission to restore truth and justice to his people, his superhuman endurance, his supernatural physical attributes and features, and the frequent and protective intervention of natural forces in his destiny place him apart in a separate company with such epic heroes as Odysseus and Sundiata.

The recurrence of the religious and Christian themes in Ngūgī's works has been frequently discussed by critics. A single publication in 1984, for instance, included three essays on the subject (*Critical Perspectives* 146-60, 201-10, 292-306). Ngũgĩ's frequent use of religious/Christian themes has more to it than the mere fact that the *Bible* was the first available book in indigenous Kenyan languages. Ngũgĩ's biblical allusions also go beyond the prominence of religion in his colonial education. The seriousness, tenaciousness, and frequency of biblical references in Ngũgĩ's works suggest that his unorthodox use of biblical motifs becomes a kind of liberation theology. The social and political equality that he advocates as a socialist writer shares much in common with the equality implicit in Christ's revolutionary advocacy of the love of one's neighbor.

Devil on the Cross is the rehearsal of a kind of hagiographic style which Ngũgĩ develops more fully, in more than just a chronological sense, in *Matigari*. While the former presents a history of a heroine, Saint Warĩĩnga, the latter tells the story of the saint *par excellence*—Christ Himself. The protagonist Matigari has been carefully and convincingly presented in every particular as a Christ-figure. Numerous parallels exist between the thematic and stylistic presentation of Christ in the Gospels and Matigari in Ngũgĩ's novel.

Matigari is prophesied as the political redeemer of his people by the local legend originated in the Kenyan Mau Mau patriotic history and post-independence disillusionment. Like Christ, Matigari is fully grown and ready when he appears in the public for the first time to commence his ministry. He is baptized by a John the Baptist figure with the name "Seeker of Truth and Justice" (62). Matigari, just like Christ, loves children who flock to him and touch his clothes (16, 155). He has his Mary Magdalene in Gũthera, a fallen Christian. He commences his ministry in the prison where he appoints his twelve apostles, among whom is a Judas who will later betray him as a government informer. He provides a fresh interpretation of religion: "The real Church of God resided in people's hearts" (33). When asked, if he is "the one whose Second Coming is prophesied," he replies: "The God who is prophesied is in you, in me and in the other humans" (156). He has a binary ethical vision of things as good or evil; he has come to repossess his house (of God) by driving away the modern-day pharisees and scribes who are desecrating it with imperialist doctrines, and he threatens the desecrators with everlasting hell fire (81). He preaches on the Mount (63) and speaks like Christ ("Open your eyes and see ... Open your ears and hear ... Let the will of the people be done! Our kingdom come ..."); he teaches, using parables; he delivers prophesies, and he is tempted in the wilderness (86). He has what seem to be miraculous escapes a number of times, and he disappears at the end of the story, fatally wounded, but uncaptured by his enemies, through what appears to be divine intervention.

A study of mythopoeia in Matigari can only compliment its presentation within hagiographic and oral performance traditions. The mystery, power, and supernatural endowments which characterize Matigari as an epic hero and a saint also qualify him as a mythic hero. The novel contains at least two clusters of major and minor thematic myths. Again there is the religious myth of Matigari as Christ. There is, also, the secular myth of Matigari as the legendary Mau Mau patriot destined to free his people from political oppression and imperialist exploitation. The two policemen with the dog and who are depicted as if they were guarding the gate to hell, and the politicians who are presented as ogres, suggest additional analogues of classical myth.

The most fascinating aspect of Matigari as myth is that the novel itself is a study in the process of myth-making, in which Ngũgĩ implicitly suggests that myth is nothing but a lie constructed for political or religious convenience. The novel subtly but self-consciously presents how a make-believe is created and elevated to the height of myth.

Oral performance, epic, hagiography, and myth, Matigari is also convincingly constructed as a traditional novel that adheres strictly to all the principles of formal realism as analyzed by Ian Watt in The Rise of the Novel. Verisimilitude of character, setting, action, and language or style are critical tests of realism and, in this respect, Matigari easily passes in every detail.

Related to a discussion of the details of verisimilitude in Matigari is the extra-textual question of the relationship of fiction to life in today's Africa. The fact that officials of the Kenyan government mistook the novel's hero for a real-life revolutionary planning to overthrow of government, issued an order for the arrest of a fictional character, and organized a man-hunt for his capture, suggest a situation in which life is stranger than fiction. Equally strange is that Matigari's presentation of individuals who have made themselves Presidents-for-life, and have so corruptly enriched themselves that their personal wealth, stacked safely away abroad, is often much larger than the combined assets of the countries over which they rule as dictators, merely reflects a mundane African reality. Matigari is a political satire with the usual tendency of satires to use the hyperbolic medium of caricature, lampoon, and disguise. However this fact does not preclude the novel's verisimilitude. The god-like Excellency Ole Excellence is not any more arrogant or presumptuous than most of Africa's life-presidents of today. The institutionalized corruption in the police, legal system, other government offices, and in the church is true to actual experience in spite of *Matigari*'s satiric exaggerations. The vicious repression of all opposition and dissidents, and the unlawful arrest, detention, and massacre of demonstrating students, all of which frequently occur in many African countries, are factors which have made what the novel calls the "philosophy of parrotology" (mindless submission and syco-phancy) the very code by which many scholars and intellectuals negotiate the conditions of survival in real life under dictatorial regimes as well as under so-called African democracies. The collaborative relationship between John Boy and Settler Williams, on the one hand, and their joint exploitation of the common man, on the other hand, are as true to life as the forceful suppression of factory strikes and the search of garbage heaps for sustenance by abandoned urban children in the Africa of the era of Structural Adjustment Program (SAP).

In spite of the caricaturing of officials like Kīrīro through the use of absurd details and actions such as the wearing of a KKK-initialed tie, the prohibition of dreams, and the institution of the so-called instant justice which amounts to a rape of justice (117, 125), the language of the novel is realistic, especially in its details of setting, action and atmosphere. In Matigari himself, Ngūgī has painted a not-so-flattering, realistic picture of the otherwise mythologized hero. When Matigari does not wear the garment of a folk hero or of a saint, he looks old, unimpressive, tired, and vulnerable. Yet considered as a whole, he remains a convincing realistic character. He is ultimately a hero by virtue of his selfless dedication to the interest of his people and not on account of any mysteries with which an approving public invests him. In other words, heroes are ordinary men who rise above mundanity by their own force of will and deification by a public that needs inspiration and leadership. Thus, Ngūgī demystifies both his protagonist and his public through realistic representation.

Including such a variety of literary modes and genre, *Matigari* is bound to harbor deconstructing, contradictory elements. The novel's particular demy-thologizing tendency is obviously deconstructive; as is its presentation of the very process of transformation which creates a legendary epic hero and the Christian myth of a messiah right before the reader's eyes. As a socialist writer, Ngūgī demystifies myth-making for ordinary people in order to liberate them from the stranglehold of any kind of myth, yet particularly the Christian. The problem, however, is that Ngũgĩ's own myth-making is so effective that it can undermine his own strategy.

Ngũgĩ also wants to create believable characterization by ameliorating the contrast between his capitalist ogres and socialist saints. Consequently, he humanizes his saints by giving them personal weaknesses and, in contrast, makes his ogres, though seriously shaken, invincible in the end. Thus, the desire to be realistic functions in a manner that undermines the obvious ideological intention to create a positive socialist hero for workers' emulation. His workers might even become disillusioned. If a hero as courageous and as supernaturally endowed as Matigari can not change the status quo, what real hope is there of deliverance? That Ngũgĩ allows this situation to remain as it is, a situation that reflects the actual reality of Africa today, shows how much he wishes his novel to be true to life and realistic.

Several self-deconstructing moments in the novel are associated with either specific images or details of language. The image of Matigari aspiring to heroic and supernatural qualities as a folk hero or a Christ-figure and the image of him as a true-to-life person with human weaknesses co-exist; yet these images work against each other in an unresolved tension. A kind linguistic deconstruction occurs at the end of the first division of the first part of the novel. Here Matigari muses to himself: "It's good that I have now laid down my arms" (5). This announcement is undermined by the immediately preceding act of carefully hiding the arms which have been supposedly laid down. The sentence connotes, on one level, surrender and, on another, a careful stowing away of weapons for future use. A third meaning is that of calling a truce by both laying down his arms and keeping them, preparatory to enjoying peace. But he does not enjoy peace, and he fails to reach the weapons when he needs them for protection. Paradoxically, the least desirable and unintended meaning of the phrase is what in the end it turns out to mean: laying down arms is surrender. The laying down of the arms turns out to be a symbolic passing on of the patriotic baton of Mau Mau love of freedom to the younger generation of Kenyans. Matigari himself has been caught unarmed and eliminated by the enemy, but his arms have been transferred to a younger fighter for freedom. The story closes appropriately and optimistically with the image of a man bearing arms to ensure freedom.

Notes

[1]Isidore Okpewho (65-66, 154-60), John William Johnson (30-38), and others have argued against earlier scholars who insisted that epics must necessarily be composed in verse. The study of African epics is steadily growing, and a valuable bibliography was recently published by David Westley in the Winter 1991 issue of *Research in African Literatures*.

Works Cited

Brown, David Maughan. "Matigari and Rehabilitation of Religion." *Research in African Literatures* 22.4 (Winter 1991): 173-80.

Chinweizu, Onwuchekwa Jemie, and Ihechukwu Madubuike. *Toward the Decolonization of African Literature*. Enugu: Fourth Dimension, 1980.

Foley, John Miles. *The Theory of Oral Composition*. Bloomington: Indiana UP, 1988.

Johnson, John William. *The Epic of Son-Jara: A West African Tradition*. Bloomington: Indiana UP, 1986.

Jones, Eldred Durosimi. Ed. *Oral & Written Poetry in African Literature Today*. London: James Currey; Trenton, NJ: Africa World, 1989.

Kebler, Werner J. *The Oral and the Written Gospel*. Philadelphia: Fortress, 1983.

Killam, G. D. Ed. *Critical Perspectives on Ngũgĩ wa Thing'o*. Washington, D. C.: Three Continents, 1984.

Lindfors, Bernth. *Folklore in Nigerian Literature*. NY: Africana, 1973.

Lord, Albert B. *The Singer of Tales*. Cambridge, Massachusetts: Harvard UP, 1960.

—. "The Gospels as Oral Traditional Literature." *The Relationships Among the Gospels: An Interdisciplinary Dialogue*. Ed. William O. Walker, Jr. San Antonio: Trinity UP, 1978, 33-91.

Mbele, Joseph. "Language in African Literature: An Aside to Ngũgĩ." *Research in African Literatures* 23.1 (Spring 1992): 145-52.

Ngũgĩ wa Thiong'o *Matigari*. Trans. Wangũi wa Goro. London: Heinemann, 1989.

—. *Decolonizing the Mind: The Politics of Language in African Literature*. London: James Currey; Nairobi: Heinemann; Portsmouth NH: Heinemann, 1986.

—. *Devil on the Cross*. London: Heinemann, 1982.

—. *Homecoming: Essays on African and Caribbean Literature, Culture and Politics*. London: Heinemann, 1972.

Obiechina, Emmanuel. *Culture, Tradition and Society in the West African Novel*. Cambridge, UK: Cambridge UP, 1975.

Okpewho, Isidore. *The Epic in Africa*. NY: Columbia UP, 1979.

Ong, Walter J. *Orality and Literacy: The Technologizing of the Word*. London and NY:

Routledge, 1988.

Sienaert, Edgard R., A. N. Bell, and M. Lewis. Eds. *Tradition and Innovation: New Wine in Old Bottles?* Durban: U of Natal Oral Docummentation and Research Center, 1991.

Watt, Ian. *The Rise of the Novel.* Harmondsworth, England: Penguin, 1977.

Westley, David. "A Bibliography of African Epic. *Research in African Literatures* 22.4. Winter, 1991.

Williams, Katherine. "Decolonizing the World: Language, Culture, and Self in the works of Ngũgĩ wa Thiong'o and Gabriel Okara. "*Research in African Literatures* 22.4. Winter, 1991: 53-62.

Lewis Nkosi

Reading *Matigari*: The New Novel of Post-Independence

1.

THE WRITING ON the margin contradicts or disturbs the poise of the prefatory dedication "To the Reader/Listener." In the dedication which marks the opening of this political fairy-tale the "Reader/ Listener" is informed that the story of Matigari takes place in an "imaginary country" without a name even; that "it has no fixed space" and "no fixed time"; and that the action may take place in the country and time of the "Reader/Listener"'s choice. A mere glance across the page, however, quickly disposes of this subterfuge for the author reveals that "Matigari, the fictional hero, and the novel, his only habitation, have been effectively banned in Kenya. With the publication of this English edition they have joined the author in exile."

As the author further tells us in the brief preface, this book was "written largely in exile in the quietness of my one-bedroom flat in Noel Road, London, in 1983". Like its author, this is in many ways an exiled book; a homeless tale, orphaned yet at home everywhere in Africa. Nevertheless, it would be foolish to deny the work's special links with the Kenya of Jomo Kenyatta and Arap Moi, or rather its contestation of their version of the country, and the claims the novel makes on the legacy of the freedom fighters, the brave men and women who imagined they were delivering their country from British colonialism only to discover, as Matigari does, that "only a handful of people profited from the suffering of the majority" (12). Yet the novel preface's suggestion that its political paradigms have an almost universal application in postcolonial Africa is surely correct.

> *Ngũgĩ's gradual relinquishment of realistic representation for the world of fairy tale and day-dream may provide us with yet another sign of the crisis afflicting the postcolonial novel in Africa generally in its attempts over these past three decades to plot the story of corruption and exploitation under the leadership of civilian-military dictatorships.*

Africa is a place of repetition. In Zimbabwe the memory is still fresh of a bloody struggle which followed Ian Smith's desperate, last-ditch attempts to thwart progress toward majority rule; and at the moment of that inconclusive victory we can still remember moving television pictures of guerrillas, some of them very young and yet unaccustomed to peace, seen marching toward collection points where they were to surrender their weapons before being demobilized. Today, unprovided for and unemployed, many roam the streets of the capital, bitterly disappointed by the miserly rewards of struggle. One has a distinct feeling that South Africa will be next.

Though set in Kenya *Matigari* is the story of many freedom fighters in Africa. On his return from the forests, Matigari buries his sword and his AK-47 under a *mūgumo* tree—alas too soon as it turns out—in order to don "a belt of peace" (5). His principal aim to which the novel devotes most of its rather insubstantial plot is to take possession of his "house" from which he had fought to dislodge Settler Williams. This struggle for possession is obviously meant to symbolize the people's bid to claim their heritage at the end of the freedom struggle; in Matigari's own words he now wishes to "blow the horn of patriotic service and trumpet of patriotic victory" (6) but is astonished to find on his return that nothing has changed very much; if anything conditions have become worse. The Anglo-American Leather and Plastic Works company runs a factory behind a wall of metal sheeting, and the workers' quarters are fenced in by barbed wire beyond which, in a garbage yard also surrounded by barbed wire, children scuffle "with dogs, vultures, rats, all sorts of scavengers and vermin, for pieces of string, patches of cloth, odds bit of leather, show soles, rubber bands, threads, rotten tomatoes, sugarcane chaff, banana peels, bones ... anything" (11).

Among these children is one fatherless boy, Mūriuki, who soon acts as Matigari's guide and to whom Matigari acts as a replacement of the absent father. The "returnee", to use the current South African terminology for returning freedom fighters, also encounters Ngarūro wa Kīrīro, a trade union leader who will later be killed leading a workers' strike against the Anglo-American company; and finally Matigari meets and earns the deep gratitude of a prostitute, Gūthera, whom he rescues from two policemen bent on sexually harassing her under the guise of performing their police duties. This is also the beginning of Matigari's quest across the country for fellow-believers whom, he hopes, will help him establish a new social order, founded on the twin ideals of Truth and Justice, for which taking occupation of his "house" would merely constitute the final test and validation. During the course of the novel Matigari's quest brings him into contact with different personages representing various social institutions: the church, the law, the prisons, the academic and the business world, the latter in the figures of two of its principal representatives, Settler Williams' son and John Boy Junior, both continuers of a tradition of exploitation in which ancestral Williams, aided by this faithful black servant John Boy, form an initial partnership. In his brief "rites of passage" Matigari is subjected to assaults by young delinquents, to imprisonment by the state, and is finally chased into a flooded river by security forces after a vain attempt to take possession of his "house."

2.

Even a brief paraphrase shows this novel to be a thinly veiled allegory about post-independent Kenya; as such the themes that the book rehearses will be news to no one, much less to those who have followed Ngũgĩ's career as he has continued to chronicle the political and moral decline of the country's leadership since independence. After all, is Matigari not simply another Kĩhĩka from an earlier novel, A Grain of Wheat? Is Kihiki not another Dedan Kĩmaathi in the play The Trial of Dedan Kĩmaathi?

Is Gũthera the prostitute not another Wanja from Petals of Blood? Without trying in any way to detract from Ngũgĩ's achievement, it may be argued that Matigari simply gathers up all the wood shavings left over from Ngũgĩ's other political novels and the play. In this narrative very little that is strange, surprising or unexpected is allowed to disturb the pure successivity of events which mark like some invincible law the story of anti-colonial struggle and the farce of postcolonial independence in Africa. Indeed, Ngũgĩ's gradual relinquishment of realistic representation for the world of fairy tale and day-dream may provide us with yet another sign of the crisis afflicting the postcolonial novel in Africa generally in its attempts over these past three decades to plot the story of corruption and exploitation under the leadership of civilian-military dictatorships. Economic decline, violence, coup and counter-coup have produced a profound disillusionment among Africa's populations which have in turn inevitably left their marks on the novel.

As early as 1976 Ngũgĩ wa Thiong'o and Mĩcere Mũgo, co-authors of The Trial of Dedan Kĩmaathi, were already asking themselves, albeit only rhetorically, whether or not "the theme of Mau Mau struggles [was] exhausted in our literature?" (1). And if the answer in 1976 was an obvious "no", nearly two decades later it is no longer certain what the answer to the same question might be. Ngũgĩ himself seems to be aware of the near-exhaustion of the soil out of which his major fiction has grown over the years. The clues are everywhere in his latest writing; satire, self-reflexive irony and repetition are only indexes of an internal struggle with form which the simplest obligations to external politics can only exacerbate without providing a ready-made aesthetic resolution. But to put it this way is perhaps to suggest that it is not so much the soil—what Ngũgĩ and Mĩcere Mũgo call the "theme of Mau Mau struggles"—that has become exhausted but the tropical hoe with which to work up that soil which has become blunted by constant use.

However, form and content are, as we have come to accept, so inextricably linked, so dialectically interdependent, the one mirroring the other, that the exhaustion of one can seem to mean the exhaustion of the other. In any case, the dominant impression left by reading too many novels of post-independence decline and inevitable disillusionment is one of a corresponding crisis and stagnation of artistic form as if the "spiritual penury" which afflicts the national middle-class had taken revenge on the very aesthetic form which traditionally is supposed to serve as a vehicle of its own class consciousness. Not surprisingly, among the most intelligent writers a desperate search commences for new methods of telling what, in fact, has become a dreary but familiar story of chronic under development and corruption. Adding to the discomfiture of a writer of fiction is the suspicion that the story of the premature decline and decay in the neo-colonial state has already been told to maximum effect, not in a work of fiction but in a political treatise which by now deserves a poetics of its own. I mean, of course, Frantz Fanon's *The Wretched of the Earth*, which we know Ngũgĩ read thoroughly and thoroughly assimilated. Are not *Matigari* and novels like it an attempt to assemble characters who would act as human agents in a narrative already outlined elsewhere many many years ago? Fanon wrote and *Matigari* repeats essentially the same story:

> Before independence, the leader generally embodies the aspirations of the people for independence, political liberty and national dignity. But as soon as independence is declared, far from embodying in concrete form the needs of the people in what touches bread, land and the restoration of the country to the sacred hands of the people, the leader will reveal his inner purpose: to become the general president of that company of profiteers impatient for their returns which

constitutes the national bourgeoisie. (Fanon 134)

This of course could constitute an almost exact paraphrase of Ngḷgḷ's novel. An increasing tendency in Ngūgī's fiction, already evident in his earlier work, has been to forge an uneasy alliance between historical materialism and religious mysticism, sometimes disclosing itself in the emergence of a Messianic hero of extraordinary, even mysterious powers, who must lead the oppressed out of their bondage. Kīhīka, Kīmaathi and Matigari are mere versions of Jesus Christ incarnate. The obvious dilemma of such an improbable marriage between materialism and mysticism is resolvable only through a renunciation of realism in favour of fable and allegory. In order to extract imaginary victories for the exploited class in a struggle in which the odds are currently stacked, as they certainly are in contemporary Africa, against workers and peasants, the protagonists of such novels can only have local and limited successes by a recourse to miracles or supernatural aids. Not surprisingly, Matigari inhabits this "timeless" world of folk tale and allegory in which the configurations of bourgeois time lie dormant and must be opportunely reactivated in order to reinsert the narrative into the Kenya class struggle.

Folk tales are not timeless but they belong to no particular place, as the dedication to the "Reader/Listener" of *Matigari* makes obvious; at the most, their historic sense is retarded. It is nearly impossible to read off their surface any particular epoch except perhaps in the sense in which one can date historical novels, for example, by the costumes the characters wear. For example, in Amos Tutuola's fragment of "The Complete Gentleman" the "ghost" (for that is what this complete gentleman is in other versions of this tale) can both wear modern suits and still move about in a transfigured world of supernatural spirits common to this folk tale throughout traditional African societies; and this is perhaps Tutuola's genius and magic. The story "has no fixed place," says the dedication in *Matigari*. A variant of Tutuola's tale is known in many African societies, including South Africa.

Quite often the folk tale relies on miracles or supernatural aids as transformative devices of the plot. In terms of the class struggle it is possible to treat such devices as mere sleights of hand; however, before we can fault Ngūgī for using such bags of tricks to promote the impossible victories of his protagonists we ought to remember that one of the triumphs of the modern, especially the postcolonial novel has been to turn fairy tales into contemporary narratives of decolonization and, paradoxically, even versions of the modern.

In her interesting commentary on *Devil on the Cross*, Eileen Julien writes that

> *Devil on the Cross* proposes different approaches to the novel... Ngũgĩ refers to his novel as a parable because he intends it as a simple story to illustrate a lesson. More precisely, *Devil* is a fable of economic and political greed. Its thieves are not the animal characters that readers usually associate with the tradition of fable but are one-dimensional beings.... *Devil* is a fantastic narrative that continually blurs the line between real and surreal. (147)

In so far as *Matigari*, like Ngũgĩ's earlier novel *Devil on the Cross*, represents a search for a solution to the problem of, or what has turned out to be, a crisis of representation for all post-independence African novels, the work bears all the hallmarks of this new stage of development. Not accidentally *Matigari* often reads like a well-known folk tale, the outlines of which are familiar to the listeners, and like many folk tales in the oral tradition depends for its originality on the ingenuity of the re-telling. From the perspective of current literary theory *Matigari*, often wry, self-consciously knowing and allusive, approximates to the category of metafiction, for *Matigari* is in many mays a self-reflexive novel in which the characters are constantly hinting at the self-knowledge of the medium in which they are implicated.

In one jokey moment in the book the characters seem to be unhappily aware of their double existence as personages in the present work as well as being mere citations in a postcolonial discourse whose preamble was written some time ago. "Cool it," Settler Williams' son tells John Boy Junior, son of his father's infamous servant and collaborator; "Remember you are playing a comic role; the tragic role was played by our fathers" (47), an obvious allusion to Marx's paraphrase of another philosopher in *The Eighteenth Brumaire of Louis Bonaparte*. Marx wrote: "Hegel remarks somewhere that all facts and personages of great importance in world history occur, as it were, twice. He forgot to add: the first time as tragedy, the second as farce." For the first time Ngũgĩ seems to be aware that it is hardly possible anymore to write another post-independence novel of disillusionment without descending into pure farce. The shock is simply no longer there; only linguistic violence can now perform that task, and Ngũgĩ is not, in my opinion, a writer temperamentally equipped to do verbal violence of the kind the late Dambudzo Marechera (*House of Hunger*) or Yambo Ouolouguem (*Le Devoir de*

Violence) thought it eminently their duty to produce. Nevertheless, few who know Ngũgĩ personally and are familiar with his earlier work—politically dutiful, grimly stoical and minding his historical materialist manners to a fault—can have expected to find him extracting so much unalloyed pleasure from the deployment of irony and satire.

Nearly every other page of *Matigari* displays examples of Ngũgĩ's mischievous satirical turn of phrase, always at the expense of the already degraded local bourgeoisie. A few of these examples will suffice to indicate the general tone of the novel. At one stage, worried by rumors which link Matigari's return with the long-awaited second coming of Jesus Christ, the state radio warns listeners: "There is no way that Jesus could return without paying a courtesy call on His Excellency Ole Excellence. Members of the public are urged to report anyone claiming to be Jesus or Gabriel to the nearest police station" (84). After Matigari has been temporarily arrested—he soon escapes—information reaches government ears that many woman are now "singing that they will give birth to more Matigari ma Njirũũngi"; a member of the ruling KKK government party warns: "Pregnancies are the result of evil and wild desires. I shall ask the government to ban dreams and desires of that kind for a period of about two years. Fucking among the poor should be stopped by presidential decree" (121).

As for political ideas which are already inflaming the population, the ruling party also has a ready antidote. The chairman of a local branch tells a meeting: "This Karl Marx is driving our students, lecturers and workers crazy. He should have his work permit withdrawn. I say that Karl Marx, Lenin and Mao should have no work permits in this country" (119). And throughout the novel the Mercedes-Benz car, emblem of success everywhere in Africa, bears the same cruel fate in Ngũgĩ's novel as the ruling elite, which is to be the butt of unending humour and satire. Walking past an hotel car park Mũriuki, the boy turned Matigari's guide, casually remarks: "This car park sometimes fills up with Mercedes-Benzes; you would think that this is where they are manufactured" (14). Another time Matigari is led through a vast plantation, the glaring symbol of greed of the new land-owning class, seemingly without any immediate prospect of reaching one end of it. This provokes someone to observe that the plantation is so big "the owner can cover it from end to end only on horseback"; to which the irrepressible Mũriuki responds by exclaiming: "Or maybe on a winged car ... Oh, how I would love to fly above this tea estate on a winged Mercedes-Benz or, better still, on a winged horse, with the leaves of these bushes softly brushing the dust off my aching feet" (42). There are many other instances when Ngũgĩ's satire just manages to stay this side of cartoon humour and comic-strip whimsy.

3.

However, there are other indicators of Ngũgĩ's dissatisfaction with the novel as it has been used so far as a vehicle of critical consciousness in post-independence Africa. In Ngũgĩ's case, the nature and the extent of that crisis are already reflected in his switch of linguistic medium from English to Gĩĩgĩkũyũ, but such a switch in mid-career is not as simple as some of the advocates for writing in African languages would make it seem and even though Ngũgĩ himself tends to gloss over the difficulties. For example, he writes in his prison diary:

> I had deliberately given myself a difficult task. I had resolved to use a language which did not have a modern novel, a challenge to myself, and a way of affirming my faith in the possibilities of the languages of all the different Kenyan nationalities, languages whose development as vehicles for the Kenyan people's anti-imperialist struggles had been actively suppressed by the British colonial regime (1895 - 1963) and by the neo-colonial regime of Kenyatta and his comprador Kanu cohorts. (8)

Nevertheless, far from what the above passage seems to imply, African languages are not innocent vehicles of national and working-class consciousness. Like the oral traditions African languages, through their historic links with traditional structures, have been used to underpin clan authority, patriarchy and gender dominance. For example, younger members of certain castes and kinship groups are prevented by religious sanction or taboo from employing various categories of speech in the presence of males, relatives, or members of religious cults. Indeed, Achebe makes this an explosive issue and a turning point in the development of his novel, *Things Fall Apart*, when an overzealous Christian convert tears the mask off one of the egwugwu: "The other egwugwu immediately surrounded their desecrated companion, to shield him from the *profane gaze of women and children*" (13, italics mine). African languages have hardly been immune to such social discriminations. If it is true that European languages are bearers of imperial codes of social and political dominance, African languages, too, constitute a veritable battleground of local ideologies which have nothing to do with European colonization.

Ngũgĩ's African past in this novel is of course problematic. A character in *Matigari* asks rhetorically: "In the past, before the whites brought imperialism here, did we ever have police and soldiers?" One is inclined to say "yes." Wherever there are kingdoms and empires there are soldiers and police. And she asks: "Were there any prisons?" Again, one is inclined to answer "yes": perhaps not as organized institutions such as we find today, but confinement nevertheless. After all, confinement is encoded in African mythology such as in the Yoruba's *The Imprisonment of Obatala.* "Was there as much crime as there is today?" Again the woman quickly answers: "No! We used to rule ourselves, didn't we?" Ngũgĩ is hardly someone likely to share in the naivety of his characters or in such a gross lack of historic sense, for this allusion to an Edenic Africa of "pure childhood" before the Fall is hard to sustain. Ingrid Bjorkman writes in her study of Ngũgĩ's work, *Mother, Sing For Me:* "Ngũgĩ was critical of those who indulged in nostalgic enthusiasm for things truly African. The main concern of the writer was social reality and the future" (1).

Finally, a more intriguing question about this orphaned text concerns its very linguistic medium. Whose text is it, in fact? How faithful is the English translation to the original Gĩkũyũ text? How much of it is Ngũgĩ's and how much Wangũi wa Goro's, the translator? What words does she use for such concepts as "imperialism"? The question is even more intriguing when one takes into account the magnificent verbal satire of the English translation. One wishes that Gĩkũyũ-speaking scholars would add to the growing Ngũgĩ scholarship by doing comparative studies of his original Gĩkũyũ texts and their translations.

Works Cited

Achebe, Chinua. *Things Fall Apart.* London: Heinemann, 1958.

Bjorkman, Ingrid. *Mother Sing For Me: People's Theatre in Kenya.* London: Zed Press, 1989.

Fanon, Frantz. *The Wretched of the Earth.* New York: Grove Press, 1966.

Julien, Eileen. *African Novels and the Question of Oralij.* Bloomington and Indianapolis: Indiana University Press, 1992.

Ngũgĩ wa Thiong'o. *Detained: A Writer's Prison Diary.* London: Heineman, 1981.

—. *Matigari.* London: Heinemann, 1987.

Moving the Center: An Interview by Charles Cantalupo

T
HE FOLLOWING INTERVIEW in English took place on the afternoon of January 23, 1993, in the living room of Ngũgĩ's home near Newark, New Jersey. Larry Sykes and I arrived there slightly early, and Ngũgĩ was not yet back from NYU, where he taught and where he enrolled himself in an intensive language course in French. While we waited for him to return, Ngũgĩ's wife, welcomed us with friend- of the new crop of refilled often, and glasses which I did not think of the world, although here. We were joined dren: Lashambi, the ter from Nelson her homemade greet- from prison; Ndũũcũ, return to Oberlin Col- mester; Wanjikũ, a stu-

...there are more voices coming from Kenya, from Africa, the Third World. The literature from Africa, from Asia, from South America, is increasingly becoming a part, an integral part, of the teaching of literature in different places.

Njeeri wa Ndũng'ũ, ly conversation, a bowl clementines, which she of a tropical fruit juice was available in this part I was born and raised by four of Ngũgĩ's chil- proud recipient of a let- Mandela, responding to ing card on his release who was just about to lege for the Spring se- dent at NYU, who was helping her mother in the kitchen; and Njooki, a student at Chad School, who was also helping her mother. When Ngũgĩ arrived, he invited Larry and me into the living room, where we spoke until we could no longer resist the aroma of roast goat, which Njeeri had prepared for us for dinner.

Cantalupo   Congratulations on the publication of *Moving the Centre*. Was it a coincidence that its publication date coincided with the holiday celebration of Martin Luther King's birthday?

Ngũgĩ   It was pure coincidence. It was supposed to come out in November, 1992, but I kept on doing corrections, and this delayed its appearance. But it was a good coincidence. Particularly just before his death, Martin Luther King was talking about moving the democratic center from its prison in the establishment to creative locations among the people.

Cantalupo Does *Moving the Centre* develop and extend any of the ideas of your last book of essays, *Decolonizing the Mind*? Since its publication in 1986, it has achieved the status of a popular, required text for non-Euro-American and multicultural literary study. Does *Moving the Centre* pick up where *Decolonizing the Mind* left off?

Ngũgĩ Some of the essays in *Moving the Centre* were written after *Decolonizing the Mind*, so obviously they do extend some of the ideas already contained in *Decolonizing the Mind*. Some of the items were papers given at confer-  ences, and often these conferences were responding to some of the issues in *Decolonizing the Mind*. *Decolonizing the Mind* as a text has become so talked about, that wherever I go, in conferences and in countries, in Africa and outside Africa, I'm obliged to answer questions about *Decolonizing the Mind*. These questions are reflected in some of the papers in *Moving the Centre*.

At the same time, *Moving the Centre* is a book that developed almost accidentally. The initial suggestion had come from my publishers, who said that since I would no longer be writing in the English language, and that I would be using Gĩkũyũ as my primary language in writing, they wanted to put together all of the articles and papers I had already given and which were not yet published. It started as a project to bring together anything which I had and which had not yet been published. Yet in the process of putting the various items together, we came to realize that a certain pattern was forming, and that certain essays and papers, whether given in 1982 or in 1991, could be grouped around certain themes. In other words, we found that actually running through all the papers and items were certain motifs which held the essays together ...

Cantalupo ... and this explains the book's being organized into four sections: "Freeing Culture from Eurocentrism," "Freeing Culture from Colonial Legacies," "Freeing Culture from Racism" and "Matigari, Dreams and Nightmares."

Moving the Centre contains an emotional essay, "Many Years Walk to Freedom: Welcome Home Mandela!" on his historic release from a South African prison, after he had served twenty-seven years of a lifetime sentence. In the book's preface, however, you note that, although the essay appeared first in English in the New York based African-American news magazine, Emerge, "the Gīkūyū original of the Mandela piece is still in ... [your] drawer ... among a good many others" (xiv). You also say that "In their different destinies, the two  pieces illustrate the difficulties in the way of those writing theoreti-cal, philosophical, political and jour-nalistic prose in an African lan-guage, moreover in conditions of exile."

Ngũgĩ What happened was this. In March—I was then at Yale—there was an announcement that Mandela was to be released. Planning a special issue on this his-toric event, Emerge asked me to write an article for it. I said to myself, I can't write about Mandela's release in English. I have to do it in Gīkūyū language, I have to do it in an African language. What does his release mean to me as an African? As a Kenyan? As a human being for whom Mandela and the South African struggle has meant so much? So, I wrote the entire piece in Gīkūyū language. And it became very interesting. The flow in the article arises precisely from that. There's a sense of engagement in Gīkūyū language.

In the preface, I was just trying to point out some of the difficulties that people writing in African languages currently have or can face. For instance, there are very few journals in African languages, there are very few forums, that wholly utilize African languages. Write an article in Gĩkũyũ language, as I do, and often it does not have an outlet, unless it is published either in translation, as in the case of the article on Mandela in *Emerge*, or with an English translation published side by side with the original Gĩkũyũ text, as happened in the case of the article on language in *Moving the Centre*, "Imperialism of Language: English a Language for the World?". It was also originally given for the BBC, but later published in both languages by the *Yale Journal of Criticism*.

In fact, the Mandela article, in Gĩkũyũ language, has not yet been published.

Cantalupo   To be asked to write suddenly on Mandela was a kind of supreme moment of theory in practice in terms of your decision to write in Gĩkũyũ, a theme which is ...

Ngũgĩ   ... very close to home, so to speak, yes.

Cantalupo   In your new book's title essay, "Moving the Centre: Toward a Pluralism of Cultures," you evoke your days as a student at Makerere University College in Uganda. Writing "I can still recall the excitement of reading the world from a centre other than Europe" (4), you remember in particular "one of the characters in George Lamming's novel, *In the Castle of My Skin*, [who] talks of his suddenly discovering his people, and therefore his world, after hearing Paul Robeson sing."Let my People Go." You go on to say, "He was speaking of me and my encounter with the voices coming out of centres outside Europe."

            Do you still experience this "excitement of reading the world from a centre other than Europe," when you read contemporary literature?

Ngũgĩ   Of course, not the same way. Obviously there are more voices coming from Kenya, from Africa, the Third World. The literature from Africa, from Asia, from South America, is increasingly becoming a part, an integral part, of the teaching of literature in different places. For me that "excitement" really came at a particular moment in history: at a particular moment in my growing up, discovering this new literature. It's a moment which is obviously difficult to repeat, for me. But it will be a moment that many other people from Africa, Asia, and South America may experience, especially if they have not been exposed to literature from a world which has molded them.

Cantalupo   Let's discuss America. In *Moving the Centre*, you cite DuBois' observation that racism is "*the* problem of the twentieth century" (150). Have the riots in Los Angeles in 1992, and/or Bill Clinton's election as President of the United States altered any of your views on racism?

Ngũgĩ   I believe that what I say about racism as an ideology in the third section of *Moving the Centre* is still pertinent today. Racism has been so much a part of the Western world, so much a part, an integral part, of the twentieth century, that it's something which has to be continually fought against consciously and deliberately. Obviously, there is a difference in a sense. Racism is recognized more and more as a social evil that has to be addressed, and that's very important. But, as I said, it's been so much part of structures of domination and subjugation that it cannot be really eliminated until those structures of economic, political, and cultural domination have been altered sufficiently to be the real base for group and social equality.

Cantalupo   American universities and academics have been attacked for advocating what has become known pejoratively as "pc" and "political correctness." Yet their efforts, at least in theory, and occasional excesses of puritan zeal notwithstanding, are primarily to become more sensitive to and, more importantly, inclusive of the many different kinds of people who attend universities today. Nevertheless, they are attacked precisely for being engaged in "moving the centre," to use the phrase with which you title your new book of essays, within our nation and between nations to "the real creative center among ... people" of equal status, regardless of any conditions of gender, economics, race, religion, sexuality, and physical ability. Repeatedly and eloquently in *Moving the Centre* you advocate "opening out the mainstream to take in other streams" (8), "moving towards a pluralism of cultures, literatures and languages" (10), "understanding all the voices coming from what is essentially a plurality of centres all over the world" (11). Your political agenda is international, yet it is distinctly applicable to American universities and the nation itself, too.

Ngũgĩ   Yes, obviously it's a healthy trend. A trend that redresses imbalances—obviously, it's important and it should be encouraged. But it has to go beyond just the universities. It has to be at the very structure of economic and political power, where the problem is. In eliminating racism, as well as sexism, we're talking about empowerment: a people's lack of empowerment. The basic question is a question of economic, political, and cultural empowerment of peoples: of creating conditions that allow for that kind of empowerment. With that corrected, there's a question of people's attitudes, individual as well as group, which will ultimately change. But the fact that a trend consciously addresses the problem is a very, very positive thing. It's the real correct thing to do.

Cantalupo   In *Moving the Centre*, I find many of your political tenets more gently expressed than in *Decolonizing the Mind*. For example, in the introduction to the latter you identify the United States as the leader of international imperialism, simply presenting "the struggling peoples of the earth and all those calling for peace, democracy and socialism with the ultimatum: accept theft or death" (3). Strong words. Do they fully and accurately describe the situation in the 1990's? How can the situation change for the better. How would you advise a new administration in Washington to begin constructive change of US policy in Africa?

Ngũgĩ   To come back to an earlier comment: both in *Decolonizing the Mind* and *Moving the Centre*, one is writing about moving the centre in essentially two ways. In the twentieth century, what you see between nations is definitely structured on inequality. There's no doubt in my mind that if you look at the world as it is today, the West, as a whole, still bleeds the Third World, the countries of Africa, Asia, and South America. This is clear. Even if you take it at the level of the burden of debt, the financial burden. Many economists now say that the Third World countries are net exporters of the capital that they so badly need—through debt servicing, through their repayment of debt. Third World countries need capital but, in fact, they end up exporting capital to the West. Because they borrow money from the IMF or World Bank, or from the West generally, many of these countries are now completely burdened by the interest they have to pay on the loans. So, they end up giving more to the West: the very capital the Third World countries actually need for their own development. There is still a structural imbalance between the West and the rest of us, so to speak. This imbalance is basically economic, but it is also political, and it has cultural implications. So, moving the centre, in an international situation, is really a movement toward correcting this structural imbalance.

Within nations themselves, within Africa, or in America, or in the West, there is also social structural imbalance between the few in all these countries who control the resources and the majority of the people in each of these areas. I talk about moving the centre *within* nations, yes, and *between* nations: this thesis runs throughout *Decolonizing the Mind*. It's also there in *Moving the Centre*. In the past, whenever countries in Africa have tried to opt for a different path of social development and to break with the colonizing or neo-colonizing structures of relationships, as in the era of the Cold War, there was hostility from the West. So, we see some of the worst dictatorships being supported by the West. I'm talking about countries like, say, Zaire, with Mobutu, Kenya with Moi, Malawi with Banda, Central African Republic, in the days of Bokassa, say, and countries like Cameroon, with Biya, or Barre in Somalia. This support of dictatorships, which repress their people internally, prevents the only possibility these countries have of getting out of this vicious encirclement. The ability to get out relies entirely on the energies of the people. But the energies of the people cannot be relied upon if they are repressed. So, my own feeling is that it's really in the interest of everybody in the world to encourage and support democratic trends in Africa, even when those democratic trends result in social and economic programs that do not necessarily meet the approval down to the details and fit the capital market economies of the West. I think if political change emerges democratically in these countries, this should be allowed to develop. Obviously the state in many African countries has to play a more active role in economic and social development, whether people like it or not. There's really no other way. The question is, what kind of state, controlled by whom? Are they just states under dictatorships, or are they democratic states that will respond to the people?

Cantalupo   Without government repression and its insistence on doing things only in its own way, the energy of a people on their own will emerge—no matter what form it takes.

Ngũgĩ   Yes, exactly. You need to release the energies of the people. You must create what one African thinker, Babu, has called enthusiasm for production! But with the dictatorships in Africa, often supported by the West, there has developed a kind of cynicism: a collective disbelief, and this is very dangerous for development. We need new people based democratic movements that will generate incentive for change and renewal.

Cantalupo   Have you just described what has happened in Somalia? Has such cynicism and collective disbelief destroyed Somalia from within? And allowed the traditional colonial powers, in lieu of any established local government, to return for the allegedly humanitarian reason of solely assuring the distribution of food?

Ngũgĩ   Look at postcolonial Africa, whether Somalia or Kenya or Zaire—

concrete examples. Moi, of Kenya, during the colonial days, was working with British colonial settlers to prevent independence for Kenya. In other words, at the height of the Mau Mau armed struggle against the British in Kenya, he was a British appointee in the colonial legislature. Yet now, in post-independent Kenya, he is the one who is wielding power, and until recently with the full support of the West, the British in particular. Mobutu of Zaire, during the colonial days, was part of the Belgian colonial army, suppressing the Zairian people. Yet post-independence, he becomes a leader. Take Uganda. Before Museveni, there was Idi Amin. Idi Amin used to be, again, part of the colonial army, fighting against African nationalism. Yet in fact when he came to power, through a military *coup d'etat*, he was immediately received

by the then French president Pompidou. He was received by the queen of England. He was given a state, red-carpet welcome in the West. Bokassa of Central Africa— he's no longer there now—used to be a friend of the French presi-dent. Barre, of Somalia, was part of the Italian co-lonial army. All of these leaders had power sup-ported by the West. They were a part of the Cold War era because they said, 'okay, we are anti-communist,' or 'we are anti-Marxist,' and, of course, it was supported. Look at these leaders very, very carefully: they never see their inspiration as coming from the people, because they know very well that their being in power is not dependent on Somalian people, on Kenyan people, on Zairian people. They don't owe a single loyalty to those people, because such leaders don't feel—and essentially it's true—their power is derived from the people. So, they don't fear that they will lose their power to rule, as long as they have the monopoly of the gun and of support of Western governments. They don't feel accountable to the people. If democracy is not allowed to flourish freely in Africa, we shall continue to have a proliferation of the same problems.

Cantalupo   Let's shift from government and democracy to writers. In "The
             Writer in the Neo-Colonial State," you state a writer's alternatives:
             "silence or self-censorship ... . Or he can become a state function-
             ary ... . Or he may risk jail or exile, in which case he is driven from
             the very sources of inspiration. Write and risk damnation, avoid
             damnation and cease to be a writer. That is the lot of the writer
             in a neo-colonial state" (71). Do you yourself feel these restraints?
             Do you know writers who feel these restraints? In some ways, you
             have overcome them, or you've been forced to overcome them. Is
             democracy going to affect that? If democracy is allowed to flourish,
             surely the role of the writer will get better, too.

Ngũgĩ   Obviously I hope for more democratic space to give writers more
             room to articulate their visions, to be themselves as writers. In
             Africa, particularly the Africa of the Cold War, the political
             climate was very hostile to writers. Indeed, it resulted in horrible
             actions: writers have been killed in Africa, writers have been
             forced into exile, and other writers who remain at home have been
             forced to side either with the government, as has happened to
             some writers in Kenya, or else to practice self-censorship. Others,
             of course, continue writing and articulating their visions, but they
             risk all of those other things: death, exile, or jail.

Cantalupo   What about women writers in particular? They too must challenge
             and break through social conventions, yet there is the imposition
             of sexual stereotypes and the politics of gender. For a man to
             challenge social conventions and break free of hopeless alterna-
             tives is sometimes easier than for a woman.

Ngũgĩ   Yes, it's true. But remember, there are prominent African women
             writers, and politically they face the same problems: speak out and
             face jail, exile, death, censorship and all that. There is also, of
             course, the habit, the problem of gender discrimination, or of
             structural discrimination, and women writers have to articulate
             all of these burdens of gender, race, and class.

Cantalupo   What happens if the democracy movement in African nations is suppressed and suppressed—to a point of extinction? Is this possible? You write in the introduction to Moving the Centre,

> Cultures under total domination from others can be crippled, deformed, or else die ... . Hence the insistence in these essays on the suffocating and ultimately destructive character of both colonial and neo-colonial structures. A new world order that is no more than global dominance and neo-colonial relations policed by a handful of Western nations, whether through the United Nations Security Council or not, is a disaster for the peoples of the world and their cultures. (xvi)

This sounds elegiac, although this feeling is mitigated at the end of your book. Do you think you have seen a culture deformed, dying and finally left for dead?

Ngũgĩ   I was giving two alternatives. Cultures that are completely dominated can die. Equally well, countries which are in complete isolation from others can fade. In fact, cultures in the past have developed through a healthy balance of give and take. For instance, African cultures during the colonial era suffered structural damage because of colonial domination. In the era of slavery, there was even greater damage, because this meant the removal of human beings who are the basis of the development of culture. There was structural damage to a people's capacity to evolve their own languages and their culture. There is a necessity of cultural give and take on the basis of economic and political equality between groups. Otherwise, as in the case of colonial or neo-colonial imbalances, the cultures of those who are the victims of imbalance are likely to be deformed. In a situation of economic and political equality between groups, cultures can develop on the basis of give and take. Countries will borrow from each other naturally those elements that are healthy to each country.

Cantalupo You make a similar point about African languages and their borrowings. In *Moving the Centre*, you confidently assert,

> African languages will borrow from one another; they will borrow from their classical heritages; they will borrow from the world—from the Caribbean, from Afroamerica, from Latin America, from the Asian—and from the European worlds. In this, the new writing in African languages will do the opposite of the Europhone practice: instead of being appropriated by the world, it will appropriate the world and one hopes on terms of equal exchange, at the very least, borrow on its own terms and needs. (23)

Your theory sounds as if it has an enormous, healthy appetite. In the same passage, you also cite Bakhtin's observation that "Latin literary language in all its generic diversity was created in the light of Greek literary language" (22), and you go on to ask "the rhetorical question: ... is it possible to conceive of the development of Greek literature and culture without Egyptian and other Mediterranean cultures?" In your view, African languages play as rich a role in the future as they have in the ancient past.

Ngũgĩ Look at the United Nations, in terms of imbalance. In my mind, it is an organization which should be strengthened. It should be the hope of the world. New and rising nations can be politically and economically strengthened by the empowerment of a United Nations. But it has to be democratized itself! The Security Council, the executive body of the United Nations, is dominated by basically Western, white, imperial nations. In other words, they can veto anything, even against the will of a majority from Africa, Asia. Look at the languages of the United Nations organization. They're nearly all Western, European languages. We want a strong United Nations organization, but we want it also to reflect genuinely the multiplicity of world cultures and peoples, and not for this organization to become an instrument of U.S. foreign policy, or an instrument of the foreign policy of Western powers.

Cantalupo   I was talking with the poet Michael Harper, and he recalled that James Joyce once said that a writer's language is his homeland. Do you feel that way? Do you feel that way about English and/or Gĩkũyũ, or just Gĩkũyũ?

Ngũgĩ   That language is one's homeland? Well ...

Cantalupo   Is that enough emotionally, or just intellectually?

Ngũgĩ   To have a language is to have a world, in more sense than one at the personal level—obviously a writer carries language in him, and he has his connection with whatever is the language of his choice. When he's writing a novel or a poem, he'll have dialogue with the voices or the characters in the language of his choice. But languages simply are not a matter of personal acquisition. They are also a matter of social communities. When languages of a group are suppressed—through whatever means, economic, military, or whatever—the language of the individual is affected. If I had a language as a writer, but that language had no community of speakers anywhere in the world, then I do not think that that language would really be my world. In other words, I am able to possess language as my world precisely because it is the language of the community.

Cantalupo   Maybe Joyce worked towards a language of no one's world. Maybe it was a solace yet a lonely world in the end, a world like *Finnegan's Wake*, that few could understand?

Ngũgĩ   James Joyce comes from Ireland. Ireland has the longest colonial history: *vis a vis* England, *vis a vis* the West, and I think he may have been avoiding the implications of that: not facing up to that reality, that Irish reality.

    If there was no community of English speakers anywhere in the world, then that language for Joyce would not have been meaningful and enough. Language becomes meaningful at a personal level precisely because that language is part of a wider community.

Cantalupo	Do you ever feel alone or frustrated in your own strong advocacy for the cultural imperative of writing in Gĩkũyũ and African languages in general?
Ngũgĩ	No, I don't worry. Throughout history languages have had to struggle, to fight. There is now a need for more literature in African languages, and eventually they will emerge out of their marginalization. In Africa, and in the West, there are now increasingly more and more debates about this very issue of languages. It really is important. I don't feel that I am very lonely, and of course, I'm not the only person who's advocating or who has ever articulated this. I'm only one of a whole series of people who have been saying, 'Look. This is important. It is crucial that people's languages are recognized. It is important that there is literature and philosophy, and so on, in these languages.' The problem is that there are often not enough financial resources given for the development of those languages.
Cantalupo	You have some remarkable stories, recalled in both *Decolonizing the Mind* and *Moving the Centre*,

> of instances of children being punished if they were caught speaking their African languages. We were often caned or made to carry plaques inscribed with the words 'I am stupid' or 'I am an ass.' In some cases, our mouths were stuffed with pieces of paper picked from the wastepaper basket, which were then passed from mouth to mouth to that of the latest offender. Humiliation in relation to our languages was the key. (33)

In another autobiographical passage from *Moving the Centre*, you also recall your youthful, "whole hearted affection" for Robert Louis Stevenson's *Treasure Island*, Charles Dickens' *Oliver Twist* and the popular series of adventure stories based on a fictional twentieth-century hero of the British empire, James Bigglesworth, nicknamed "Biggles."

Was the English language a kind of "first love" who betrayed you?

Ngũgĩ   There's nothing wrong with the English language. There's nothing wrong with French. There's nothing wrong with any language in the world. It's very important that what has been produced in these languages—in Chinese, in Japanese, in Finnish, in Swedish, in whatever—is a part of human heritage. They're all very important. Equally well, what's produced in African languages—in Swahili, in Gĩkũyũ, in Yoruba—is also a part of human heritage. Suppressing the languages of three fourths of humankind, we are suppressing three fourths of human heritage. For persons growing up in Africa, fully in the world of their languages, in the literature of their languages, there's nothing wrong with them acquiring other languages as well, and enjoying fully whatever has been produced in those other languages. There's even nothing wrong in African languages appropriating whatever is best that has been produced in and through other people's languages. There would be nothing wrong with ancient languages appropriating the best that has been developed in African languages in a healthy give and take. When economic structural imbalance is corrected, these borrowings from each other would be a natural, organic, healthy development without competition, if you like. Acceptance or rejection would be a part of a healthy dialogue ...

Cantalupo   ... which is a point you make repeatedly in *Moving the Centre*.

I'd like to turn from the issue of what language to choose to a specific word. "Struggle" is a word that recurs often in your essays. In the preface to *Moving the Centre*, you cite Hegel's principle, "Without struggle there is no progression" (xiv), and you go on to state that "Culture develops within the process of a people wrestling with their natural and social environment. They struggle with nature. They struggle with one another ... . What is ... often officially paraded as authentic African culture today is virtually a repeat of the colonial tradition: tourist art, dances, acrobatic

221

contortions emptied of the content of struggle" (27). When did you discover that "struggle," "the content of struggle," is a major theme in your writing? In your youth? At Makerere?

Ngũgĩ It was gradual. "Struggle" is a part of nature and part of our history and cultures. As a central concept in my aesthetic or cultural vision, "struggle" has been developing, I think, starting from my essays on writers and politics. One can see this theme become more and more dominant in my cultural theory and aesthetic theory. "Struggle" is central to nature, to human art and to my history.

Cantalupo In *Moving the Centre*, you say that *Devil on the Cross* was "an attempt to reconnect myself to the community from which I had been brutally cut by the neo-colonial regime in Kenya" (106). You observe the same about yourself, though more generally, in another passage: "Writing  has always been my way of reconnecting myself to the landscape of my birth and upbringing" (156). Described in this way, writing sounds like a kind of religious act, if we consider that the word "religion" is derived from the Latin "*re*," meaning "back" or "again," and "*ligare*", meaning "to bind" or "connect." For writing to be an act of reconnecting—to a kind of happiness, solace, truth—yet also to be primarily about struggle seems paradoxical.

Ngũgĩ There is a connection between the organic development of a language and the organic development of a culture. Each form of development is not one-sided and both are developed through struggle. As biological creatures who are human beings, we live in two conditions. We develop under conditions of internal development within our own biological structures. But we also live in conditions of an external environment, say, the air we breathe, and so on. Our external life is an integral part of ourselves. None of us can live without breathing in air, for instance. Yet at the same time, air is out there, external to us. It's give and take or die. By emphasizing the ideal of organic development, I mean that whatever comes from outside, say, the air we breathe, must not deform internal development. Taking in air supports our internal organs, yet if there is too much, like a blast of air, it can hurt one as much as a lack of air. This is a kind of healthy struggle and a system which must not be deformed by either external circumstances or by such internal imbalance so as to completely deform the possibilities of development.

Cantalupo   This almost sounds mystical.

Ngũgĩ   Not quite. If you examine nature, that's how people develop; that's how even trees develop. When there are floods, for instance, or hurricanes, there is a kind of overdose from the external environment, so that trees break, and so on. But the same air, under normal circumstances—the air that trees and human beings breathe—helps their own development.

Cantalupo   Let's discuss Moving the Centre's last essay, "Matigari, and the Dreams of One East Africa". It derives from a trip you made to Tanzania in 1987. Could your return to Kenya be on the horizon?

Ngũgĩ   Not as long as Moi is in power. Anything can change, obviously, although it's been very disappointing that the Moi dictatorship continues in Kenya. There have been, of course, some healthy advances, and we hope that this will continue to develop. But I still would find it very difficult at present to go back under the Moi regime because what is really happening is that, although there have been some advances, some very important advances—I don't want to deny that—I do not think that the cultural, political climate has really changed. As long as Moi and his regime are there, the same distortions that created a community of Kenyan exiles will continue.

Cantalupo   Another "structure of domination and subjugation," to use your words from before.

Ngũgĩ   This is a clear-cut dictatorship, and it continues. The Moi regime is one of the problems, and as long as Moi is there, we shall continue to have those problems. What we want in Kenya, in Africa, is not simply democratization in terms of having political parties. We're talking about a democratic culture. We're talking about the right to organize: not just political organizations, but cultural organizations, social organizations. We're talking about the right of people to move freely within their own countries. We're talking about whether they be workers, or peasants, their being able to organize freely. This is what some of us mean by a democratic culture in the country, which is not like life in a country like Kenya where, for instance, even now people cannot meet without a legal license. The right to move freely, the right to organize freely, the right to assemble freely, are the basis of creativity. The moment that that is affected, obviously, it also affects individual creativity.

Cantalupo   In the preface to Moving the Centre, irrespective of any particular economic or political power, you evoke as the greatest power "the real creative centre among the working people in conditions of gender, racial and religious equality ..."(xvii)

Ngũgĩ   ... of the people, wherever they are. And that we can actually do, to get real, genuine national and international creativity.

Cantalupo   If that was the case, would East Africa—East Africa in its entirety—become one country?

Ngũgĩ   My own hope, quite frankly, is that. When I travel, say, from Kenya to Tanzania, or Uganda, or Somalia, or Sudan, I see their problems as so similar that I feel that these countries would be better off uniting. I don't have any mystical notions about nations. Nations definitely do grow, do change. There's nothing that says that nations cannot change and that they cannot combine. So my belief, my hope, is that African nations will come together, and that people will come together under one form of umbrella unity.

Cantalupo   "Matigari, and the Dreams of One East Africa" offers an embodiment in East Africa itself—its "kalaidoscope of colours, cultures, and contours of history" (161)—of the book's recurring theme: the "plurality of centres" (10) and the "pluralism of cultures, literatures and languages."

Ngũgĩ   A united East Africa would of course have its own individual characteristics: again, all those particularities are very, very important. But there really is no reason why Tanzania, Kenya, Uganda, Somalia, Ethiopia, Sudan cannot be one political region.

Cantalupo   Does this last essay signal a new stage of development in your work? When you say that there's no reason why these countries can't be one, and, in the same essay, that an "awareness of the land as the central actor in our lives distinguishes East African literature" (163), you sound less ideological than you sometimes do in your more recent work.

Ngũgĩ   You mean the last essay wasn't as polemical?

Cantalupo   It was very beautiful, emotionally and visually.

Ngũgĩ   More reflective.

Cantalupo   The political theory is perfectly embodied in vignettes of eating, fishing at night, or dress, and this is a style which is different from, though not necessarily unconnected to, most of the writing in *Decolonizing the Mind*.

Ngũgĩ	I occasionally use that style. Come to think of it, it's also partly there in *Decolonizing the Mind*. *Decolonizing the Mind* has a lot of personal recollection: childhood days, capturing this type of moment, but it is put in a wider, polemical, intellectual context. My essay on East Africa is a development of that. *Detained* uses it an awful lot—this personal life.
Cantalupo	Yes, but with not simply as much natural beauty, an "awareness of the land," as you say, and its domestic scenes.
Ngũgĩ	It's in my novels a lot. Certainly in *A Grain of Wheat*, the landscape is beautiful; I am very conscious of the landscape. Some of the more interesting pieces in *Petals of Blood*, especially at the end, are actually pure description: of changing seasons, the season of harvest, the season of planting, the season of things growing. There's quite a lot of that. In my last two novels, *Devil on the Cross* and *Matigari*, the actual landscape is not so dominant. But even that's not true in *Matigari*: when Matigari is moving across the land, the hills and valleys, and when he dies—or rather, when he meets his fate, whatever it is—in the river, and when he's being hunted. In visual terms, you can see him as part of the landscape. Many times you don't see him as a figure but as almost part of the landscape.
Cantalupo	Do you have any new books that you're working on, any new novels?
Ngũgĩ	Not at the present, you know, but there's always something, obviously.
Cantalupo	Would you ever think of putting on some of your plays again, in connection with the Performative Studies position you now have at NYU? Including students, the great wealth of musicians in New York, its large and diverse artistic community?
Ngũgĩ	I've only been at NYU since June of last year. I'll have to see how things work out. I'll see how I fit in New York, before I know

exactly what to do.

Cantalupo   It was just an idea. I think it would be great.

Ngũgĩ by Telephone

W E WERE READING Ngũgĩ's play, *I Will Marry When I Want*, in English class. My teacher, Mr. Gern, proposed a number of questions to help us explore the play and its author's intentions. I thought what better way to know what Ngũgĩ was thinking than to ask him directly. I would telephone him.

It took me a week to find his telephone number. First I called Kenya and spoke to an operator who said he had moved to England. Then I called England. The operator there looked for him all over England, in all the different cities, but couldn't find him. Then I called a friend from Kenya. She told me that he was now in America. I got hold of his son's number and he gave me Ngũgĩ's number. Finally I tracked him down.

> *He seemed so willing and happy to talk with me. I remembered that he had written a book about why he stopped writing in English. What was it called?*

"Hello. This is Tami Alpert and I am a student at Stuyvesant High School in New York City. Your play, *I Will Marry When I Want*, is very interesting and I was wondering if you could just answer a few questions about it for me."

"O.K. Yes. You know the play? You do many books by African writers?"

"We are studying Africa right now. We read your book and Achebe's *Things Fall Apart*."

"What do you want to ask?"

I looked at my sheet of questions, which Mr. Gern had helped me with.

"I was wondering what the significance of the title is—'I Will Marry When I Want'—and if it has a different meaning in Gĩkũyũ."

Ngũgĩ replied, "As you can see from the play, it is taken from the song sung by the drunk character at the beginning and also by Kĩgũũnda at the end when he loses his land and he is out of work like the other one. Obviously it is meant to remind people of the similarities in the situations of the two characters. When you hear the song at the beginning and then at the end sung by somebody else, you think about the two situations. But it is also an idea of rebellion. In many countries people are expected to marry. This idea that I will not necessarily do as I'm expected to do—there is an element of rebellion there. The song itself was very popular in Kenya some time ago among young people when they were slightly rebellious against tradition and authority. But not in a criminal way. Just in sentiment. So the title was taken also as a reference to that very popular song. Remember in the play that the idea of marriage is one of the central themes. Kīgūūnda and his wife marry according to their national ways. They also have to marry according to the church. The play is about marriage, but is also about the idea of cultural differences. The Christian marriage connotes one kind of value system. The national wedding ceremony connotes another type of value system. The title has a number of suggestions and the reader can look for them. Even the author may not be in the position to tell everything about his work."

What was my next question? He seemed so willing and happy to talk with me. I remembered that he had written a book about why he stopped writing in English. What was it called?

Ngũgĩ answered, "*Decolonizing the Mind*. In addition to explaining why I stopped writing in English, the book also discussed the politics of language in Africa. The idea is important for African writers and African literature to develop in African languages. This is so the majority of the people in each of the language groups can have access to and can read the works of those writers. The idea is for African writers to help in the development of their own languages. I thought that since I am a writer telling others what they should do, I must put that into practice myself."

I was amazed when Mr. Gern told us that Ngũgĩ went to jail as a result of his writing. I couldn't understand this, so I asked, "What happened to you? Why did you leave Kenya?" I wondered if he would want to talk about it. He did.

"I went to jail in 1978. I have also written a book about this called *Detained*. It is by the same publisher as *I Will Marry When I Want*. The play was part of a community activity in a place described on the cover of the book. What happened is that the Kenyan government did not like very much the people speaking about their own problems in a play."

"Why?" I asked again.

"Because the Kenyan government at that time and still now is repressive. It is sort of not democratic. They like to speak on behalf of the people instead of letting the people speak for themselves. When a play makes people speak for themselves, they feel uneasy. They punished me by stopping the play, arresting me and putting me in jail. It was not only to punish me but also as a warning to others not to follow in my footsteps. I was in jail for a year."

When I asked Ngũgĩ if the play was still done today in Africa, he told me "Yes. In some places, but not in Kenya, although the book is still on the book shelves." I remembered that we weren't able to buy the books in New York, and my teacher had to get them sent from England. When I told Ngũgĩ this, I was surprised to hear him say that the distribution of African books in the United States was very poor. He said that he was sad because this denies a whole generation of Americans access to a crucial literary tradition in the understanding of the twentieth century!

He asked me if I had any more questions I wanted to ask. Remembering the classes in which we argued about the politics of the play, I said, "Yes. *I Will Marry When I Want* seems to be very Marxist. With the collapse of the Soviet Union and the other countries that were Marxist, have your politics changed at all?"

Ngũgĩ answered, "When one looks at a word like *Marxist* , particularly in relation to literature, it can be very misleading. It is just a label. When it comes to art, theater and novels, one must experience the works themselves. What I tell people is this. Do you know Marx? Karl Marx? History did not learn from him. It is he who learned from history. Do you get the idea? Meaning that people live. They work; they struggle; they eat; they marry; they quarrel; they fight. That is the reality. Marx and others observed this and they drew lessons or conclusions from this daily struggle that we all face. We are all dealing with the same issues, the same history. If some ideas look like some others, it is all very fine, but the main idea is to look at the reality itself. This is very important, especially when it comes to art and literature. You should look at the plays and try to understand what the people do. How they live and how power is expressed in that society. How is power organized in that society? How are wealth and power distributed in that society? How does that affect people in the areas of culture, in their psychology, in their values and how they relate to one another?"

Ngũgĩ's answer reminded me of another discussion we had in class. My teacher and some students were wondering if the play wasn't a little too polemical against foreigners, so I asked Ngũgĩ what he thought about this interpretation.

He replied, "Of course when it comes to art, different people interpret things differently. My play is not anti-foreigner as such. But it is very important for people wherever they are, whether it is in Africa or here, to see how their particular situation is affected, not only by conditions in their own country but also by relationships between their own country and other countries. Those relationships can be one of domination or dominating. Those internal relationships, as well as external relationships, affect people's lives, even when they don't

231

see them directly. It is quite important for art and literature to examine all those relationships because they affect us wherever we live."

I listened to Ngũgĩ and he seemed to understand his country *and* to love his country so well. I was curious if he had been back to to Kenya recently, and when I asked him if he had, I was stunned by his reply. His voice remained gentle as he told me that he was still in exile. He had left Kenya for England in 1982 after his other play, *Mother Sing for Me*, was also stopped by the Kenyan government. When he came from prison in 1978, he went to continue working in the community in Gĩkũyũ at Kamĩrĩĩthũ. But after the second play was stopped, the theater itself at Kamĩrĩĩthũ, where the original *I Will Marry When I Want* was performed, was razed to the ground by the police. For ten years he had been away from his country. He was now a professor of comparative literature at NYU.

I had one more question. "If you ever have any free time, would you come visit us at our school?"

"Yes," he replied, "and if you ever have any more questions, just give me a call."

Frank Chipasula

Singing Like Parrots*

> I call on all minsters, assistant ministers and every other
> person to sing like parrots.
>
> —An African Head of State

And so the mind, emptied, rots
into a parrotry of sing-song praises:
You dance to the rattle of your chains
—on your arms, on your legs—
You wail from lips split by constant whips
Necklaces of your tears adorn your necks.
You have pawned your lies for the right
to sing in the beak of a hawk. Your
Disciplined thighs sigh open
and dish out rewards
to murderers, firm-beaked cocks
with fire crested on their heads
poke and poke and poke at
the Loyal forbidden fruit whose juice
leaks into the toxic Kachasu gin
and the Carlsberg beer that turns their heads.
Obedient breasts unleash a torrent
of milk and bittersweet honey
that drown the country under floods of songs.
And they sing like parrots while envious men
fondle their thoughts like rosary beads, afraid
to breach the false Unity, while
the sour cassava of poisoned slogans
brews a whirlwind in the earthen vessel.
Ministerial mouths perpetually open,
swallow the morsels of power that drop
from the peak of the paternal beak.

Inflamed, they sing like parrots also
Praises to the impotent wolf-faced hawk
with talons dipped in our blood.

*from Frank Chipasula, Whispers in the Wings (1991), by permission of Heinemann
Educational Books

The Water of Light

to search once more for the light that sings
inside of me, the unwavering light.

—Pablo Neruda

The fragrant fingers of the island breeze
swept stars onto my sharpened tongue
and perfumed my speech with the star dust
glowing on the head of each verb that fired
and scorched the trash of lies, mounds upon
mounds upon the market counters of base coins.
For awhile I feared that night had collected
in my mouth and smothered my singing light,
but the ring of stars barred it
like a surreptitious cat stealing into my throat.
A secret truth is rooted to my tongue
like a familiar rocky island
anchored in the sweet water of light.
With my dark fingers I squeeze
light from the floating stones,
from my lips and my spear-pointed pen
flows the sweet water of light.
I moult out of a nightmare
and mold myself into a dream
and mold the nightmares into dreams,
from my silence and my solitude,
cassava from the stones, fish from the sand.

When the water lifted its palms against my island
of grey stones tumescent with water songs
ripening in the sleepy silent mangoes
filling with the sap of light from the dark earth,
and when they snatched the nipple of the mango
from the starved lips of the island urchin,
I proffered a light. It was this light that you drank,

my land, my island, from the calabash of my hands,
to stop you from reeling, drunken on blood,
feet fettered ever by memories of faded glory.

Because silence is death, and solitude is death,
I rose from the shell of night, light sparks upon my wings
and shouted into the silent well, scooped a handful
of raging light with which I anoint the seven-headed,
fork-tongued snakes. With this blue water of light
I baptize the limp tricolored flag soaked
with so much blood, like a bird in downpour,
it cannot freely fly and laugh in the wind.

With the sacred water of light I cleanse
the hawks' claws caked in clotted blood.
With this water of light I cleanse
the swollen cheeks of the one who kneels at the feet
of power for his daily slap.

With my water of light I fumigate the roaches
out of the crevices where they feast on darkness,
And where the thirsty rocks drink the lake,
I hand them a chalice brimming with my watery light.
With my scalpel of tapering light I scrape
the gangrene off the yawning wound of our land,
and bathe her in my balmy fragrant water of light.

The Dance Has Entered the Streets

for the dead in Nairobi and Blantyre

Suddenly, the big dance lit
the misty May streets:
calloused feet weary
from pounding pavements,
hands like fins stirred
the silenced air into fiery songs
that fired blood
into moribund hearts,
and lips worn by stale slogans
bloomed into new songs
as the dawn dance entered
the drowsy streets,
Met by incendiary roses
and the trigger-
happy blinding fog
of lies, promises spewed
by the new masqueraders.

Columns of blood drained veins,
and fueled awakened limbs
marching to the new drum-
taps of their hearts:
they held up traffic
and ordered the city to halt;
from morning to night
the city stood still, bemused,
and emptied its pockets
of our looted promises,
avenues filled with false
revenue, and slowly filled them
with forgotten nuggets of truth.

Hearts now as fearless

as tested old shields,
Hearts filled with the new
water of love, advanced, dancing,
on those boisterous streets,
ready to spill it
into the gullies of the streets
where new feet danced on fear
and ground it into dust.

Was it the Shire's anger that erupted
and fueled the new dance
that freely meandered past
the Clock Tower in Chilembwe's footsteps?
Was it the new fire that unfurled
the petals of the forty or two hundred
open to the burning gifts
that plucked those tender flowers
nipped the corolla and collected
the scorching sap that flowed, red,
into the stormy tea cup
in the demented tyrant's hands?

What new spirit moved stealthily,
surreptitiously, through the angry
and joyous thousands deaf to insult,
deaf to the hoarse drum, as they danced
to the rattle and chorus of the tarmac?

It is a new dawn. The big dance is here.

Tanure Ojaide

Ivwri: Invoking the Warrior Spirit

I

If the healer's favourite child dies,
know that he has expended his resources.

If the eagle fails to soar to the sky,
what feathers will perch on the iroko tree?

If the champion swimmer dies in water,
who will recover the body from the depths?

If the hunter runs away from night,
who will bring us secret power?

II

Some cries pierce the soul, others
stifled to shame the torturer

Hysteria consumed the land.
In bed the sick dined
with their departed families,
the pregnant delivered monstrosities
that they ran away from,
those who ventured out with cheerful faces
encountered rabbits in daylight,
sustained shivers from hair-root down.

The invisible ogre broke every fence
and swept those hiding behind
into its compulsive trail of peril.
Many children born into the house
choked the earth before they walked,
the youths that spiced life

collapsed from fever, *unburied*.

Cultic membership built no granite
fortification, no guns gave cover
from the bugs roaming the air
to bite with poisonous teeth.
The paddles we called spears
fragmented before we launched them.
The wind blew against us and to spite us
sent back our missiles to strike us.

Looking out before raising the foot
in a chameleon habit,
we still fell into holes;
the sun shone over our missteps.
The mahogany to be leaned on
melted into a spiderweb when touched,
the cutlass we wielded
once raised exploded into dust.

And so every other person
prowled in a leopard
that leaped from the dark;
in the undergrowth,
a puffadder on our heels.
And the louder the howls,
the more the suspects.
And this is the land
fabled for the tortoise!

We sold bereaved mothers
for witchcraft,
we sold the *yellow* ones among women
for witchcraft
(we lost the fair shade
of the cotton tree),
we stoned toothless grannies
for witchcraft.

We wanted to flush
bad blood from our body
without throwing away family genes.
We sold the owls
to rid the land of an ugly face.

The fowl breaks its own eggs,
mindless of the reckless act...

Survivors of the arsonist's
unquenchable fire
contested their own bodies
with carrion birds,
who flew in to collect their dues.
Every year a record dirge—
we lost to the pit,
we lost to the sea,
we lost to neighbours,
we lost to our own gods.

The sky has remained over
cast for generations...

III (Odjugo's Example)

Each dirge brings us to
a crossroads, a tryst
with the disembodied voice
that we sent to rest
with divined sacrifice.

Odjugo might have chewed
the very herbs and barks
that immortalize healers, but
without invoking the spirits
outside their vegetable selves,
he remained more exposed—
with open eyes, he walked into

the net cast over his life.

The body crumbles fast
without the soul's wedge.
Muscles make no defence
where the murmur of words
deflects fatal shots!

IV (Rivers)

Divine courier
sent into Olokun's
under-water mansion,
let your course
fill new acolytes
with cheerful tales...

Offerings at river beaches
mirrored coins and icons
of cults and devotees.
Red/white-robed priestess
and her press of women
from land of the iroko
went to the Ethiope
for their yearly bath.

Boat driver
that made the Delta
a family of creeks,
fish provider
that filled every mouth,
you were the greatest
of many friends.

On your back of currents
and from sea-ward where
fish had poured into nets
and into kitchen racks
came ships, foreign carriers;

they were fitted with cannons,
they knocked away matchets
and raised warrior hands—
I do not know what supplication:
prayer to poor gods
or surrender to fire-balls.

Rivers of pirates,
rivers of kidnappers!
How soon habits change
from coercion, how fast
the friend's defaced!
Conquistadors planted a curse
in our waters.
We never looked again
to the sea to Olokun;
we saw an armada
rivetting our phalanges.

Who knew how farther than Ughoton
would our people go against currents?

V (The Forest)

Evergreen magnate
whose close weave
catches the sun
and leaves leftovers
of light to slip
through its sieve!
You leave parent Earth
too little to live with.

Many of your thorns
have brought tetanus
upon the tribe,
the poison of briars
has raised rashes,
blamed on rivals.

Puffadders and scorpions
refuged under the leaf-
mat of your tangled locks
have made fame for healers.
Colonies of bees,
wasps and tailor-ants have
had their peace breached
by adventurous soles—
the omens stirred
have inflicted insomnia
on tireless heads.

From the palm tree
the tapster fell, dead.
The iroko tree whose bark
brews into an elixir
but also accomplice
of evil medicines.
And night turns
the mahogany
into a coven
that only the fortified
can afford to approach...

Before overbreeding
tore the tangles
with matchets and matches,
before Shell BP flared
the forest into a wasteland,
the hyrax cried *aghwaghwa*
all night—who knew what
spirit kept it sleepless?
In the shrubbery, moist
from copious downpours,
ritualists stalked bushfarers
to behead the weak and unwary
for skulls to toast prowess.

Monkeys leap-frogged
to elude the smartest hunters.
The chimpanzee surprised
the lonely woman, pawed
about and raped her—
how like men, animals;
how like animals, men;
primates in their tastes.
The civet cat cried foul—
even animals recognized ugliness
when flaunted at them!

And the iguana of slit tongues
came on leave into town
to steal eggs, and if
it chanced to be crushed,
it received human burial.
Orogun, warrior clan,
conferred on the iguana
totem status.

Those trapped within
knock from inside.
I am learning
to come out of the forest
and retain its tapestry
of sunlit evergreen.

VI (Necessary God)

And my father told the remote healer
how he feared for my life,
though I felt sound. Suddenly
I fell sick from the cryptic complaint.
Was there a plot to auction me away
for a gold stool in coven, blood promotion
that broke loose on cast kola-nuts?

And the marks inflicted remain,

tattoos to dispel vagabond spirits.
I must be the chameleon
that nobody would consciously attack,
I would be forgotten in evil councils.
No hunger so harrowing to desire a toad...

I have seen people without disability
leaning on a tree fall with it,
I have seen property laid in the sun
blown away without any wind,
I have seen the town's wealth
melt away without any hardship sun
(Agbadamashi left with a singlet
of his far-famed empire!)

Many exposed despite roofs overhead
have gone to bed to be ridden
over potholes, cast into graves
and wake a hysterical wreck—
malaria was a house demon masked
to compete with Eshu in their lives.
And the succubus almost pressed tripes
out of the warrior's guts.
And who could overcome the awe
of waves of flying blows and missiles
that sought you awake or asleep?

Must we not stay the hand of lightning
hired by rivals to cut down erect ones?
Must we not burn the owl, mouthpiece
of malefactors, with whatever fire?
Must we not keep away the dread
of leprosy, tuberculosis and smallpox
that explodes at us from nowhere?

Mother has delivered me,
Father has done his own part.
It is left with me to make good

the rest of my life.
That's the adult song nobody taught me.
Unspoken at the shrine I know why
they added Ivwri to the pantheon
from the beginning without a warrior.

VII

I have ridden the iguana
and mounted the hornbill,
brought together two spirits
into one necessary god.
I have called Ivwri to the shrine.

What snout, what horns
rear their presence in my body,
once the mirror of the pursued!
Buffalo that drives bushfarers
from its dominion of leaves,
Crocodile that polices the water
from the river to the sea,
Eagle, marshal of the sky,
that supervises our airspace,
from your conglomerate of power,
Great Ivwri, you who cannot
be fully known, give me
enough to be firm and free.

VIII (Aftermath)

Now that we have summoned countless forces
into one body,
now that we have dispersed one formidable spirit
into our multifarious selves
and consecrated into a god the craft
we would like to wield over others,
we can invoke Ivwri to drive harm
from our way.

Ivwri waits at the bottom of the precipice
to cushion us against a hard fall,
Ivwri fortifies the threatened with *utiri*
that blunts the blades of matchets,
Ivwri keeps the gun from firing at his devotees,
Ivwri snatches his favourites from peril
and throws them into safety.

And those possessed by Ivwri, headstrong
annihilate their raiders—
don't try the patience of the impatient;
it is not there, too consuming;
don't raise dust that will be your shroud,
don't stir water that will drown you.
Ivwri's clan of children conjure hurricanes
to sweep their blocked way,
they raise bees to smite those who taunt them,
they have forced hostile gods to flee the land.

Afraid for myself at home and abroad,
I have gone to the grove like others
to imbibe Ivwri's draughts, ruled
on the forehead with the sacred chalk.
I have become an irrepressible rebel,
a warrior against myself in the head
as against thousands of strangers.
All the ropes that tied me to myself
have snapped and my restless soles
chase the horizon on its blue heels.

Who is surprised now that I sleep
with one eye closed and the other open
and my people die with a clenched fist?

Ivwri is a sculpture of various powers that the Urhobo people of the Delta part of Nigeria
invoked in the days of slavery to fight slave merchants and to free those already captured
from slavery.